Abortion Politics

Abortion Politics
Private Morality and Public Policy

by
Frederick S. Jaffe
Barbara L. Lindheim
Philip R. Lee

McGraw-Hill Book Company

New York   St. Louis   San Francisco   Auckland
Bogotá   Singapore   Johannesburg   London
Madrid   Mexico   Montreal   New Delhi
Panama   São Paulo   Hamburg
Sydney   Tokyo   Paris
Toronto

This book is dedicated to
Phyllis, Paul, David, and Richard Jaffe

363.46
JAF

Library of Congress Cataloging in Publication Data
Jaffe, Frederick S
    Abortion politics.

    Includes index.
    1.   Abortion—United States.   I.   Lindheim, Barbara L., joint
author.   II.   Lee, Philip R., joint author.   III.   Title.
HQ767.5.U5J33   363.4'6'0973   80-17035
ISBN 0-07-032189-2

 234567890   DODO   8987654321

The editors for this book were Robert A. Rosenbaum and Carolyn
Nagy, the designer was Mark E. Safran, and the production super-
visor was Sally Fliess. It was set in Palatino by David E. Seham
Associates, Inc.

Printed and bound by R. R. Donnelley & Sons Company.

Contents

Preface

The Supreme Court abortion decisions of 1973 have so far failed to settle public policy on abortion in the United States. The use of tax funds, the issue of parental or spousal notification or consent—the very legality of abortion—are still matters of controversy, dramatized by mass demonstrations, pro and con, calls for a Constitutional Convention, picketing and sit-ins at abortion clinics, firebombings of abortion facilities, petitions, state laws and policies, and challenges to them in the courts, and the liberal distribution of roses and coathangers to legislators every January 22nd, the anniversary of the 1973 decisions. One might despair that this issue will ever be resolved in the manner traditional in a pluralistic society where there are deep-seated differences about matters affecting morality, i.e., by allowing each person to make his or her own conscientious decision about what to do.

A similar controversy boiled for decades over the issue of contraception. Today, there is an extraordinary consensus among Americans, reflected in governmental law and policy, that the use of contraception is a private affair between couples, and that the government should help poor people who want to plan their births by paying for family planning services, including all available methods, to use or not use, according to their own consciences and wishes.

A Ford Foundation grant in 1975 enabled the authors to begin to gather research on the development of public policy on abortion in the United States since the 1973 Supreme Court decisions, as well as to examine the parallels, and differences, with the evolution of public policy on contraception. This book is the result of those efforts.

The principal author, Frederick S. Jaffe, died suddenly and tragically in the summer of 1978 after completing a draft of all but the concluding chapter. His coauthors—Barbara L. Lindheim of The Alan Guttmacher Institute and Philip R. Lee of the University of California Medical School—attempted to complete the book in the spirit in which Fred Jaffe conceived it. Editorial assistance was provided by David Zimmerman; and Rachel Gold, Richard Lincoln, and Jeannie I. Rosoff updated the manuscript in the light of rapid new developments. The research assistance of Maureen Cotterill and the secretarial help of Enos Hernandez and Cecil Wyatt were invaluable.

Introduction

This book takes as its starting point the fact that individuals and religious groups have sharply divergent and irreconcilable views on the morality of abortion. These differences did not emerge in 1973, when the Supreme Court ruled on abortion—they had long been argued by theologians, philosophers, doctors, and ordinary people.

We do not believe our personal views would add much to this debate. So we shall not attempt to assess whether abortion always is wrong or the circumstances under which it is justifiable. A spate of books in the last decade has dealt with these questions; the interested reader is urged to consult them.[1]

We do not think that the different beliefs about abortion will be reconciled in the foreseeable future. Nor need they be, in a pluralistic democratic society like ours, since this form of government was framed specifically to enable individuals and groups to live together *despite* deep-seated differences on fundamental matters of religion, morality, and conscience. In the face of these irreconcilable differences, the operative social question is not whether abortion is right or wrong but what kind of public policy is tenable and desirable. This question is the focus of the present volume.

Public policy is forged from many elements. We will try to delineate the main factors in the crucible of abortion policy. In a society that values equity, for example, it is a matter of public concern whether abortions are equally available to all women who need and want them, in all parts of the country, and in all socioeconomic and age groups. This public-policy issue does not disappear just because some citizens regard abortion as an anathema.

1

In a society that spends enormous sums for medical care, and in which government and the professions have been given great responsibility for regulating the quantity and quality of medical services, it is a question of public policy whether or not abortions are performed with maximum safety. There is a similar public interest in whether sufficient effort is invested in preventing the unwanted pregnancies that create the need for abortion and in whether the cost of abortions is reasonable. In a society that values self-determination and freedom of choice, finally, public policy should be concerned with the kinds and amounts of information available to women about their options in coping with pregnancy.

Our method in addressing these questions is primarily empirical. We have been able to make use of the wealth of information that has been gathered on abortion since 1975, when this study of U.S. health, professional, and political institutions' responses to the Supreme Court decisions started, with the help of a grant from the Ford Foundation.

Based on the evidence of what has in fact happened, we will address policy questions regarding the abortion responsibilities of government, the health professions, and educational and social-service institutions. Implicitly and explicitly, we seek to illuminate courses of action for government and private nonsectarian institutions that will best serve the public interest.

In our view, the 1973 Supreme Court abortion decisions foreshadow the only sort of public policy that ultimately is tenable in a democratic society like our own. Everyone's right to have or help perform abortions is protected, as is everyone's right not to participate—if he or she chooses. Any other decision by the Court necessarily would have meant that the morality of certain groups and individuals would have been imposed upon others who conscientiously believe differently, as indeed it had been for many years.

Beliefs aside, like most Americans we see abortion as one means to prevent unwanted births: not the preferred means, and not one that all persons will choose for themselves—but a means that has been, and will continue to be, used by millions of women to cope with their personal crises. This outlook doubtlessly offends many who approach the question theologically or metaphysically. But it is one we share with many other Americans, whose attitudes and practices cannot be interpreted in any other way.

Our views on abortion policy also are shaped by our research experience in health and fertility control. The most obvious fact about abortion is that, regardless of what the law has said, many millions of women have had recourse to it, even when they still had to obtain it illegally and at great risk to their lives and health. Millions of their spouses and partners participated in these decisions.

The prevalence of abortion in the United States and throughout the world makes clear that, to a very large degree, the public issue is not whether abortions should be allowed but whether they should be safe and under some degree of social control rather than risky and illegal, unmonitored and invisible.

Americans have not been alone in facing up for the first time to the public-policy consequences of legal abortions. By 1979, two-thirds of the world's population lived in countries where abortion was legal either without restriction or on broad moral, social, or medical grounds. In 1971, the comparable proportion had been 38 percent.[2] "Few social changes have ever swept the world so rapidly," concluded one study of this global trend.[3]

The countries where abortion now is legal include the world's four most populous ones—the United States, the Soviet Union, China, and India—as well as Japan and the Eastern European and Scandinavian nations where restrictive laws long ago were removed. Many nations, like our own, changed their laws within the last decade, including Great Britain, France, Austria, West Germany, Cyprus, Israel, Iran, South Korea, Tunisia, Zambia, and, recently, Italy. We are not alone in perceiving the need—or meeting it.

Clearly, potent factors must exist for a world-wide change of this magnitude to occur in so short a period of time and in such diverse countries. Increasing concern over the deaths and illness associated with illegal abortion is one factor that frequently is cited. So is the movement of women in many nations toward greater equality in rights and status.

Data from the World Health Organization and other sources were used in 1976 to construct a rough estimate that 50 million abortions are performed each year throughout the world—35 million of them legally. This indicates that abortion is one of the principal means of birth limitation.[4]

Restrictive laws do not stop abortions: in Brazil, it is estimated that half of all pregnancies end in abortion, despite that country's highly restrictive abortion law. The largest maternity hospital in Bogotá, Colombia, uses half its beds for women suffering the complications of illegal abortions. In Spain, where a woman can be jailed for six years for having an illegal abortion, between 300,000 and 500,000 procedures are performed each year.[5] Considerations of this kind have led many national legislatures to repeal restrictive laws and to improve public health by bringing abortion into the open, under medical supervision and scrutiny.

The importance that women's-rights organizations place on the repeal of restrictive abortion laws is evident in industrialized countries like the United States, France, Spain, and Italy. But the same theme was echoed by leaders from developing nations at the International Women's Year Conference (IWY) sponsored by the United Nations in Mexico City in 1975. While the IWY World Plan of Action avoided any specific reference to abortion because of opposition from many Catholic countries, an informal caucus of more than 1,000 delegates from many nations called on the United Nations and individual nations to insure women's access to safe legal abortion and provide free family-planning services, abortion, and maternity care when needed.[6] The official Plan of Action did declare:

> Individuals and couples have the right freely and responsibly to determine the number and spacing of their children and to have information and the means to do so. The exercise of this right is basic in the attainment of any real equality between the sexes, and without its achievement women are disadvantaged in their attempt to benefit from other reforms.[7]

If the IWY articulated some of the reasons for the world-wide trend toward legalized abortion, the individual human elements in the equation were cogently stated by France's president, Valéry Giscard d'Estaing, during the intense struggle that led to legalization in his country in 1974, despite vigorous opposition by France's Catholic hierarchy and center and right-wing political parties. Recalling that nearly a thousand illegal abortions were performed daily under the old restrictive law, resulting in an estimated four hundred deaths each year, Giscard d'Estaing appealed to his countrymen to "examine their consciences" and determine honestly whether "the realities of daily life justify clinging to an absolute purity that is too often a rejection of charity."[8] In 1979, the country reaffirmed its commitment to legalization of abortion.

Many opponents of abortion nevertheless still speak of abortion as a luxury that enables irresponsible women to escape punishment for their sins. They imply that many women decide to have abortions on trivial grounds, simply as a matter of convenience. Underlying this assertion is an image of women as wanton and irresponsible.

In our judgment, this image bears little resemblance to reality. The extent to which American women and men already seek to act responsibly in their sex lives is demonstrated by the fact that contraception is more widely practiced in the United States than in virtually any other country. But even if everyone were to practice contraception, and use the most effective medically prescribed methods, there would still be a very large number of unwanted pregnancies. None of the current reversible methods—not even the pill or intrauterine device—is failure-proof. These methods have failure rates that are high enough to result in a very large number of unwanted pregnancies each year, to which must be added the additional pregnancies that follow inconsistent or ineffective use of the methods.

The need for abortion services in the United States thus reflects limitations of current contraceptive methods and practices. These limitations exist not only among the "wicked" but among us all.

Abortion is a subject many people would prefer not to think about. It also is a subject on which decent and sincere people can—and obviously do—have sharply conflicting views. Our focus is not on whether a particular woman should have an abortion; in our view, that judgment is best left to the woman herself, weighing her own circumstances and values, in consultation with her physician.

Our focus rather is on the public policy that our society should adopt—which in some ways is an even more complicated issue. Our effort has been sustained by two convictions: first, that public policy on abortion is a consequential matter that affects many Americans personally and directly, and all of us indirectly; second, that our pluralistic society, given its democratic traditions, has the capacity to develop a public policy that will allow us to agree to disagree—even on the bitterly contested question of ending unwanted pregnancy.

References

1 We particularly recommend *Abortion: Law, Choice and Morality*, by Daniel Callahan, (New York: Macmillan, 1970), an ethicist writing from a Catholic background. He has painstakingly assessed the legal, medical, social, biological, and religious evidence underlying the abortion argument in a manner that facilitates reflection and independent judgment. Callahan's evenhanded treatment, and the approach to public policy that flows from it, unfortunately have gone largely unheeded.

2 C. Tietze, *Induced Abortion: 1979*, New York: The Population Council, 1979; updated by C. Tietze, Jan. 10, 1980.

3 L. R. Brown and K. Newland, "Abortion Liberalization: A Worldwide Trend," Washington: Worldwatch Institute, 1976.

4 Ibid.

5 "Stiff Abortion Laws in Spain Ineffectual," *Los Angeles Times*, June 20, 1976.

6   "Free Access to Fertility Control Measures Endorsed by Two IWY Bodies," *Planned Parenthood Washington Memo,* July 25, 1975.

7   World Conference of the International Women's Year, *Declaration of Mexico, Plan of Action,* United Nations: December 1975, p. 17.

8   F. Dupuis, "Abortion Now Legal Two Years, France Looks Back and Sighs," *Los Angeles Times,* Nov. 17, 1976.

CHAPTER ONE

The Most Frequent Operation in the United States

In 1972, the year before the U.S. Supreme Court's historic abortion decisions in *Roe v. Wade* and *Doe v. Bolton*, the Center for Disease Control (CDC) of the U.S. Department of Health, Education and Welfare (now called the Department of Health and Human Services) reported that 586,760 legal abortions were reported in the 28 states that already had to some extent liberalized their abortion laws.[1] Most of these procedures were performed in New York and California, which had legalized abortion on broad social and medical grounds before 1973. There also were an unknown number of illegal abortions.

By 1978, the number of legal abortions had more than doubled to 1,374,000.[2] Some legal abortions were performed in each of the 50 states, and the prevalence of self-induced and other illegal abortions apparently had plummeted. More abortions now were being performed each year than diagnostic dilatation and curettage, hysterectomy, or tubal ligations, the three operations that previously had topped the list of surgical procedures for adults. Termination of pregnancy had become the most frequently performed operation on adults in the United States.

The rapid increase in reported legal abortions starting in 1973 surprised many, shocked others. The rise was particularly surprising to people who were unaware of the large number of unwanted and accidental pregnancies that occur in the United States each year and the many illegal abortions that previously were performed to end them.

The rapidly rising number of abortions seemed to some people to confirm that the Court had established a right to "abortion on demand," whenever a woman wants it and for whatever reason—

including convenience, whim, or caprice. Increasingly, the fear was expressed that abortion was replacing contraception as the preferred way of regulating childbearing. This in turn was interpreted to be a wholesale abandonment of responsibility by American women. President Jimmy Carter expressed some of these fears in the summer of 1977, when he told reporters: "I am afraid that to take a very permissive stand on abortions, paying for them—which puts them in the same category, roughly, as other contraceptive means—will be an encouragement to depend on abortions to prevent pregnancy."[4]

In fact, the evidence of what happened in the five years following the 1973 decisions provides little support either for the contention that "abortion on demand" had been written into law or that abortion is replacing contraception. The Court indeed went out of its way to state, unequivocally, "a pregnant woman does not have an absolute constitutional right to an abortion on her demand."[5]

Since the meaning of the Court's decisions frequently is misunderstood, it may be helpful to summarize them at the outset, so they can serve as a framework for assessing subsequent developments. In its principal opinion, *Roe v. Wade*, invalidating a Texas statute that prohibited abortion except to save a woman's life, the Supreme Court held, by a 7-2 majority:

> This right to privacy . . . is broad enough to encompass a woman's decision whether or not to terminate her pregnancy. . . . [But] the privacy right involved . . . cannot be said to be absolute and must be considered against important state interests in regulation. . . . It is reasonable and appropriate for a State to decide that at some point in time another interest, that of the health of the mother or that of potential human life, becomes significantly involved. The woman's privacy is no longer sole and any right of privacy she possesses must be measured accordingly.[6]

Under this principle, the Court held that a state may not make special regulations to govern the performance of abortions during the first trimester of pregnancy, except to require that it be done by a licensed doctor, because the mother's risk of death early in pregnancy is less than the risk in normal childbirth. In the first trimester, which usually is defined as the first 13 weeks, the Court ruled, "the attending physician, in consultation with his patient, is free to determine, without regulation by the State, that in his medical judgment the patient's pregnancy should be terminated."

During the second trimester, the Court said, a state may regulate abortion "in ways that are reasonably related to maternal health." It may, for example, require that in this period an abortion be performed in a hospital.

The state's "important and legitimate interest in potential life," the Court held, begins at the point of viability—which normally occurs at between 24 and 28 weeks of gestation—when the fetus is potentially capable of life outside the womb. At that point, a state may prohibit abortion, except when necessary to preserve the life or health of the pregnant woman.[7]

One of the most crucial aspects of the *Roe v. Wade* decision, it has since turned out, involves the role assigned to doctors. The justices held that the doctor is a critical participant in the abortion decision, both prior to and after those points in time when the state attains its compelling interest in the woman's health, and later, in the fetus' potential life. The Court said: "The abortion decision in all its aspects is inherently and primarily a medical decision, and basic responsibility for it must rest with the physician."[8]

Whether and to what extent the medical profession is making these decisions and is fulfilling the responsibilities that are implicit in this language is one of the principal points of inquiry in this book.

In the companion case, *Doe v. Bolton*, dealing with a Georgia statute, the Supreme Court outlined the considerations it expected doctors to take into account when women came to them for abortions:

> The medical judgment may be exercised in the light of all factors—physical, emotional, psychological, familial, and the woman's age—relevant to the well-being of the patient. All these factors may relate to health. This allows the attending physician the room he needs to make his best medical judgment.[9]

Far from establishing "abortion on demand," the rulings created a complex decision-making process for abortion. The pregnant woman, the doctor, and the state all are participants in this process. Particularly striking is the Court's delegation of responsibility for abortion to the medical profession and its institutions. Doctors are expected to employ their professional judgment in advising and assisting abortion-seeking women—a responsibility that the record shows doctors have been reluctant to accept.

The Court surely did not contemplate—and certainly did not intend—that doctors and their institutions would deny women *de facto* the very right that it was establishing for them de jure. In this light, it is instructive to reread a passage in *Roe v. Wade*, in which the justices dissect the injury done to women by a legal ban on abortion, bearing in mind that the real-life consequences are exactly the same if she is denied the procedure through the intended or unintended acts of doctors:

> The detriment that the State would impose upon the pregnant woman by denying this choice altogether is apparent. Specific and direct harm medically diagnosable even in early pregnancy may be involved. Maternity, or additional offspring, may force upon the woman a distressful life and future. Psychological harm may be imminent. Mental and physical health may be taxed by child care.
>
> There also is the distress, for all concerned, associated with the unwanted child, and there is the problem of bringing a child into a family already unable, psychologically and otherwise, to care for it . . . . |T| he additional difficulties and continuing stigma of unwed motherhood may be involved.[10]

The Court surely then did not intend that the medical profession—a woman's putative partner in the abortion decision—would deny her the rights it was supposed to help her achieve. But this, in fact, is what all too often has occurred.

What has happened since 1973 to women who want abortions—those who get them as well as those who do not—has been the sum of interactions between women, doctors, the health institutions doctors work in and may control, the legislatures and courts, and a variety of government agencies. In each successive year more women have been able to terminate pregnancies, as more health facilities and physicians have begun to perform abortions. But many women still are denied the option of abortion.

There has been a gradual diffusion of abortion services into all regions of the country. In 1973, half of all legal abortions were performed in New York and California. Few or no abortions were performed in Louisiana, Mississippi, North Dakota, Utah, and West Virginia. By 1977, only three in 10 abortions were performed in New York and California. By 1977, only one woman in 11 had to travel outside her home state to obtain a legal abortion, compared to more than one in four in 1973.[11]

Greater availability brought other changes. The proportion of all abortions performed in the first 12 weeks climbed, year by year, from 83 percent in 1973 to 91 percent in 1977—and half of all abortions now were done in the first eight weeks.[12] These were important developments, for even though first trimester abortion has proved to be exceptionally safe, the risk of major complications increases by 91 percent and the risk of death rises almost fivefold between the eighth and twelfth week of gestation.[13] In the same period, the proportion of procedures performed using suction curettage, far and away the safest method, also increased, from 65 percent to over 90 percent.[14]

The typical abortion patient now, as in 1973, is young, white, and unmarried. In each year, about one-third have been teenagers, another third between the ages of 20 and 24, and the remainder 25 or over. About one woman in four is married, half have no children, a third have one or two, and the rest three or more.[15] About 191,000 teenagers obtained legal abortions in 1972, compared to more than 413,000 in 1977.

The percentage of pregnant women who obtain abortions (i.e., the number of abortions per 100 abortions and live births) is a standard measure that is used to compare the extent to which different groups of pregnant women employ abortions to resolve their unwanted pregnancies. These data show that three in 10 pregnancies in the United States now are terminated by abortions.[16]

In each year since the 1973 Supreme Court decisions, the highest percentages of abortions to total pregnancies have been found among women under age 20 and above age 35. In 1977, for example, abortions were obtained by 58 percent of pregnant girls below age 15; by 44 percent of those between 15 and 17; by 20 percent of pregnant women between 25 and 29 and by 47 percent of those over age 40. While 67 percent of all unmarried pregnant women obtained abortions, only 10 percent of pregnant married women chose to do so.[17]

Many young, unmarried, pregnant women thus appear to have abortions in order to complete their education, find jobs, and marry before beginning a family. Many older pregnant women, who probably feel they have completed their families, also have abortions—apparently to avoid having additional children. In each year since 1973, the percentage of pregnant women in these age groups obtaining abortions has increased, indicating that greater availability has allowed an increasing proportion of them the choice of avoiding unwanted births.

One notable change since 1973 has been an increase in the number of blacks and other nonwhites who obtain legal abortions. One-third of all women who obtained abortions in 1977 were nonwhite, compared to just 23 percent five years before; in absolute terms, the number rose from 135,000 in 1972 to 429,000 in 1977.[18]

Four out of 10 pregnant black women in 1977 obtained abortions, compared to one out of four pregnant white women. This is to be expected, given the higher rates of unintended pregnancy among blacks.[19] Since blacks are disproportionately poor, the changes since 1973 also indicate that greater availability has enabled more low-income women to obtain abortions. In the years preceding the Supreme Court decisions, an important argument advanced for the repeal of restrictive abortion laws was to give poor women the same opportunity to obtain safe abortions that affluent women long had enjoyed through their ability to travel to places where abortion was legal or to pay the high prices demanded by skilled clandestine abortionists.

The religious affiliations of women who obtain abortions is of interest, given the significant doctrinal differences that exist among religious groups regarding the morality of abortion. This information however is difficult to obtain. Hospitals often ask "religion" on admission forms, but the data rarely are tabulated or reported; ambulatory health facilities, such as abortion clinics, usually do not ask.

It is difficult to extrapolate from the fragmentary published reports that are available. But most of them seem to indicate that the proportion of abortion patients who are Catholic is equal to—or even greater than—the proportion of the community's population that is Catholic.[20]

Those opposed to abortion complain that a principal effect of the Court's decision has been to enable American women to engage freely in sexual activity while avoiding its natural consequence. Yet judged by their own surveys and published reports on abortion and its emotional sequelae, it is difficult to imagine *any* abortion patient getting off "scot free"—which seems to be one of the particular worries of abortion opponents.

The fear that abortion will lead to sexual irresponsibility also contributes to the concern of many people—including some health professionals who readily accept abortion as a backup measure for contraceptive failure—that abortion is replacing contraception as the primary means of birth control. President Carter expressed this concern when he declared (without citing any evidence) that "it is very disturbing how many of the recipients of Federal payments for abortion in the past have been repeaters!"[21] The issue is important, because most people agree that abortion is less desirable than contraception as a means of controlling fertility.

Of reported abortions in 1977, 20 percent were performed for women who had one previous induced abortion; an additional 6 percent were for women who had two or more.[22] These percentages have increased year by year since the Supreme Court decisions, which is to be expected since each year there are more women who already have had a first abortion, thereby increasing the pool of those at risk of a second. But these figures do not substantiate the belief that abortion is being widely substituted for contraception.

Christopher Tietze, senior consultant with The Population Council, explains that there are several factors that increase the likelihood that a group of women who already have had one abortion will, over time, have another. Most are in their prime reproductive years. Almost all are fertile. All are sexually active at the time of their first conception, and all have accepted abortion as an option to avoid unwanted birth. Yet if just 6 percent of these highly fertile women shunned all contraception the following year and aborted the resulting pregnancies, Tietze estimates they could account for *all* the repeat abortions in that year. This calculation suggests that a large majority of women who obtain abortions must subsequently practice contraception, and with a high degree of success.[23]

A recent study supports this impression. Researchers at the University of Hawaii found that women who had undergone an abortion had about the same success in avoiding a subsequent pregnancy as did all women of childbearing age. The researchers also concluded that there was no evidence that the availability of abortion in Hawaii has led to relaxation of contraceptive vigilance.[24]

Other analyses confirm this conclusion. A detailed study in New York City showed that the *pregnancy* rate per 1,000 women of reproductive age declined 7.5 percent between 1971, the first year of legalized abortion in New York, and 1973, the third year—an impossible result if contraception had been neglected.[25] Perhaps the most telling evidence comes from a series of four surveys of contraceptive use by U.S. married couples between 1965 and 1975.[26] The average annual increase in use was only 0.2 percent in the last half of the 1960s when there were few legal abortions, but it jumped to 3 percent per year after 1973. The proportion of sexually active unmarried teenagers using contraceptives at their last encounter also increased, from 45 percent in 1971 to 64 percent in 1976.[27]

One important—but elusive—factor that must be taken into account in assessing the abortion statistics since 1973 is the degree to which legal abortions are replacing abortions that previously would have been obtained on an illegal basis. There is of course no precise information on the number of abortions performed illegally prior to 1973. For many years, the best available estimate was extrapolated from Alfred Kinsey's studies in the 1950s. But, given the unrepresentative sample he used, a committee of statisticians and demographers concluded that a plausible estimate "could be as low as 200,000 and as high as 1,200,000 a year."[28]

Abortion's legalization in New York in 1970, while it remained illegal in most of the rest of the country, provided an opportunity for researchers to estimate reliably the number of illegal abortions prior to 1970 by analyzing changes in the number of live births and abortions to New York City residents during the transition years. They showed that approximately 70 percent of the legal—and safe—abortions obtained by New York City residents from 1970 to 1972 replaced abortions that before 1970 would have been performed illegally—and at far greater risk.[29] Using data for the nation as a whole, other researchers have produced similar estimates that suggest that about two-thirds of all legal abortions in the early years of legalization replaced formerly illegal procedures.[30]

Between 1972 and 1978, the annual number of births increased slightly; if all or many of the reported abortions had been "new," there would have been a very large decline in births. The proportion of abortions that substitute for previously illegal procedures would have had to decline by 1978, if only because the number of reported abortions had increased substantially. But most analysts conclude that current abortions still include a sizable proportion—perhaps half—that substitute for procedures that formerly were illegal.

Another approach to putting the number of legal abortions into context is provided by a recently derived estimate that more than two million unintended pregnancies occurred annually to U.S. women early in the 1970s, when contraceptive use already was widespread but legal abortion was much less available. These unintended pregnancies comprised close to half of all pregnancies experienced by American women in these years, and it is estimated that about one-third of them were aborted legally or illegally.[31] The one factor that has changed significantly since then is the increasing accessibility of legal abortion. This seems to have made it possible for a larger proportion of these women to end unwanted pregnancies safely and legally since the birth rate has fallen, while the number of women in their reproductive years has risen. In this context, the actual number of legal abortions performed each year suggests that many women still carry unwanted pregnancies to term because they are unwilling or unable to obtain abortions.

Given these data, informed social analysts can only conclude that *unwanted pregnancy* was not called into existence by the Supreme Court rulings in 1973 but has been part of our collective experience for a long time. In fact, in view of improvements in contraceptive efficacy and practice in the last two decades, they have reason to believe that in the past the incidence of unwanted pregnancy was, if anything, much greater than at present.

This conclusion threatens our customary ways of looking at the world. It raises questions that are both intensely personal and broadly social: How did our parents cope with unwanted pregnancy? In what ways has it—or fears of it—shaped, or warped, our emotional growth and our marriages? What did it do to women and their lives? What has it done to their children? Clearly, the necessity of developing more positive bases for personal and familial relationships is a major challenge that is frightening to many people.

Abortion figures for the nation as a whole mask significant regional variation in the delivery of abortion services. Despite the diffusion of abortion services after 1973, the majority of abortions are still performed in a relatively small number of clinics and hospitals concentrated in the more populous cities. A greater number of American women have been able to obtain abortions in the years since the Supreme Court decisions. But the opportunity to make that choice has not been equally available.

A 1977-1978 nationwide survey could not identify a single hospital, clinic, or physician that performed an abortion in 2,387, or 77 percent, of all U.S. counties. In four of 10 of the counties that did have abortion facilities, fewer than 100 abortions were performed in the year.[32]

Providers were few and far between in the Central and Midwestern states. Women had to travel to facilities hundreds of miles from their homes to obtain abortions. In most states, the vast majority of all abortions were performed in one or two large cities, and there were no identified providers in 47 sizable metropolitan areas, including Shreveport, Louisiana; Canton and Lorain, Ohio; Beaumont, Texas, and Huntington, West Virginia.[33]

Poor distribution of health resources is endemic in the United States. But the delivery pattern for abortion services that has emerged since 1973 is distorted beyond precedent. Open-heart surgery and other procedures that require high skill and massive technology may be concentrated in a few, highly sophisticated hospitals, located for the most part in large cities. But medically simple procedures like abortion usually are provided by physicians and hospitals near the patient's home. To require hundreds of thousands of patients to travel far from home to obtain tonsillectomies, for example, would be cited as proof that the U.S. health system had failed to meet the nation's health needs. Yet the paucity of abortion services fails to elicit a comparably harsh judgment.

It is necessary to transform the raw numbers of reported abortions into standardized indices if one wishes to compare geographical areas of different sizes. One index that has been found to be particularly useful for health planners is the ratio of reported abortions to an area's estimated need for abortion services. This measure is derived by applying to each community's population of reproductive-age women the abortion utilization rates for six geographically diverse states in which legal abortion is widely available and accessible. It thus reflects the assumption that if all U.S. women had equal information about, and access to, safe, legal abortion, there would be only small differences between areas in its use. The rapid local increases in abortion use when services are introduced into previously unserved areas support the wide applicability of this index of need.

In 1978, more than 1.8 million American women were estimated to need abortion services. Since almost 1.4 million women obtained abortion that year, the *percent met need,* as this index is called, for the nation as a whole thus was 74 percent. The remaining unmet need, for 479,000 abortions, means that more than one woman out of four estimated to want an abortion was unable to obtain it.

The state-to-state variations in met need were substantial: in 18 states and the District of Columbia in 1977, as well as in 106 of the nation's metropolitan areas, the met need was 67 percent or above. These states included Colorado, New York, Kansas, and Florida. At the low end of the scale, the met need was less than 33 percent in nine states and in 41 percent of the nation's 260 metropolitan areas. This low percent-need group included Indiana, South Carolina, and Mississippi.[34]

Another standardized index is the *abortion rate,* the number of abortions per 1,000 women of reproductive age. For the United States as a whole in 1978, this rate was 27.5. In metropolitan areas it was 35.1, in rural ones 5.8. The available data are imperfect since they are often overstated in areas to which women travel to get abortions and understated in the areas from which they come. But they still are revealing. The rate in New York State was 46.2, which is eight times higher than the lowest rate, of 6.0 in Mississippi.[35]

This extraordinary range does not occur in the delivery of other health services. One could ask if there are comparably wide differences among women in different communities to account for these extremes. The fact is, however, that there are not large differences among U.S. women in the factors relevant to the abortion decision: rates of unintended pregnancy, contraceptive practice, and desired family size. In addition, industrial and rural states in all regions can be found among the "high" rate areas, as are cities in the traditionally conservative Deep South and Midwest. Clearly, any simple explanation, such as the "conservatism" of Middle America, compared to the cosmopolitan characteristics of the two coasts, cannot be sustained. In fact, the only major difference between areas with high and low abortion utilization is the availability of abortion facilities.

By 1976, abortion, which was a crime in virtually all states in 1966 and in most states in 1972, had become the most frequently performed legal operation in the United States. From 1967, when abortion statistics first began to be collected, to the end of 1978, about six million American women obtained legal abortions—one for every eight women of reproductive age. This high incidence points to the first important conclusion to be drawn from the experience of the first five years of legalized abortion: it is not happening to "them" and "their" wives, daughters, sisters, lovers, and friends—whatever nationality, ethnic, religious, or income group "they" may be—but to "us" and "ours" as well. Unwanted pregnancy remains a regrettable fact of life even in a highly contracepting society like our own.

References

1 Center for Disease Control, *Abortion Surveillance, Annual Summary, 1977*, Atlanta, 1979, table 1 (hereinafter referred to as *Abortion Surveillance 1977*).

2 J. D. Forrest, S. Henshow, E. Sullivan, and C. Tietze, *Abortion 1977–1979: Need and Services in the United States, Each State and Metropolitan Area*, New York: The Alan Guttmacher Institute, 1980 (hereinafter referred to as *Abortion 1977–1979*).

3 In 1978, there were 963,000 diagnostic D&Cs, 643,000 hysterectomies, and 551,000 tubal ligations performed in hospitals on adults over age 15. National Center for Health Statistics, unpublished data from the National Hospital Discharge Survey, DHEW.

4 Office of the White House Press Secretary, press conference, Yazoo City, Miss., July 21, 1977, p. 14.

5 *Doe v. Bolton*, 410 U.S. 1979 (1973), p. 9.

6 *Roe v. Wade*, 410 U.S. 113 (1973), pp. 39, 44.

7 Ibid., p. 48.

8 Ibid., p. 50.

9 *Doe v. Bolton*, op. cit., pp. 11–12.

10 *Roe v. Wade*, op. cit., p. 38.

11 *Abortion, 1977–1979*.

12 Ibid.

13 *Abortion Surveillance 1977*, pp. 9, 47, and W. Cates, K. Schulz, D. Grimes, and C. Tyler, Jr., "The Effect of Delay and Method Choice on the Risk of Abortion Morbidity," *Family Planning Perspectives*, 9:266, 1977.

14 *Abortion Surveillance 1977*, Summary Table.

15 Ibid., p. 1.

16 *Abortion 1977–1979*.

17 Ibid.

18 Ibid.

19 Ibid. In 1977, the ratio for blacks and nonwhites was 405 abortions per 1,000 live births, compared to 250 for whites. The higher incidence of unwanted and mistimed pregnancies among blacks is reported in C. F. Westoff and N. B. Ryder, *The Contraceptive Revolution*, Princeton: Princeton University Press, 1977, table X-18, p. 307; J. E. Anderson, L. Morris, and M. Gesche, "Planned and Unplanned Pregnancies in Upstate New York," *Family Planning Perspectives*, **9**:4, 1977, table 6; M. L. Munson, "Wanted and Unwanted Pregnancies Reported by Mothers 15–44 Years of Age," *Advance Data from Vital and Health Statistics*, National Center for Health Statistics, Aug. 10, 1977, table 10.

20 For example, in the early 1970s, the proportion of abortion patients who were Catholic was 18 percent in Maryland, compared to 11 percent of the state's population; 21 percent in Colorado, compared to 13 percent of the population; and 42 percent in Connecticut, compared to 30 percent of the population. In Milwaukee, 43 percent of women seeking information at a pregnancy counseling service in 1973 were Catholic, compared to 36 percent of the city's residents. At an abortion clinic in central Florida in 1977, the disparity was even greater—38 percent of the clinic's patients, compared to 22 percent of the area's population. In San Diego in 1977, Catholics constituted more than 36 percent of women seeking referrals for abortion but only 20 percent of the population. Similar reports have come from such diverse places as the Boston Hospital for Women and the Wheeling, W. Va., abortion clinic. In Hawaii, a unique, study linking the state's birth and abortion records showed that between 1970 and 1973 the proportion of pregnant Catholics who obtained abortions was only a few percentage points lower than that of pregnant non-Catholics. Among those who became pregnant in August and September of 1973, 17 percent of Catholics and 22 percent of non-Catholics had abortions; the comparable proportions among those becoming pregnant in July and August of 1970 were 17 and 20 percent, respectively.

Sources:

H. Osofsky (ed.), *The Abortion Experience*, New York: Harper & Row, 1973, p. 211.

M. Haines, "Some Social Factors Associated with Elective Abortions: A Preliminary Report," thesis, University of Wisconsin–Milwaukee Urban Affairs Department, June 1973.

Reported in M. Winiarski, "Abortion, The Issue No One Wanted So Catholics Took It On," *National Catholic Reporter*, Feb. 24, 1978.

Planned Parenthood Association of San Diego County, unpublished statistics of referrals in June 1977.

Chicago Defender, Sept. 13, 1975.

Wheeling News–Register, Sept. 23, 1976.

J. Palmore, M. Furlong, P. Steinhoff, and R. G. Smith, "Measuring the Success of Legalizing Induced Abortion," presented at Population Association of America annual meeting, Montreal, April 1976.

21 Office of the White House Press Secretary, op. cit.

22 *Abortions 1977–1979* (excluding unknowns).

23 C. Tietze, "Repeat Abortions—Why More?", *Family Planning Perspectives*, **10**:286, 1978.

24 P. G. Steinhoff, R. G. Smith, J. A. Palmore, M. Diamond, and C. S. Chung, "Women Who Obtain Repeat Abortions: A Study Based on Record Linkage," *Family Planning Perspectives*, **11**:30, 1979.

25 C. Tietze, "Contraceptive Practice in the Context of a Nonrestrictive Abortion Law: Age-Specific Pregnancy Rates in New York City, 1971–1973." *Family Planning Perspectives,* **7**:197, 1975.

26 C. F. Westoff and E. F. Jones, "Contraception and Sterilization in the United States: 1965–1975," *Family Planning Perspectives,* **9**:153, 1977.

27 M. Zelnik and J. F. Kantner, "Sexual and Contraceptive Experience of Young Unmarried Women in the United States, 1976 and 1971," *Family Planning Perspectives,* **9**:55, 1977.

28 M. S. Calderone (ed.), *Abortion in the United States,* New York: Hoeber-Harper, 1958, p. 180.

29 C. Tietze, "Two Years' Experience with A Liberal Abortion Law: Its Impact on Fertility Trends in New York City," *Family Planning Perspectives,* **5**:36, 1973.

30 P. C. Glick and A. J. Norton, "Marrying, Divorcing and Living Together in the U. S. Today." *Population Bulletin,* vol. 32, no. 5, Washington, D.C., 1977.

31 C. Tietze, "Unintended Pregnancies in the United States, 1970–1972," *Family Planning Perspectives,* **11**:186, 1979.

32 *Abortion 1977–1979.*

33 Ibid.

34 Ibid.

35 Ibid.

CHAPTER TWO

The Impact of Legal Abortion

Amid the emotion and cant of the moral and political debate over abortion, the impact of legalization on the health and well-being of American women and their families seldom is discussed. Yet, for the majority of Americans who favor legal abortion—and who have indicated that they or their family members would use it under certain circumstances—questions about the effects of legal abortion on health and social welfare have both personal and social relevance.

There already is wide agreement that the single most important effect of legalization has been the substitution of safe, legal procedures for abortions that formerly were obtained illegally. This substitution quickly led to a dramatic decline in the number of women who died or suffered serious, someti.nes permanent, injury from botched, clandestine abortions.

These were the main findings of a comprehensive report on the health aspects of abortion prepared by the Institute of Medicine (IOM) of the National Academy of Sciences.[1] The IOM report found that

> many women will seek to terminate an unwanted pregnancy by abortion whether it is legal or not . . . . Evidence suggests that legislation in proper medical surroundings will lead to fewer deaths and a lower rate of medical complications than restrictive legislation and practices.

A second, equally important result of legalization concerns *equity*: before abortion was legal, it was poor women, minority women, and very young women who suffered most, since their only options often were delivery of an unwanted child or a back-alley or self-induced abortion.

The number of illegal abortions performed each year before legal reform began in 1967 can only be guessed, as we noted in Chapter 1. In the 1950s, knowledgeable researchers produced estimates that ran from 200,000 to over one million illegal procedures per year.[2] Clearly, many women resolved their unwanted pregnancies in this way.

By the 1960s, the illegal abortion business was flourishing. Puerto Rico and Mexico had become widely known abortion centers. Many large U.S. cities had underworld abortion rings. In some states, clergymen formed problem pregnancy consultation services that referred women to competent, though illegal, practitioners. These consultation services were used primarily by women of means, not the poor. Most illegal abortions continued to be performed under unsafe—usually degrading—conditions.

Illegal abortionists apprehended in this period following the deaths of their clients included a boatyard worker, a real-estate salesman, a hospital orderly, and an automotive mechanic. These operators often worked under unsanitary conditions and avoided anesthesia, so they could speed women who had just been aborted on their way.[3]

As awful as illegal abortions were, the self-abortion methods that many desperate women used were even more dangerous; these included lye, soap, Lysol, and iodide douches, as well as self-inserted catheters, knitting needles, and goose quills.[4]

No records were kept of these clandestine procedures. They are known from hospital and coroners' reports on women who died from abortion complications. There were 320 such deaths recorded in 1961.[5] This toll dropped steadily during the 1960s, as a result of advances in contraception and medical care and of the increased availability of legal abortion after 1967. By 1972, when 587,000 legal abortions were reported nationally, only 39 women died from illegal or self-induced procedures. In 1973, the year of the Supreme Court decisions, illegal abortion deaths fell to 19 and then to an average of fewer than five a year since 1974.[6]

Information from hospitals on admissions for septic and incomplete abortion corroborate this trend. At Grady Memorial Hospital, Atlanta's large public hospital, admissions for complications of illegal abortion dropped from 33 per calendar quarter in 1970 to five in the final quarter of 1973.[7] Between 1967 and 1970, the Los Angeles County/University of Southern California Medical Center reported a decline of more than 50 percent in admissions due to septic abortion and a 78 percent reduction in the ratio of septic abortions to live births.[8]

The rate of admissions for septic and incomplete abortions in New York City's municipal hospitals declined by more than 40 percent between 1969 and 1973.[9] Before legalization, large public institutions like Harlem and Kings County hospitals reserved beds for these cases because they were so common. In about one case in four, the instrument used to induce the abortion still was present in the uterus and had to be surgically removed. Many women misplaced a catheter in the urinary bladder, rather than in the uterine cavity; these required cystoscopic removal. Septic abortion patients often were critically ill and required intensive medical and nursing care for up to a month.[10]

A few years brought dramatic change. In 1976, it was reported that when a patient was admitted to a large New York municipal hospital with a diagnosis of "septic abortion," the entire resident staff was brought in to see what had become a "rare event." Only seven years earlier, 6,524 cases of septic and incomplete abortions had been admitted to municipal hospitals during the year.[11]

The federal Center for Disease Control (CDC) in Atlanta has conducted extensive studies of the safety of legal abortion. They confirm that legal abortion, particularly early abortion, is one of the safest surgical procedures. Eight deaths from legally induced abortions were reported in 1978, or 0.5 per 100,000 abortions. The number of deaths attributable to legal abortion procedures has dropped each year since 1973, while the number of procedures has increased. Researchers believe this reflects the higher percentage of abortions that are being performed at earlier gestational periods, the wider use of safer techniques, and the increasing skill of doctors who perform the procedure.[12]

To put abortion mortality of 0.5 per 100,000 into perspective: in 1974 and 1975, the risk associated with other common procedures was 9 deaths per 100,000 tonsillectomies, 110 deaths per 100,000 hysterectomies, and 225 deaths per 100,000 appendectomies.[13] Deaths from pregnancy and childbirth, in 1977, totaled 11.2 per 100,000 deliveries.[14] Thus, in terms of risk of mortality, childbirth is 14 times more dangerous than legal abortion, and tonsillectomy is nine times more dangerous.

Deaths from abortion have been found to increase with length of gestation. In the first eight weeks of pregnancy, when half of legal abortions now are performed, the mortality rate is only 0.6 deaths per 100,000 abortions. Between the ninth and the tenth week of pregnancy, when an additional 27 percent of abortions are performed, the rate rises to 1.7 deaths per 100,000 procedures. At the far end of the spectrum, after 21 weeks, when less than one percent of abortions are performed, the death rate jumps to 20.5.[15]

Using aggregated mortality data, CDC researchers point out that the abortion death rate increases 40 to 60 percent per week for each week of delay after the eighth week. Abortions performed at 9-10 weeks are nearly three times more dangerous, in terms of deaths, than earlier ones; the small number of abortions performed after 20 weeks' gestation are about 45 times riskier. Clearly, while the overall risk of death is very low, it increases sharply later in pregnancy.[16] The widespread availability of abortion services, and the reduction of geographical, procedural, and financial barriers resulting from legalization have allowed women to obtain earlier abortions, thereby reducing legal as well as illegal abortion mortality.

Death resulting from legal abortion is a very rare occurrence and easy to measure. Nonfatal complications occur more frequently but are difficult to monitor in a uniform manner. To determine the incidence of such complications, CDC conducted a four-year study in 32 hospital centers that performed more than 80,000 abortions. Morbidity was found to be influenced by length of gestation, the abortion method, the woman's race and age, and the number of children she had borne.

In the first trimester, less than half of one percent of all abortion patients experience major complications. The main risks result from delay: between the eighth and twelfth weeks, the risk of major complications doubles from two per thousand to four per thousand, while at 17 weeks, it rises to 17 per thousand. The most common complications are bleeding, infection, and injury to the cervix or uterus.[17]

Since 1973, the proportion of women obtaining abortions before the eighth week—and using the safest method, suction curettage—has steadily increased. By improving availability and accessibility, legalization thus has also contributed to a significant decline in complications.

The second major consequence of the shift from illegal to legal abortion has been to increase equity. Before legalization, there was in fact not one illegal abortion market, but two. Women with knowledge and means could usually obtain a reasonably safe abortion, performed by a physician, at a cost of $500 to $1,500, and up. For women without information and funds, this option was unavailable.

Biostatistician Christopher Tietze of the Population Council has noted that one effect of the increasing availability of safe illegal and legal abortion for middle-class American women in the 1950s and 1960s was a dramatic rise in the *differential* abortion mortality experienced by black and white women. In 1933, when abortion was generally unavailable and unsafe for all, black women suffered twice the abortion mortality reported for whites; by 1966, when safe abortions were more easily available for those who could pay, the death rate from abortion was six times greater among blacks than among whites.[18]

A study conducted in poverty neighborhoods in New York City in the mid-1960s suggests why this was so. One woman in 12 in the sample reported an abortion attempt. Eighty percent of the women who had attempted abortion had tried to terminate the pregnancy themselves; only 2 percent said a doctor had been involved in any way![19]

The inequities persisted even after some states passed a form" laws in the late 1960s. These laws allowed abortions t of medical and psychiatric indications, which had to be verifi eral physicians or hospital abortion committees. Not surpri was overwhelmingly the more educated and affluent women w able to obtain legal abortions under these circumstances. In 1967, obstetrician Robert Hall pointed out that "hospital abortions are performed four times as often on the private services as on the ward services." He added, "The rate of therapeutic abortions per live births among white women in New York is 1 per 380; among nonwhites 1 per 2,000."[20] Even recently, the lack of access to legal abortion in different parts of the country and in different socioeconomic strata was reflected in a concentration of illegal abortion deaths among poor and minority women; between 1972 and 1974, the national rate was 12 times greater among nonwhite than among white women.[21]

The 1973 Supreme Court abortion decisions, and subsequent diffusion of abortion services to smaller communities, have resulted in dramatic decreases in cost. A medical procedure that cost $1,500 when abortion was illegal could be obtained for $500 in a hospital soon after the Supreme Court decisions and for $150 after free-standing (nonhospital) abortion clinics were established. These changes have helped to alleviate these former inequities—but they have not eliminated them.

The increased availability of safe, legal abortions has had other positive social consequences. These more lasting effects are difficult to measure, but some conclusions can be drawn. A series of studies show how legal abortion has led to a reduction in out-of-wedlock births;[22] many of these births are to teenagers. And the greater health risks to mother and infant resulting from early childbearing have been well documented.[23] The social and economic costs are staggering: teenage parents are more likely to drop out of school, to have more children, and to have more births that are closely spaced, out-of-wedlock, and unwanted than those who defer childbearing until their 20s. When they marry, teenage parents are more likely to end up in the divorce courts. Because they lack education, they are less likely to hold skilled, well-paying jobs, and their incomes and savings are permanently reduced; they are more likely to depend on public welfare.[24]

Not only do the children of teenage parents risk greater likelihood of damage at birth, but also there is evidence that they too are likely to suffer long-lasting educational and economic deprivation.[25] The web of negative health, social, and economic consequences associated with early childbearing suggests that the use of legal abortion by more than 400,000 teenagers annually to avoid unwanted births has benefited themselves, their children, and society.

The health benefits associated with legal abortion have been widely acknowledged. Concern has been expressed, however, that over the long run abortion will replace contraception as the fertility-control method of choice. The opposite in fact may be true; access to legal abortion may result in improved contraceptive practice, particularly among young women. For many of these women, the abortion facility is their first contact with a source of medical contraception. At present, contraceptive counseling, education, and prescriptions are offered by almost all abortion clinics and many hospital abortion programs. In 1976, clinics reported that more than 90 percent of their patients received contraceptive counseling and over half obtained contraceptive prescriptions or devices.[26]

Studies have confirmed that women are better—not worse—contraceptors after having an abortion. One follow-up study found that 93 percent of women contacted four months after their abortions were using birth control, compared to 59 percent using it before the abortion. More important, almost 80 percent were using highly effective methods, while previously only 15 percent had done so.[27]

The availability of legal abortion also has made possible the birth of healthy, normal children to couples at high risk of having congenitally abnormal babies. It makes feasible prenatal diagnosis of fetal defects, followed by abortion when indicated and desired by the parents. (This development is discussed more fully in Chapter 10.)

Because one-third of abortions are obtained by teenagers and half are obtained by childless women, great concern has been expressed that long-term complications will affect these women's ability to bear children in the future. Cervical incompetence, scar tissue from infection, and other trauma to the reproductive organs are among the complications that it has been suggested might lead to subsequent spontaneous abortion, prematurity, ectopic pregnancy, or infertility. In 1975, after examining all the available evidence, the IOM report noted that most of the studies that gave rise to these concerns were conducted outside the United States and were methodologically flawed. The report found no conclusive evidence linking legal abortion to subsequent infertility.[28]

Some recent studies by researchers in the United States, Europe, and Asia suggest, however, that induced abortion may increase somewhat the risk of problems in subsequent pregnancies. An association between two or more abortions and miscarriage, prematurity, and low-birth-weight babies in later pregnancies appears fairly certain. But the magnitude of this risk cannot yet be ascertained, and evidence as to the risk of one abortion is contradictory.

In studies conducted at the University of Washington Hospital in Seattle, the Boston Hospital for Women, and the state of Hawaii, for example, researchers found no link between previous induced abortion and various unfavorable outcomes of pregnancy, such as prematurity, stillbirth, ectopic pregnancy, complications of delivery, low birth weight, ill health, or congenital malformations in the newborn, or increased neonatal deaths. Teenagers and women who had never given birth did not appear to be at greater risk than other women as a result of abortion. But the Hawaii study showed an increased risk of miscarriage in the fourth and fifth months of pregnancy among women previously having induced abortions. On the other hand, the Seattle and Boston studies and another conducted in three New York City hospitals failed to confirm this finding.[29]

Two newer studies, one conducted in the United States the other undertaken by the World Health Organization (WHO) in eight countries, have reported an increased risk of unfavorable pregnancy outcomes among women having *repeat abortions*. The WHO study concluded that these women are significantly more likely to have premature deliveries or low-birth-weight infants than are women who have had one abortion or none. The study at Boston Hospital for Women found a higher incidence of first and second trimester miscarriages among women who have had repeat abortions but not among women who have had one abortion.[30]

Preliminary findings from several studies suggest that there may be an increased risk of subsequent second-trimester spontaneous abortions and premature births among women who have had only one abortion. These results are not definitive.[31] But they underscore the need for further research on the long-term consequences of abortion, as well as the urgent need to insure that adolescents who obtain their first abortions are told of the importance of avoiding subsequent ones—and are offered the contraceptive means to do so.

Concern has been persistently expressed in the popular media, as well as among some professionals, that women who obtain abortions will experience severe psychological disturbance. After an exhaustive review of the literature, the IOM report concluded:

> Emotional stress and pain are involved in the decision to obtain an abortion and there are strong emotions that surround the entire procedure. However, the mild depression or guilt feelings experienced by some women after an abortion appear to be only temporary . . . and to be outweighed by positive life changes and feelings of relief.[32]

An in-depth study, in 1975, of women who obtained abortions found, similarly, that while the decision to terminate a pregnancy is neither casually made nor easy, most view abortion as a difficult but necessary alternative to an unwanted baby. It concluded that, despite their ambivalence, most women manage to resolve their negative feelings soon after the procedure.[33]

The ambivalence theme is explored by journalist Linda Bird Francke in a book in which she interviews women from diverse backgrounds on their feelings about their abortions.[34] She finds that the circumstances prompting the abortion decision and the women's relationship with the male partner are the most powerful factors that shape her reaction to the abortion. Many women report that the abortion caused serious problems in their relationship with the man.

Although they could not be described as being clinically disturbed, some of these women experienced persistent feelings of guilt, loss, or depression. But others, particularly the younger women, found that their ability to handle the crisis was "a positive experience and a period of personal growth."[35] Author Francke concludes that the complex emotions that women experience when unexpectedly pregnant make it inevitable that abortion will produce "a period of great stress for every person involved. There is indecision, there is pain. There is regret and there is relief."[36]

References

1 Institute of Medicine, *Legalized Abortion and the Public Health*, Washington, D.C.: National Academy of Sciences, 1975.

2 M. S. Calderone (ed.), *Abortion in the United States*, New York: Hoeber-Harper, 1958, pp. 178–180.

3 L. Lader, *Abortion*, Boston: Beacon Press, 1966, pp. 64–67.

4 Ibid., pp. 67–69.

5 C. Tietze, *Induced Abortion 1979*, New York: The Population Council, 1979, p. 95.

6 Center for Disease Control, *Abortion Surveillance 1977*, p. 12; and W. Cates, personal communication, Jan. 21, 1980.

7 R. S. Kahan, L. D. Baker, and M. G. Freeman, "The Effect of Legalized Abortion on Morbidity Resulting from Criminal Abortion," *American Journal of Obstetrics and Gynecology*, 121:115, 1975.

8 P. Seward, C. A. Ballard, and A. Ulene, "The Effect of Legal Abortion on the Rate of Septic Abortion at a Large County Hospital," *American Journal of Obstetrics and Gynecology*, 115:3, 1973.

9 Institute of Medicine, op. cit., p. 65.

10 B. Barley, "Legalized Abortion," *Medical World News*, Jan. 23, 1978.

11   W. M. Hern and B. Andrikopoulis (eds.), *Abortion in the Seventies*, New York: National Abortion Federation, 1977, p. 75.

12   Center for Disease Control op. cit., p. 7, and W. Cates, personal communication, Jan. 21, 1980.

13   National Center for Health Statistics, *Monthly Vital Statistics Report, Final Mortality Statistics 1975*, **25**:11, Feb. 11, 1977; and Commission on Professional and Hospital Activities, 1974–75 PAS Hospital Mortality data, personal communication, June 27, 1978.

14   National Center for Health Statistics, *Monthly Vital Statistics Report, Final Mortality Statistics 1977*, May 11, 1979, p. 33.

15   Center for Disease Control, *Morbidity and Mortality Weekly Report*, Vol. 28, No. 26, July 6, 1979, p. 302.

16   Ibid., p. 7.

17   W. Cates, Jr., K. F. Schulz, D. A. Grimes, and C. W. Tyler, Jr., "The Effect of Delay and Method Choice on the Risk of Abortion Morbidity," *Family Planning Perspectives*, **9**:267, 1977.

18   C. Tietze, "Abortion on Request: Its Consequences for Population Trends and Public Health," in R. B. Sloane (ed.), *Abortion: Changing Views and Practice*, New York: Grune and Stratton, 1971.

19   S. Polgar and E. S. Fried, "The Bad Old Days: Clandestine Abortions Among the Poor in New York City Before Liberalization of the Abortion Law," *Family Planning Perspectives*, **8**:126, 1976.

20   R. E. Hall, "Abortion in American Hospitals," *American Journal of Public Health*, **57**:1934, 1967.

21   W. Cates, "Legal Abortion: Are American Black Women Healthier Because of It?", *Phylon*, **38**:267, 1977.

22   See J. Sklar and B. Berkov, "Abortion, Illegitimacy and the American Birth Rate," *Science*, **185**:909, 1974; K. E. Bauman, J. R. Udry, and R. W. Noyes, "The Relationship Between Legal Abortions and Birth Rates in Selected U.S. Cities," reported in *Family Planning Perspectives*, **7**:12, 1975; K. A. Moore and S. B. Caldwell, *Out-of-Wedlock Pregnancy and Childbearing*, Washington, D.C.: Urban Institute, 1976, and "The Effect of Government Policies on Out-of-Wedlock Sex and Pregnancy," *Family Planning Perspectives*, **9**:164, 1977; and North Carolina Department of Human Resources, *The Right to Abortion: Its Impact in North Carolina*, Raleigh, 1976, p. 9.

23   See The Alan Guttmacher Institute, *Eleven Million Teenagers: What Can Be Done About the Epidemic of Adolescent Pregnancies in the United States*, New York, 1976, pp 22–23; and J. Menken, "The Health and Social Consequences of Teenage Childrearing," *Family Planning Perspectives*, **4**:45, 1972.

24   See for example, F. F. Furstenberg, Jr., "The Social Consequences of Teenage Parenthood," *Family Planning Perspectives*, **8**:148, 1976; K. A. Moore, "Teenage Childbirth and Welfare Dependency," *Family Planning Perspectives*, **10**:223, 1978; T. J. Trusell, "Economic Consequences of Teenage Childbearing," *Family Planning Perspectives*, **8**:184, 1976; and J. J. Card and L. L. Wise, "Teenage

Mothers and Teenage Fathers: The Impact of Early Childbearing on the Parents' Personal and Professional Lives," *Family Planning Perspectives*, **10**:199, 1978.

25 W. Baldwin and V. S. Cain, "The Children of Teenage Parents," *Family Planning Perspectives*, **12**:34, 1980.

26 Data from AGI Special Abortion Provider Survey, 1976–1977.

27 E. W. Freeman, "Abortion: Subjective Attitudes and Feelings," *Family Planning Perspectives*, **10**:150, 1978.

28 Institute of Medicine, op. cit., pp. 60–63.

29 See "5 Studies: No Apparent Harmful Effect from Legal Abortion on Later Pregnancies; D & C Possible Exception," *Family Planning Perspectives* **10**:34, 1978; J. R. Daling and I. Emanuel, "Induced Abortion and Subsequent Outcome of Pregnancy in a Series of American Women," *New England Journal of Medicine*, **297**:1241, 1977; S. C. Schoenbaum, R. R. Monson, P. G. Stubblefield, P. D. Darney, and K. J. Ryan, "Outcome of the Next Delivery After an Induced Abortion," *American Journal of Obstetrics and Gynecology* (forthcoming); C. S. Chung, P. G. Steinhoff, M. P. Mi, and R. G. Smith, "Long-Term Effects of Induced Abortion," paper presented at the 1977 annual meeting of the American Public Health Association, Washington, D.C.; T. H. Lean, C. J. R. Hogue, and J. Wood, "Low Birth Weight After Induced Abortion in Singapore," paper presented at the 1977 annual meeting of the American Public Health Association, Washington, D. C.; and J. Kline, Z. Stein, M. Susser, and D. Warburton, "Induced Abortion and Spontaneous Abortion: No Connection?", *American Journal of Epidemiology*, **107**:209, 1978; S. Harlap, P. Shiono, S. Ramcharan, H. Berendes, and F. Pellegrin, "A Prospective Study of Spontaneous Fetal Losses After Induced Abortions," *The New England Journal of Medicine*, **301**:677, 1977.

30 "Repeated Abortions Increase Risk of Miscarriage, Premature Births and Low-Birth-Weight Babies," *Family Planning Perspectives*, **11**:39, 1979; A. Levin, S. C. Schoenbaum, R. R. Monson, and K. J. Ryan, "Induced Abortion and the Risk of Spontaneous Abortion," paper presented at the 1978 annual meeting of the American Public Health Association, Los Angeles; and World Health Organization, *Special Programme of Research, Development and Research Training in Human Reproduction: Seventh Annual Report*, Geneva, November 1978.

31 D. Maine, "Does Abortion Affect Later Pregnancies?" *Family Planning Perspectives*, **11**:98, 1979.

32 Institute of Medicine, op. cit., pp. 98–99.

33 E. W. Freeman, op. cit.

34 L. B. Francke, *The Ambivalence of Abortion*, New York: Random House, 1978.

35 Ibid., p. 63.

36 Ibid., p. 11.

CHAPTER THREE
The Mainstream Abdicates

The Supreme Court's 1973 rulings freed women to choose, in accordance with their own beliefs and values, either of two means of coping with pregnancy: delivery at term or abortion. Both are medical procedures, and their availability is legally and in practice controlled by doctors. The Court thus created a decision-making process in which women and the medical profession are coparticipants, and implementation of a woman's choice hinges on her ability to find a doctor or health institution willing to perform the abortion.

The Court could hardly have ruled otherwise, given the small but real risk of injury and death associated with both childbearing and early termination of pregnancy. Abortion, if not childbirth, remains a surgical procedure and requires knowledge and skills that are almost exclusively within the medical domain. Most babies are delivered by doctors, and doctors perform almost all legal abortions.

Implicit in the Court's 1973 decisions is the assumption that doctors and health institutions—except those with religious objections—would respond to women's need for safe termination of pregnancies in a manner that reflects society's delegation to doctors of virtual monopoly control over the delivery of health services. Any other assumption would have made the Court's delineation of women's newly defined constitutional right a mockery. If the justices had expected most doctors to refuse to meet this need, its assignment to the profession of coresponsibility for abortion would have been a Catch-22.

But the anticipated, responsible response has not been forthcoming from the mainstream of American medicine in the years since the

Court's ruling. The many legal abortions that have been obtained since then have, of course, been performed by doctors, in shared health facilities or in their private offices. Yet only a minority of all American doctors, about half of the obstetrician-gynecologists who specialize in women's health care, and only a few non-Catholic hospitals provide abortion services.[1]

The medical mainstream, in effect, copped out. By doing so, it has produced great disparities in the availability of abortion services in many parts of the country. This has led to the creation of an entirely new system of specialized clinics, which now account for most U.S. abortions.

The best evidence of mainstream medicine's dereliction of responsibility comes from questionnaires sent annually to 7,000 hospitals by the American Hospital Association (AHA),[2] which ask whether abortion services are provided, and from annual surveys of all abortion providers, including those identified by AHA, and by The Alan Guttmacher Institute (AGI). These studies include privately run non-Catholic general hospitals and public hospitals owned and operated by federal, state, or local governmental bodies. Catholic hospitals are excluded from this discussion because they are not considered to be potential abortion resources.[3]

In 1977 and the first quarter of 1978, at least *one* abortion was performed in 1,661 non-Catholic short-term general hospitals—1,251 private and 410 public institutions—all of which we call *provider hospitals*, even though almost 59 percent of them performed, on average, less than two procedures weekly. These provider hospitals represent only 31 percent of all U.S. non-Catholic short-term general hospitals. The remaining private and public hospitals reported no abortions.

The provider hospitals accounted for 393,000 abortions during 1977, 30 percent of the national total. An additional 879,000, or 66 percent, were performed in 533 specialized clinics. There were 51,000 abortions, or 4 percent of the total, performed by 522 doctors in their private offices. By the first quarter of 1978, 69 percent of all abortions were performed in clinics, only 27 percent in hospitals. The hospital proportion declined substantially in each year after the Supreme Court decisions.

In many localities, the role of hospitals in the provision of abortions varied significantly from the national average. For example, 47 percent of non-Catholic hospitals in metropolitan areas performed at least one abortion, compared to only 16 percent in nonmetropolitan areas. *No* hospitals in North Dakota or South Dakota reported any abortions in 1977-78. In 19 principally Midwestern and Southern states, fewer than 15 percent of non-Catholic hospitals performed any abortions. In 61 metropolitan areas, in which there are 2.4 million women of reproductive age, there were no public *or* private hospital providers of abortion services.

The failure of 7 in 10 U.S. non-Catholic hospitals to respond appropriately to the Supreme Court's decisions is extraordinary and shocking. The hospitals' grudging response to legalization was predictable, given their performance in the era of restrictive abortion laws: the growing use of hospital abortion committees, after 1945, to evaluate abortion requests, in theory made the procedure more equitably available; judgment now was vested in several senior medical staff members, rather than in two individual doctors as formerly was the case. In fact, the opposite occurred: it is estimated that at least 30,000 hospital abortions were performed in 1940. But by the mid-1960s, there were only about 8,000 annually.[4]

The arbitrary and discriminatory manner in which the abortion committees worked has been well documented.[5] The committees used both formal and informal quotas and often based their decisions primarily on committee members' personal or religious views. At many hospitals, a low abortion rate was sought; one physician from Philadelphia remarked, "The fewer abortions, the better we look."[6] In 1965, Carl Goldmark, Jr., president of the New York County Medical Society, summed up the committees' function when he said: "The abortion committee is just something for a hospital to hide behind."[7]

Several studies have attempted to explain the difference in hospitals' provision of various health services. Larger hospitals with teaching affiliations, and those that offer more types of care generally, have been shown to be more likely to adopt new techniques and services.[8] A pioneer research effort, using diverse data sources from the entire state of Maryland, recently shed more light on the determinants of hospitals' abortion policies. The investigators found that organizational and structural factors and the attitudes of the medical staff members together account for three-quarters of the variation in hospitals' provision of abortion services. The psychosocial attitudes of staff obstetricians toward fertility control and abortion explain almost 30 percent of the variation between hospitals, in terms of the numbers of abortions performed. The study concludes: "Unless there is a major institutional commitment to abortion services . . . it is the attitudes and feelings of these individual private physicians that ultimately determine the hospital's role in abortion-service provision."[9]

These findings help explain the fact that hospital abortion services are concentrated in large urban hospitals, which more commonly have made such an institutional commitment. Yet it is in the public and private general hospitals in the smaller communities throughout the nation that hospital abortion services are most needed—and are most lacking. The Maryland study confirms that these hospitals' failure to offer abortions is largely attributable to the attitudes and practices of their staff doctors.

Hospitals are the only institutions in the U.S. health system with sufficiently broad geographical coverage to ensure the availability of frequently utilized services in all parts of the nation. There are of course important differences between private and public hospitals. Private hospitals, for the most part, as the workshops of doctors in private practice, typically admit patients at the request of their doctors. Public hospitals, on the other hand, are created and owned by government bodies to ensure that services are available to "poor and unsponsored patients," for whom these hospitals "stand today as the principal source of (medical) services."[10]

The failure of a public hospital to provide abortions, while it also may result from physicians' unwillingness to perform abortions, sometimes reflects as well an explicit policy of the hospital's officials or governing body. Patients who depend on the public hospital for their medical care usually are poor, lacking resources to obtain abortions elsewhere.

Several studies have demonstrated clearly that the burden of travel is an important determinant of whether a woman will or will not obtain a legal abortion. Information on the residence of women obtaining abortions available from 17 states indicates the following:

Of pregnant women who lived in counties with identified abortion facilities, 29 percent obtained abortions in 1976 compared to 12 percent in counties without abortion facilities. The same relationships hold when metropolitan and nonmetropolitan counties are examined separately: 28 percent of pregnant women living in metropolitan counties and 20 percent in rural counties with providers had abortions, compared to only 15 percent in metropolitan counties and 11 percent in nonmetropolitan counties without abortion facilities.[11]

Researchers from HEW's Center for Disease Control (CDC) demonstrated this relationship using 1974 data for Georgia's 159 counties, when virtually all of the state's abortion facilities were located in or near Atlanta. For every 10 miles of distance from Atlanta, they found white women had six fewer abortions per 1,000 live births and black women had almost eight fewer. White women living 100 miles from the city thus had 63 fewer abortions per 1,000 live births, black women 79 fewer. Increasing distances particularly discouraged teenagers, whose abortion rates fell by 11 per 1,000 live births for each additional 10-mile distance they lived from Atlanta.[12]

In a remarkably short time after the 1973 ruling, millions of American women discovered that they could not obtain an abortion from their regular doctor or community hospital. For many, this proved to be only a minor obstacle, because they also learned quickly that competent early abortions can be obtained at specialized nonhospital abortion clinics. In the wake of the hospital default, some 533 of these free-standing abortion clinics had been established by early 1978. Collectively they now perform more than two-thirds of U.S. abortions.[13]

Free-standing abortion clinics were nonexistent before 1970. They now form a network for the delivery of ambulatory surgery that is entirely separate from mainstream health care institutions—except that they take referrals from nonprovider doctors and hospitals and almost all have back-up arrangements with hospitals to admit their patients when medical emergencies arise.[14]

More than one-quarter of these clinics are operated by nonprofit organizations, women's health groups, Planned Parenthood affiliates, or other voluntary organizations. The rest are owned and operated on a profit-making basis by physicians, individuals, or corporations. Despite these structural differences, most clinics offer services of comparable quality, at generally low fees, with a minimum of bureaucratic delay. They also have an admirable record of safety in carrying out millions of procedures.[15] Close to half of these clinics already are licensed by a state or local health agency.

As specialists, these clinics depend on large case loads; half perform 1,000 or more abortions a year. They are found in diverse places—office buildings, storefronts, and professional office complexes. Owners and managers have taken pains to make these facilities attractive. The medical personnel who perform the abortions usually are physicians in private practice; some are residents from nearby hospitals who earn extra money "moonlighting" in the clinics at night or on weekends. The incentives include adequate—or even more than adequate—remuneration and, for some clinic doctors, fulfillment of a deeply felt commitment to meeting women's needs.

The clinics usually employ trained counselors to provide information and emotional support to their clients, although in practice most women who come to an abortion clinic already have decided to terminate their pregnancies. Contraceptive counseling and prescriptions also are offered by most clinics.

The free-standing clinics offer primarily first-trimester abortions on an ambulatory basis using suction curettage. About one-fourth of clinics do some second-trimester operations, on fewer than 5 percent of their patients—usually by means of dilatation and evacuation procedures in the 13th to 15th week of pregnancy.

Almost all clinics offer—and most require—pregnancy tests, pelvic examinations, standard presurgical laboratory tests, and Rh screening *before* the abortion is performed. Two-thirds of clinics perform abortions under local anesthesia only. About one-quarter use both general and local anesthesia, while less than 10 percent use general only. Almost all ask patients to return within six weeks for a checkup. Most offer contraceptive prescriptions and supplies at the time of the abortion and at the follow-up visit.

The majority of clinics do not require teenage patients to have the consent of their parents—although most encourage them to involve a parent in the decision to end the pregnancy.

Clinics usually are listed in the telephone book. About half advertise in the press. Referrals are received from community agencies, schools and colleges, former patients, and private physicians—but few come from hospitals and public-welfare agencies.

A clinic abortion typically takes three to five hours. Virtually all clinics require payment at the time the procedure is done, although most say they allow deferred payments or reduce charges in some cases. This practice may have increased in states that have restricted public funding of abortion.

Most clinics charge a flat fee, which includes payment for the doctor, pregnancy and lab tests, anesthesia, Rh immuneglobulin if indicated, contraceptive prescription, sometimes the contraceptives themselves, and the follow-up visit. In half the clinics, the fee is $185 or less. In almost all it is less than $235.

These services differentiate the abortion clinics from the many hospitals that offer little in the way of counseling. Another difference is that most clinics, unlike hospitals, schedule patients on weekends and at other times that meet women's convenience.

Hospital abortion services differ from clinics' services in several other respects. Very few hospitals have an organized abortion service program; abortions are treated like other surgical procedures. Some hospitals place abortion patients in obstetrical units, which can be painfully difficult for everyone involved. Occasionally abortion patients in hospitals encounter rude treatment from staff opposed to abortion. More importantly, accessibility to services is limited because most hospitals do not make the existence of their services widely known and require patients to be admitted by a private physician.

Clinic fees are markedly lower than hospital charges: for an outpatient first-trimester abortion, the average hospital charge in 1976 was $250, exclusive of the $100-to-$300 fee for the doctor who performed the operation. Only about half of all hospital providers offer outpatient abortions—and inpatient procedures are far more costly.

In view of the cost differential, it is not surprising that clinic patients tend to be young; about 330,000 were estimated to be below age 20 in 1977. Almost nine-tenths of all U.S. teenagers who obtain abortions use these clinics. About 40 percent come from a different community or state from the one in which the clinic is located.

The establishment of this new service has not been without difficulties. Although abuses in clinic referral arrangements, medical care practices, and charges were more common just after legalization—when desperate women in need of abortions were particularly vulnerable to exploitation by unscrupulous operators—some big-city clinics that serve significant numbers of poor and nonresident women still offer substandard care and engage in shady and dishonest practices. These abuses, while infrequent, reflect the failure of mainstream public and private health care institutions and agencies to participate in the provision and regulation of abortion services. Some of this failure stems from uncertainty over exactly what the 1973 decisions permit, but it results primarily from the desire of health professionals and public officials to avoid the abortion issue to the extent possible.

The emergence of the free-standing clinics nevertheless is regarded as a salutary development by many people who believe that hospitals, with their impersonality and lack of supportive services, are a poor setting for a sensitive service like abortion. There is no doubt that the clinics make it possible for many women to obtain safe abortions with less difficulty and at lower cost than in hospitals. But the 533 clinics do not fully make up for the hospitals' default—nor could they.

Half of all clinics are found in the 30 largest metropolitan areas.[16] This concentration is easy to understand: a free-standing clinic of any type is economically feasible only when it has a large population from which to draw its case load. The number of specialized abortion clinics has increased since 1973 and may continue to increase somewhat in the future. But there are economic limits on the number that can be opened.

In smaller cities and rural areas, an increasing number of doctors are performing early abortions in their offices, and some see this as a possible solution to the lack of hospital-abortion provision outside cities. In 1977-78, only 4 percent of abortions were performed in private doctors' offices nationwide but in nonmetropolitan areas over 13 percent were.[17] This potential alternative is problematic, however, on several counts: first, some medical experts question the wisdom of offering even a relatively simple surgical procedure like abortion in a private office where there is little special equipment. Second, the doctors involved tend primarily to serve their regular patients and thus are unknown as an abortion resource to other women and doctors in their area. Last, it still is not known whether enough doctors will be willing to provide abortions in their offices to constitute a significant service resource.

Geography aside, clinics cannot entirely compensate for the hospitals' default, because women who use them are different from women who use hospitals. The clinics' clients are more likely to be middle class. Prior to the restriction of public funding for abortion, about one woman in four who obtained an abortion was eligible for government assistance through Medicaid. Yet fewer than one-third of these women obtained their abortions in clinics, and most clinics report only 10 to 15 percent of their patients were Medicaid recipients.[18] In addition, although clinics increasingly are performing some second-trimester procedures, most women needing second-trimester abortions continue to obtain them in hospitals. These women are disproportionately young and poor and therefore are particularly disadvantaged by lack of local hospital facilities.

The reasons low-income women tend to be underrepresented in the case load of the free-standing clinics remain unclear in the absence of a definitive study. What is known is that few clinics are located in low-income neighborhoods, yet geographical accessibility often is an important factor in poor people's utilization of medical care.[19] The poor also tend to seek care from familiar providers; even after the introduction of Medicaid, for example, many of them continued to seek much of their medical care from the hospital outpatient clinics they long had relied on, even though their Medicaid cards entitled them to services from private physicians.[20]

Ironically, one factor that undoubtedly helped establish this pattern in the past was the ability of Medicaid-eligible women to obtain hospital abortions. Unlike many private health-insurance plans, Medicaid pays for most fertility-related health services. Since Medicaid covered the bill, these women were not deterred by the sometimes much higher cost of hospital abortions, as more affluent women were. This means, of course, that the congressional restriction of Medicaid abortion funding was a particularly severe blow to poor women relying on hospitals for abortions.

The clinics thus have compensated for the scarcity of hospital services primarily for middle-class women needing first-trimester abortions, who live in or can travel to the cities where these clinics are located. They are much less likely to serve poor women, even those who live in these cities.

Public hospitals provide medical care primarily to the poor, and many poor people have no alternative source of surgical care. More than one-fourth of all U.S. births are delivered in public hospitals.[21] A large proportion of poor women of reproductive age thus are in contact with and dependent on public hospitals.

After 1973, it would have been reasonable for these women to expect these institutions to offer abortions. But half of public-hospital births occur in hospitals that provide *no* abortions. In almost all states, the percentage of all deliveries in public hospitals is two to three times higher than the percentage of all abortions.[22]

Whether a public hospital has a legal obligation to provide at least some abortions is uncertain, as the result of a 1977 Supreme Court decision that a public hospital is not required to pay for "nontherapeutic" abortions.[23] Whatever the legal situation, however, public hospitals still are medical institutions; their *professional* responsibility is to provide health services in accordance with professional criteria.

There is considerable evidence that political and religious criteria—not professional ones—are the major reasons for the abortion ban in many public hospitals. Abortion policies often are decided behind closed doors. In some communities, however, these decisions have provoked public controversies. Bitter confrontations have occurred when there has been unequivocal evidence of political or religious interference with the publicly operated health system.

One such instance was the case before the Supreme Court in 1977, which involved the two public hospitals in St. Louis. According the the *National Catholic Reporter*, the Catholic archdiocese there was "more mobilized as a political force on the abortion issue" than anywhere else. Both city hospitals prohibited abortions except to save the mother from grave physical injury or death. In fact, no abortions at all were performed in these hospitals after the 1973 Court decisions, because Mayor John H. Poelker had so ordered.

The U.S. Court of Appeals for the Eighth Circuit found that "the only reason advanced by the mayor . . . was his own personal conviction that abortion was tantamount to murder."

The situation was complicated by the fact that one of the two hospitals is wholly staffed by doctors and residents from St. Louis University Medical School, a Jesuit institution. City officials asserted that none of the staff doctors were willing to perform abortions, which is hardly surprising in view of the school's policy, stated in the faculty manual, that tenured appointments and nontenured contracts may be terminated if a "grave offense" is committed against any "well-established principle of Catholic morality." The obvious remedy—to hire doctors not associated with the medical school—seemed to elude city officials until the federal Circuit Court of Appeals ordered them to do so.[24] But the Supreme Court overruled the Appeals Court, saying that the city was not required to provide funds for nontherapeutic abortions.

In Milwaukee, meanwhile, Dr. Richard Mattingly, chairman of obstetrics and gynecology at the Milwaukee County General Hospital, was similarly unembarrassed to report that he could not find one doctor who was willing to perform abortions, although Wisconsin has 242 specialists who are Fellows of the American College of Obstetricians and Gynecologists among its thousands of doctors.[25] The hospital is the only public facility in an area that serves 25,000 reproductive-aged women who are poor enough to qualify for Medicaid coverage. It also is a teaching hospital of the Medical College of Wisconsin, now a secular institution but until 1967 a part of Marquette University, a Catholic school.

Under the hospital's rules, an abortion could be performed only to save a woman's life. But none were performed for two years after the Supreme Court's 1973 abortion rulings. In that period, hospital and county officials repeatedly resisted federal court orders to change the policy. The county even agreed, under court pressure, to pay for abortions in private hospitals while it sought a doctor willing to do them in the county hospital. The quest proved futile, albeit doctors at three private hospitals and five clinics in Milwaukee regularly perform abortions.

"We're like Diogenes, looking for an honest man with a lantern," John R. Devitt, assistant county-corporation counsel, told reporters. "We're still looking for a doctor. They're asking us to try to be a magician and pull a doctor out of a hat like a rabbit."[26]

Corporation counsel Devitt acknowledged that he had discussed the case with two priests from the Catholic archdiocese, who had urged him to continue representing the county in the litigation because if he withdrew he might be replaced by someone less fervently opposed to abortion.[27] A willing doctor was not found until just four days before a special fact finder, appointed by a federal judge, recommended that fines of $123,600 be levied against Dr. Mattingly and nine other hospital and county officials for contempt of court. The fact finder also recommended that the hospital's ob/gyn department be shut down if the abortion ban continued.[28]

Episodes like these have not contributed to public confidence that public-hospital policy decisions on abortion are based on professional medical considerations rather than on political expediency or sectarian belief. Before the restriction of Medicaid abortion funding, four out of five Medicaid abortions occurred in private facilities.[29] After the restrictions, many, if not most, of these women became dependent upon virtually nonexistent public hospital services if they were to obtain legal abortions at all. But in its narrow and perfunctory unsigned opinion of 1977 that a public hospital is not obligated to pay for "nontherapeutic abortions," the court left open the question of whether a public hospital, financed by taxes from citizens of all faiths, constitutionally can prohibit abortions that doctors determine to be necessary for the health and well-being of poor women who seek them. It is highly likely that the Court will be called on to address this question directly through future litigation.

References

1 Data on the proportion of all obstetricians and gynecologists who perform any abortions are difficult to find. The few available sources suggest that between 45 and 60 percent perform abortions. A 1976 AGI survey of a small national sample (N=1628) of ob-gyns found that 9 percent perform abortions in their own offices and an additional 36 percent perform them in hospitals only (J. D. Forrest, E. Sullivan, and C. Tietze. *Abortion 1976–1977, Need and Services in the United States, Each State, and Metropolitan Area*, New York: The Alan Guttmacher Institute, 1979). On the other hand, a Maryland survey in 1975–76 found that 57 percent of the state's obstetricians perform abortions (C. A. Nathanson and M. H. Becker, "The Influence of Physicians' Attitudes on Abortion Performance, Patient Management and Professional Fees," *Family Planning Perspectives*, 9:158, 1977); and a Connecticut study found that 61 percent of the state's ob-gyns performed abortions in 1974 (G. Affleck and A. Thomas, "Connecticut Ob-Gyns on Abortion," *Connecticut Medicine*, 42:179, 1978).

2 The AHA's survey is reported each year in the association's annual *Guide to the Health Care Field*, usually published in August.

3 The AGI studies are reported in: *Provisional Estimates of Abortion Need and Services . . .*; C. Tietze, F. S. Jaffe, E. Weinstock, and J. G. Dryfoos, *Abortion 1974–1975: Need and Services in the United States, Each State and Metropolitan Area*, New York: Alan Guttmacher Institute, 1976; E. Sullivan, C. Tietze and J. G. Dryfoos, "Legal Abortion in the United States, 1975–1976," *Family Planning Perspectives*, 9:116, 1977; and *Abortion 1977–1979*. The specific data in the chapter on the number of abortions and abortion providers are drawn from these studies for the respective years.

4 L. Lader, *Abortion*, Boston: Beacon Press, 1966, p. 24.

5 See, for example, A. Stone, "The Psychiatric Dilemma," *Human Sexuality* 4:29, 32, 1970; B. Sarvis and H. Rodman, *The Abortion Controversy*, New York: Columbia University Press, 1974, pp. 35–40, and numerous studies cited in L. Lader, op. cit., pp. 24–31.

6 S. Boulas, R. H. Preucel, and J. H. Moore, "Therapeutic Abortion," *Obstetrics and Gynecology*, 19:222, 1962.

7 L. Lader, op. cit., p. 26.

8 See, for example, A. D. Kaluzny, J. H. Glasser, J. T. Gentry, and J. Sprague, "Diffusion of Innovative Health Care Services in the United States: A Study of Hospitals," *Medical Care* 8:474, 1970; M. M. Rosner, "Economic Determinants of Organizational Innovation," *Administrative Science Quarterly*, 12:614, 1965; A. D. Kaluzny, J. E. Veney, and J. T. Gentry, "Innovation of Health Services: A

Comparative Study of Hospitals and Health Departments," *Milbank Memorial Fund Quarterly,* **52:**51, 1974; and M. K. Moch and E. V. Morse, "Size, Centralization and Adoption of Innovations," *American Sociological Review,* **42:**716, 1977.

9   C. A. Nathanson and M. H. Becker, "Obstetricians' Attitudes and Hospital Abortion Services," *Family Planning Perspectives,* **12:**26, 1980.

10   A. E. Hess, "The Future of Publicly Owned Hospitals," *HCFA Forum,* January/February 1978.

11   This analysis is derived from data on 1976 abortions by residence and occurrence published by state health departments in Georgia, Illinois, Indiana, Kansas, Maryland, Minnesota, Missouri, Montana, Nebraska, Vermont, and Virginia.

12   J. D. Shelton, E. A. Brann, and K. F. Schulz, "Abortion Utilization: Does Travel Distance Matter?", *Family Planning Perspectives,* **8:**260, 1976.

13   *Abortion, 1977–1979.*

14   Data in this section on nonhospital abortion clinics are derived from a sample survey of abortion provider agencies conducted by AGI in 1976–1977 (hereinafter referred to as AGI Abortion Provider Survey). This survey obtained information on the practices of different types of agencies and the characteristics of the patients they serve.

15   A careful follow-up of all reported abortion-related deaths in the United States in 1974–1975 conducted by the Center for Disease Control showed that the death-to-case rates per 100,000 abortions were 1.1 in hospitals and 1.0 in nonhospital clinics. D. A. Grimes, W. Cates, and C. W. Tyler, Jr., "Comparative Risk of Death from Legally Induced Abortion in Hospitals and Nonhospital Facilities," *Obstetrics and Gynecology,***51:**323, 1978.

16   *Abortion, 1976–1977.*

17   Ibid.

18   R. Lincoln, B. Döring-Bradley, B. L. Lindheim, and M. A. Cotterill, "The Court, the Congress and the President: Turning Back the Clock on the Pregnant Poor," *Family Planning Perspectives,* **9:**207, 1977.

19   See, for example, J. E. Weiss and M. R. Greenlick, "Determinants of Medical Care Utilization: The Effect of Social Class and Distance on Contacts with the Medical Care System," *Medical Care,* **8:**456, 1970.

20   K. Davis, "A Decade of Policy Development in Providing Health Care for Low-Income Families," in R. Haveman (ed.), *A Decade of Federal Anti-Poverty Programs,* New York: Academic Press, 1977, pp. 204–206; and S. B. Thacker, E. J. Salber, C. Osborne, and L. H. Mulbaier, "Primary Health Care in an Academic Medical Center," *American Journal of Public Health,* **9:**853, 1978.

21   Derived from AHA hospital survey tape.

22   Ibid.

23   *Poelker et al. v. Doe, U.S. Law Week,* **45:**4794, June 21, 1977.

24   "Public Hospitals Ordered to Provide Abortion Services," *Family Planning/Population Reporter,* **4:**48, 1975.

25 For a discussion of this episode, see L. Ambrose, "The Milwaukee Story: A Public Hospital's Resistance to the Supreme Court Abortion Rulings," *Family Planning/Population Reporter*, **4**:68, 1975.

26 "County Stalled in Doctor Quest," *Milwaukee Journal*, Nov. 28, 1974.

27 Ibid.

28 "Stiff Fine Urged for Abortion Delay," *Milwaukee Journal*, Mar. 17, 1975.

29 R. Lincoln, B. Döring-Bradley, B. L. Lindheim, and M. A. Cotterill, op. cit.

CHAPTER FOUR

The Leadership Equivocates

Decisions are not made by hospitals. They are made by the people who run the hospitals and the physicians who practice there, who are influenced in turn by many other people and organizations. It would be a mistake therefore, to view the hospitals' default on abortion as solely the hospitals' responsibility.

Hospitals in the United States are part of a complex health infrastructure, in which decision-making is shared by national, state, and local agencies, and are included in both the private and governmental sectors. Some elements in this system are professional organizations and institutions—medical and specialist societies, hospital associations, schools for health professions. Others are regulatory bodies, public-health departments, hospital boards, planning agencies, and peer-review organizations. The political establishment—from Congress to the city councils—plays a role, as do Blue Cross, Medicaid, and other sources that pay a large part of America's health bill.

Each agency has its ascribed and perceived role. Whether this diffuse network works efficiently is a question that is beyond the scope of this study. But the fact that it exists and has influenced the availability of health services, including abortion, cannot be disputed. Yet the picture that emerges from a review of the health-system's response in the period following the Supreme Court's 1973 abortion decisions is one of indifference and neglect.[1]

As an example, of 36 major national professional associations in health and related fields that responded to a 1976 survey, 22 reported taking *no* action at all on abortion following the Supreme Court's ruling: no policy statements were adopted, guidelines or standards formulated, educational programs conducted for members, or testimony offered before governmental bodies.[2] Groups that ignored the subject in its entirety include the Association of American Medical Colleges, National Health Council, Joint Commission on Accreditation of Hospitals, National League for Nursing, American Association for Hospital Planning, Health Insurance Association of America, National Board of Medical Examiners, and the American Public Welfare Association. Yet many policy issues related to abortion fall squarely in the jurisdictions of these organizations.

The lack of hospital abortion services was one such issue. Others included abortion-education and -training programs for health professionals, referral needs, program standards, private-financing arrangements, public information and education, the integration of abortion into existing health-delivery programs, and the persistent issue of public funding to meet the needs of welfare recipients.

Nevertheless, these 22 organizations did not find anything in abortion legalization that they deemed worthy of comment, nor did they find it necessary or desirable to modify their own programs in any way to meet the changed situation. The medical examiners' board, for example, explained that it takes no positions on issues other than "programs of evaluation of competence in medicine." It thereby sidestepped the question of how doctors' competence in performing abortions can be evaluated if not through licensing and specialty examinations.

Some national professional organizations did react. Their decisions ranged from the narrowest expressions of territorial imperative to serious efforts to set forth broader professional approaches to the new situation. Less than three weeks after the Supreme Court ruled, for example, the American Hospital Association (AHA) voted to recommend legislation that would give member hospitals, as well as individual professionals, a right of conscience to refuse to participate in abortions.[3] Neither then, nor subsequently, has AHA addressed other aspects of the subject, such as the professional responsibility of nonsectarian hospitals to provide the abortions that community residents of all creeds require.

The American Nurses Association, which had supported abortion reform in 1968, did better. It sponsored a panel at its 1974 convention that dealt with the differing perspectives of nurses and abortion patients—an important issue that affects the quality of nursing care. The American College Health Association recommended, in October 1973, that abortion counseling and referral be made a part of all university health services.[4]

The American Medical Association (AMA), in June 1973, urged that abortions be performed only by licensed physicians in accredited hospitals and that physicians with conscientious objections to abortion be free to withdraw from these cases.[5] The AMA's only other official action on abortion was to answer a request for information during the 1977 congressional debate on the Hyde amendment to curtail Medicaid payments for abortion. In response to a query from Senator Edward Brooke, the AMA's executive vice president, James H. Sammons, replied for the organization, "The determination of whether or not a proper medical procedure should be performed should not be defined by Congress."[6]

The consortium of professional medical organizations responsible for training and certifying the next generation of physicians has responded half-heartedly to abortion legalization. Although certification requirements for obstetrician-gynecologists specifically include abortion as a subject to be covered in examinations and clinical experience, there is no formal check on whether residents actually receive this training. A 1976 survey of ob-gyn residency programs revealed that between 20 and 50 percent of obstetrics residents receive no clinical experience in abortion, despite the fact that it is likely to be the operation they most often will be called upon to perform.[7]

The most comprehensive responses have come from the American Public Health Association (APHA) and the American College of Obstetricians and Gynecologists (ACOG), among the health professional organizations, and from the National Association of Social Workers (NASW). In 1973 APHA adopted a *Comprehensive Program Guide for Abortion Services* that covered most aspects of abortion that might be of concern to public-health professionals; it covered public education, referral, counseling and consent, postabortal contraceptive prescriptions, safety factors, and standards to govern the performance of these medical procedures. The *Guide* stresses the need for full implementation of the Supreme Court's decisions "in order to make abortion readily available in the community of residence of all patients in need of the service." It also points out the professional obligation of physicians and hospitals who do not perform abortions to refer patients to others who do, "as with any other specialized medical services."[8]

In subsequent years, APHA's annual meetings have featured panels on abortion research. The organization has consistently taken positions on abortion-policy issues. After the restriction of public funding for abortion, APHA convened researchers to discuss ways to systematically evaluate the public-health impact of the policy change and made public funding of abortion one of its priority "action issues." The APHA's president was a featured speaker at the 1977 Washington, D.C., memorial service for a Texas woman who, refused a Medicaid abortion, died after an illegal procedure. In 1978, APHA sponsored a task force on abortion services to update and expand its 1973 *Guide*. In 1979, it strongly endorsed women's right to obtain abortions through the 24th week of pregnancy and affirmed that late abortions were safe if clinicians were properly trained in later abortion techniques.

The ACOG, which already was on record as favoring abortion reform, issued an official statement a few weeks after the Supreme Court acted, urging that first-trimester abortions be performed either in hospitals or in licensed clinics with hospital backup. The ob-gyn organization outlined its view of the equipment, procedures, and facilities that the clinics should provide.[9]

While one might differ with some of the specific provisions of the ACOG statement, it was a serious effort to deal with the medical dimensions of abortion; the statement was incorporated into the 1974 edition of ACOG's *Standards for Obstetric-Gynecologic Services*. The college also has issued technical bulletins on prostaglandins, saline, and other abortion techniques and presented educational programs at its meetings. It issued a statement defending Kenneth Edelin, the Boston obstetrician accused of manslaughter in 1975 after he performed a late second-trimester abortion. During congressional debate on the Hyde amendment in 1977, ACOG vigorously opposed "the interposition of a third party—the government—without medical expertise between the patient and her attending physician."[10]

The social workers, through NASW—which also had supported abortion reform prior to the Court decisions—adopted a new policy statement in 1975 that stressed their belief that each woman be free to choose abortion in accordance with her personal values. It called for public programs to pay for abortions for poor women wishing them[11] and opposed passage of the Hyde amendment.

Like the national organizations, the reactions of state professional societies also were mixed. Prior to 1973, 19 state medical societies had voted to recommend liberalization of their state's abortion laws. Following the Court's decisions, 17 state societies—out of 42 survey respondents—formulated guidelines or adopted statements on the new situation. Six adopted the ACOG guidelines; others formulated their own. Several societies, including those in Maryland, Michigan, and Washington, worked with their state health departments or legislators in drafting abortion guidelines and regulatory legislation. But only four state societies conducted professional educational programs or developed material on abortion for their members.

The Maryland medical society prepared detailed guidelines covering doctors' responsibilities and conditions for the performance of outpatient abortions. Its officials testified in the legislature against restrictive abortion bills. The Michigan State Medical Society went further, adopting a resolution calling on nonsectarian community hospitals to allow doctors with privileges to perform abortions. Sixteen state medical societies, on the other hand, took no action on abortion after the 1973 decisions. Nine others confined their statements to narrow issues like the right of individual physicians and hospitals to refuse to perform abortions on grounds of conscience.[12]

The reaction of state hospital associations was even more limited. Of 42 respondents to the 1976 survey, 27 took no action at all; five adopted statements recommending only that objecting hospitals and physicians be exempted. The remaining 10 state hospital organizations confined their actions mainly to issuing legal opinions to their members on the implications of the 1973 decisions.[13]

In short, a large part of the national and state leadership of American medicine passed up the opportunity to educate physicians and health institutions on how to meet their new responsibilities. They also neglected their responsibility to advise legislators and other lay decision-makers on what policies were appropriate to the new situation.

The leadership also avoided grappling with the obvious underlying differences between religious groups on the morality of abortion itself—differences that take on added significance because an important segment of the health system is operated by religious institutions. Since the underlying conflicts have not disappeared, ducking the issues has meant simply that most of the U.S. health leadership has done nothing to formulate constructive solutions that could respect the minority's deeply held religious opposition to abortion, while ensuring that the system as a whole carried out its responsibilities to the majority who believe abortion sometimes is the most moral recourse—and one to which they are legally entitled.

A vivid picture of what the health leadership could have done, compared to what it actually did, can be seen by contrasting the actions of two very influential organizations, The Institute of Medicine of the National Academy of Sciences and the Joint Commission on Accreditation of Hospitals. The institute quickly assembled a committee of 11 prestigious doctors and scholars to examine how legalized abortion would affect public health. In its 168-page report, issued in 1975, it reviewed objectively the available evidence and concluded that legalization would significantly advance public health by reducing deaths and complications associated with illegal abortion.[14] The report found little evidence to support the widely promoted notions that abortion would replace contraception or lead to psychiatric and emotional problems. Since health risks increase markedly when abortions are delayed, the report strongly urged that "laws, medical practices and educational programs should enable and encourage women who have chosen abortion to obtain it in the first three months of pregnancy."[15] High priorities were set on research into possible long-term medical complications of abortion and the effects of abortion and denied abortion on mental health and social welfare.

The joint commission, on the other hand, acted as though nothing had happened to require it to modify its practices. The commission is a private nonprofit body, composed of representatives from six major medical organizations. It inspects hospitals on a voluntary basis and grants accreditation if they comply with its standards. These ostensibly require hospitals to provide the quantity and quality of health care their communities need. The commission has taken on quasipublic functions since 1965, when Congress voted to certify automatically for Medicare reimbursement any accredited hospital—a certification that in many states also extends to Medicaid.

Although the commission revised its *Accreditation Manual* in 1973 and 1975, none of the changes dealt with hospitals' responsibilities in regard to abortion.[16] But the questionnaire used by the commission to audit individual hospitals asks the number of abortions performed, as well as the number of births, so its evaluators must be well aware that many accredited hospitals provided no abortions. In 1975, for example, only 39 percent of accredited hospitals did so.[17]

There is no evidence that in determining whether to accredit a particular hospital, commission evaluators consider either abortion case load or community need for the service. Since the accreditation process is essentially secret, there is no way of knowing if the commission has ever specifically requested or encouraged nonprovider hospitals to change their policies. The commission's policy, according to its response to an Alan Guttmacher Institute survey, is that "each hospital's medical staff may define its own rules and regulations with respect to the performance of abortions."[18] In other words, the question of whether community hospitals carry out their professional responsibility to meet the community's abortion needs appears to be one the commission does not care to ask.

The Institute of Medicine clearly saw legalization as a social responsibility that required tapping the knowledge and expertise of the medical and scientific communities for policy and planning activities. Just as clearly, the Joint Commission—the health system's only institutionalized mechanism for evaluating the quality and adequacy of hospital services—did not provide any leadership for its constituents on abortion issues. The commission specifically failed to spur community hospitals and their physicians to accepting professional, rather than religious or political, criteria as the determinant of whether to perform abortions.

The private foundations—which provide considerable support for new activities in the health field—also have to a large extent avoided the abortion issue. Between 1971 and 1973, The Council of Foundations' data bank was able to retrieve only six foundations—out of 900 reporting grants of over $5,000—that supported abortion-related projects.[19] These six awarded nine grants for a total of $341,000; the data bank then had information on 21,600 grants in all fields worth $1.7 billion. Only two of the many foundations with major program interests in the health field made abortion-related grants.

Four years later, the situation had changed somewhat. The council's data for 1973-78 showed that 17 foundations had made 28 abortion-related grants for a total of $627,000.[20] Some grants went to help start local abortion facilities; several supported litigation; a few funded research.

Only after Congress restricted public funding for abortion did foundations begin to show greater interest in the subject. Several now are supporting research on the effect of the funding ban. Others are helping to underwrite litigation contesting it. Some funds are helping poor women pay for legal abortions they otherwise could not afford.

Yet foundations continued to fund important health projects that perpetuate the isolation of abortion from the mainstream of U.S. health care. A most striking example of this is a $30-million program initiated in 1976 by the Robert Wood Johnson Foundation, which is the second-largest U.S. foundation in the health field, with assets of over a billion dollars.

The program at issue funds primary-care group medical practices affiliated with community hospitals, as part of the foundation's continuing effort to improve the availability and quality of ambulatory care. The program's criteria for funding stress that a primary-care group practice should "provide or arrange for *all* basic services required" by the whole family.[21]

In February 1977, the foundation announced that 26 hospitals in 22 states and the District of Columbia had been awarded grants to start group practices.[22] Of the grant-winning hospitals, only 11 had performed any abortions since the Supreme Court decisions; only six of the nonproviders were Catholic hospitals. The program designers clearly did not consider access to abortion an element of the "primary care" that group practices are supposed to provide—although abortion, predictably, would be the most frequently required surgical procedure in most communities. Under any reasonable definition of "primary care," the provision of abortion, or formal referral arrangements should be included. Yet the program did not concern itself with where the patients in nonprovider hospitals would get abortions.

These considerations were brought to the foundation's attention. It replied that the program's advisory board felt its principal objective was

> to assist community hospitals and their medical staffs [to] further develop their existing commitments to ambulatory care . . . . [T] hey concluded that no attempt should be made to require any specific medical services of the groups. The Board members feel such decisions should be made at the local level by the participating physicians and their patients.[23]

Nevertheless, many other requirements *were* imposed by the program: and its *raison d'être* was articulated in these terms:

> In contrast to the episodic patient-care typically provided in the hospital emergency room or outpatient clinic, the primary care group practice must develop mechanisms whereby its physicians assume continuing responsibility for managing the care of their patients. . . . In cases where specialty referrals are indicated, the primary care physicians should maintain responsibility for the ongoing care of their patients.[24]

The foundation's lack of interest in assuming that women served by the groups are assured access to abortion, directly or through formal referral relationships, is clearly inconsistent with these stated principles.

The private health-insurance industry has done better than the foundations in recognizing that abortion is now a commonly sought health procedure. It has increased coverage for abortion in the last several years, although serious inadequacies remain. A 1976 study found that almost four-fifths of commercial insurance companies and nine out of ten Blue Cross basic contracts cover abortion.[25] In most of these plans, however, abortion continues to be part of maternity coverage, which is not always offered to unmarried employees and dependents. In addition, it frequently is optional and may be expensive since such coverage was designed primarily to cover costly prenatal and delivery care. These reasons explain why abortion clinics, which serve a large number of young and unwed women, report that less than 15 percent of their patients have private health insurance coverage.[26] Some women, of course, may feel that it is worth paying cash to avoid having *abortion* written into one's permanent health record.

State health authorities immediately were faced with concrete legal and administrative questions after the 1973 Supreme Court decisions. So they tended to react more directly than their private-sector counterparts did. By 1978, 17 state health departments had issued guidelines, regulations, or standards to govern abortion services, while an additional 13 had obtained authority to license outpatient gynecologic surgery centers in general or abortion facilities in particular.

These state efforts varied widely. Some had the force of law, while others merely recommended what the department and its advisers considered to be the elements of quality abortion care. Some guidelines were long and detailed—Michigan's was 44 pages—while others were brief and general. Although the Supreme Court had largely barred states from making special regulations or restricting abortions performed by physicians during the first trimester, it did not prohibit state health authorities from issuing professionally sound requirements for adequate abortion services at any stage of gestation. In some cases, however, some state regulations included provisions that obviously were designed to circumvent or negate aspects of the *Roe* and *Doe* abortion decisions. These rules have been invalidated by federal courts.

In about half the states, the official health agency still has not issued any guidelines at all, even for later procedures—which the state clearly can regulate in the interests of maternal health after the first trimester and for fetal protection after the second. Moreover, only about four in 10 state health departments have made arrangements to provide referral information on available facilities to women seeking abortions. Only 12 have undertaken educational or informational activities for health professionals or the general public.

Three-quarters of the state health departments have requirements for the statistical reporting of abortions. Although some systems still are incapable of yielding usable information for monitoring and evaluation purposes, abortion nevertheless has become one of the best-documented health services as the result of these reporting programs.

Even in states that have laws and regulations for abortion services, elimination of substandard abortion practices is not assured. Illinois, for example, has comprehensive regulations for ambulatory surgical facilities on its books. Yet, an investigative series in the *Chicago Sun-Times* revealed that a number of fraudulent, unsafe abortion clinics were operating on Michigan Avenue. When state inspectors, on an unscheduled visit, were refused admittance, they meekly went away—and the clinics continued their unregulated operation.[27] The widely known existence of substandard facilities, unchallenged by the state, is an unfortunate if predictable by-product of health leaders' reluctance to participate constructively in the provision and regulation of legal abortion.

Such an attitude is not inevitable, as was shown by a model collaborative regulatory effort in Washington, D.C. The local medical society, city health officials, and Planned Parenthood launched an areawide voluntary clinic inspection program that has inspected facilities, issued detailed reports, and publicized its activities.[28]

The federal government's response to the Supreme Court's legalization of abortion is at once the least and the most important of all: the *least*, because, as U.S. officials never tire of saying, "The federal government does not regulate the practice of medicine." The *most*, because in recent decades the federal government has made massive inroads into almost all other areas of health research and the delivery and financing of health care—so that today there are few transactions between patient and health system that are not shaped in some way by federal programs and policies.

Legalization initially posed a challenge, and provided an opportunity, to many agencies of the Department of Health, Education and Welfare (HEW) and other federal departments to articulate through professional example and practice the meaning of law. For the most part, however, these federal agencies have avoided involvement when possible.

HEW's actions in the several—potentially exemplary—health care delivery programs that it does operate directly were particularly irresponsible. These programs include some 60 Public Health Service (PHS) hospitals and clinics, and the Indian Health Service. In a telling report on the abortion policies of federal departments, the American Civil Liberties Union (ACLU) was forced to declare, in 1975, that these agencies still were not complying with the Supreme Court decisions.[29]

Rather, ACLU discovered, a 1971 presidential order by Richard Nixon remained in effect, which said that federal installations' immunity from state and local laws would *not* be invoked in the case of abortion. This matter should have been moot in light of the 1973 Supreme Court decisions, but a number of states had yet to rewrite their obsolete abortion statutes, which in the absence of court challenges, remained on the books. In the confusion created by the coexistence of these conflicting regulations, some government health care providers were reluctant to perform abortions. HEW did little to clarify the situation or to put the PHS facilities in compliance with the Court's decisions. So, in 1975, an Indian woman still might be refused an abortion in an Indian Health Service facility if an unconstitutional state law prohibited or restricted the procedure. The situation in PHS facilities was similar.

It is difficult to accept the explanation for this situation given by the director of the HEW health services branch in March 1975, more than two years after the Supreme Court rulings, when he wrote that, "There is no way at the present time that HEW can set up a standard national policy which would abridge state law."[30]

This foot-dragging policy nevertheless finally came to an end. Several months later, partly in reaction to the ACLU report, a new policy was promulgated. It stated:

> While it continues to be the policy of the PHS to comply with applicable state laws, there need not be compliance where state law has been struck down by the Courts or clearly is inconsistent with principles enunciated by the Courts.[31]

The federal government has moved only grudgingly to set a forthright and positive example for the states and individual health-care providers. In the years between the 1973 decisions and the enactment of the first ban on federal funds for abortion in 1976, HEW took *no* steps to clarify abortion's place in the Medicaid program, although large numbers of welfare women, its primary adult beneficiaries, could have been expected to seek abortions. In fact, HEW delayed issuing regulations to implement the Medicaid family-planning provisions of the Social Security Amendments of 1972, primarily because it could not resolve how—or whether—abortion was to be treated under these amendments. The result was to leave each state to determine the conditions governing Medicaid coverage of abortions.

Nor did HEW actively involve itself in abortion-related legislation subsequent to the 1973 decisions. In response to requests from Congress in 1974, the department prepared a comprehensive statement assessing—with some concern—the probable social and health impact of a cutoff of Medicaid abortion reimbursements, which infuriated antiabortion congressmen. Perhaps because of this—or more likely because it occurred during a presidential campaign in which both of the candidates opposed public funding of abortion—HEW's statement in 1976 on the proposed Hyde amendment had to be edited and cleared by the White House political staff before it could be sent to House and Senate conferees.[32] In other words, what Congress received from HEW in 1976 was less a full professional assessment of the health, economic, and social consequences of a cutoff of Medicaid abortions than a drastically shortened statement that did not conflict seriously with the president's perceived political needs.

Beyond these few incidents, HEW's post-1973 role is almost entirely one of omission. After Congress barred both its family-planning and maternal-health programs from providing abortions, HEW permitted considerable uncertainty to develop as to whether these programs—which serve millions of low-income women—could provide even abortion counseling and referral. And HEW failed to clarify what, if anything, the community and migrant health centers that it funds were supposed to do about abortion. HEW's health planning apparatus, which has been gearing up to carry out the 1974 Health Planning and Resources Development Act, intentionally avoided dealing with abortion in its 1978 *National Guidelines for Health Planning.* Yet, as will be seen in Chapter 10, these guidelines provide an opportunity to move toward solving the difficult issue of how to safeguard the interests of sectarian hospitals whose staffs and administrators oppose abortion, while meeting citizens' needs for the service.

HEW's manpower-training agencies have been similarly remiss, apparently finding nothing in the post-*Roe* and *Doe* situation to require changes in their programs for educating future health professionals. The department did undertake a study in 1978 to find out if medical and nursing schools discriminated against applicants on the basis of their views on abortion.[33] The study was mandated by legislation sponsored by a prominent antiabortion senator, who was concerned that applicants opposed to abortion were discriminated against. Most schools answered that abortion attitudes were not an admissions criterion. It is noteworthy that this survey constitutes HEW's sole effort with regard to health manpower training and legal abortion.

The HEW secretary's Advisory Committee on the Rights and Responsibilities of Women conducted a study in 1976 of the department's actions on abortion. A draft was completed just before the Carter administration took office. Since it recommended vigorous departmental efforts to ensure full implementation of the 1973 Supreme Court rulings, it is not surprising that nothing more has been heard about this endeavor.

The National Institutes of Health of HEW gave abortion limited attention, funding 15-to-20 small-scale projects each year, principally to evaluate the medical effects of abortion and for attitudinal research. In the critically important early years of abortion legalization, about $500,000 annually was committed for all medical and social-science abortion research. There since has been little change in these patterns, although overall funding levels have increased slightly.[34]

Some of these funds were sought for studies on abortion complications under the aegis of the Center for Disease Control (CDC). By 1975, almost 30 percent of all federal money going to abortion-related research was being spent by CDC: over 80 percent of all biomedical research funds for abortion were expended on projects undertaken by CDC.[35] CDC's pioneering work in developing comprehensive information on the epidemiology of abortion has been of great public-health benefit. But the narrow involvement of other research agencies indicated by these figures suggests that in the absence of the CDC commitment, little scientific evaluation of abortion would have occurred.

CDC is the one HEW agency that seems to have acted in accordance with its mission, when, on its own initiative, it began epidemiologic surveillance of legal abortion several years *before* the 1973 decisions. Since 1972, it has published annual statistical reports on abortions and the characteristics of women obtaining them. CDC staff have encouraged and aided in the development of the state reporting systems that collect these data. CDC has also conducted studies on mortality associated with both legal and illegal abortion and on the complications associated with different abortion procedures.

These findings have been a major information resource for physicians and other health professionals and have helped lower morbidity and mortality by enabling doctors to make more informed treatment choices in abortion cases. The CDC's findings have contributed to understanding the consequences of restricting access to abortion. Its monitoring efforts, for example, called public attention to the death of the Mexican-American woman who was denied a Medicaid abortion and to delays in obtaining abortions experienced by Medicaid recipients after funding was cut off in 1977.[36] CDC has demonstrated how an agency charged with furthering public health can work professionally and constructively to evaluate a major new development in health care. Because of its involvement with abortion, CDC has come under attack from congressional abortion opponents.

The U.S. Commission on Civil Rights, a quasi-independent agency, has been similarly censured for its stance on abortion rights. In April 1975, the commission issued a 101-page report opposing efforts to enact a constitutional amendment outlawing abortion.[37] The commission opposed any ban on the use of federal funds to pay for abortions for the poor. It noted that a constitutional amendment would violate the separation of church and state established in the Bill of Rights by "establishing one religious view (of when a fetus becomes a person entitled to legal protection) and thus inhibiting the free exercise of religion of others."[38] Congressional opponents of abortion responded to the report by threatening to cut off the commission's appropriations and in 1978 succeeded in barring it by law from conducting further abortion studies.

HEW's overall failure to respond constructively and positively to the Supreme Court's decisions in the early years after 1973 might charitably be attributed to bureaucratic inertia and a nonactivist orientation. But the department's vigorous implemention of *restrictions* on federal abortion funding are inconsistent with this interpretation. Indifference has been replaced by a vigorous concern to insure that the limitations are scrupulously observed.

The department did not get around to bringing its health service programs into compliance with the Supreme Court decisions for almost three years. It then exhibited great reluctance in informing states that Medicaid funding might *not* be terminated. In 1976, Congress added the Hyde amendment to the DHEW labor appropriations bill banning the use of federal funds for abortion except when the woman's life was endangered. Enforcement of the ban was stayed by a federal court before it could take effect, on October 1, 1976. But HEW issued no policy statements to its regional offices or grantees for a full week and refused to answer inquiries from frantic state administrators who did not know whether or not to reimburse abortions obtained by Medicaid recipients. The judge's order, however, explicitly forbade HEW from refusing to pay for abortions. Eventually, confusing telegrams were sent out. HEW cited technical legal language from both the ban and the court order, without explanation of their implications for whether or not state programs could pay for abortions.

A similar delay of 12 days followed the judge's second injunction, although he went so far as to specify in clear language which HEW was to send out "forthwith." Department lawyers reported they feared being found in contempt of court for the lapse, and notice finally was released—on the day *after* the presidential election.[39]

The situation was very different, one year later, when HEW Secretary Joseph Califano made a nationwide announcement of HEW's policy restrictions *within one hour* of Judge John F. Dooling's ruling lifting his restraining order, allowing enforcement of the Hyde ban, in the wake of the Supreme Court decision upholding the constitutionality of state laws prohibiting Medicaid reimbursement of nontherapeutic abortions.

Not only was HEW assiduous in its enforcement of the Hyde amendment, but Califano ignored the professional views of his top advisers and committees when setting administration policy on abortion. Two major departmental task forces in the first year of the Carter administration called for a more balanced, realistic approach to abortion. The leader of a task force on Alternatives to Abortion eventually recommended that the task force be disbanded because of HEW's lack of direction, funding, and authority to continue the effort. She noted that while there were positive steps the government could take to deal with the incidence of unwanted pregnancies, once they occurred, the alternatives to abortion "are suicide, motherhood, and some would add, madness."[40] A departmental study group on teenage pregnancy shortly thereafter released a report that said that it "considers abortion information, counseling, services and research essential to reduce the numbers of high-risk adolescent births."[41]

This disdain for expert opinion—and for women—was most apparent in the department's handling of the Medicaid-funding ban. The regulations released by HEW implementing the 1977 Hyde language were conceded by most observers to be essentially evenhanded. They certainly contained little room for abuse, since they called for the reporting of cases of rape and incest within 60 days and set stringent verification requirements on abortion certifications as required by the ban. The regulations apparently had the desired effect: data gathered by HEW for the first seven three-month quarters of the restriction show that publicly funded abortions decreased by approximately 99 percent in states that adopted the language of the federal ban. The data show further that only 15 percent of the abortions for which reimbursement was claimed and for which a justification was reported by the state were funded under the exception for "severe and long-lasting physical health damage." Yet, despite this evidence from his department, Secretary Califano publicly recommended dropping this provision and issued tighter regulations governing certification, cynically citing the potential for widespread "abuse."[42]

Indifference to and avoidance of the implications of legalization of a critical, widely sought health service were replaced by open hostility on the part of the preeminent public health official and agency in the United States.

References

1 The material in this chapter is drawn from several surveys and other sources. The Alan Guttmacher Institute mailed questionnaires in 1976 to 41 major national medical, health, and related organizations, as well as to the medical societies and hospital associations of each state and the District of Columbia. There were 36 responses among the national organizations (hereinafter referred to as "1976 AGI national organization survey"), including:

American Medical Association
American Hospital Association
American Nurses' Association
American College of Obstetricians and Gynecologists
Council on Postsecondary Accreditation
Council of Teaching Hospitals of the AAMC
Blue Cross Association

Association of State and Territorial Health Officers
Association of Schools of Public Health
American Public Welfare Association
American Academy of Family Physicians
Association of American Medical Colleges
American Academy of Medical Administrators
American Association for Hospital Planning
American Association for Maternal and Child Health
American Association of Obstetricians and Gynecologists
American College Health Association
American College of Hospital Administrators
American Osteopathic Association
American Osteopathic Hospital Association
American Protestant Hospital Association
Federation of State Medical Boards of the United States
Group Health Association of America
Health Insurance Association of America
Joint Commission on Accreditation of Hospitals
National Association of Blue Shield Plans
National Association of Social Workers
National Board of Medical Examiners
Society for Public Health Education
American Health Foundation
American College of Nurse-Midwives
Family Service Association of America
National Health Council
National Conference on Social Welfare
Child Welfare League
National League for Nursing

The most important nonrespondents were the National Medical Association, The American Board of Obstetrics and Gynecology, and the American Gynecological Society. Forty-two state medical societies responded (hereinafter referred to as "1976 AGI state medical society survey"), all except Colorado, the District of Columbia, Florida, Montana, Nevada, North Carolina, Rhode Island, South Carolina, and Wisconsin. There were also 42 responses from state hospital associations (hereinafter referred to as "1976 AGI state hospital association survey"); no responses were received from Florida, Illinos, Kentucky, Maine, Minnesota, Missouri, Montana, Ohio, and South Dakota.

Information on the post-1973 actions of the nation's foundations was obtained from special tabulations of the Foundation Center Data Bank, maintained by the Council of Foundations, in 1974 and 1977, as well as from the annual reports of foundations with primary program interests in the health field and from personal correspondence. The actions of state health and welfare departments have been monitored through annual surveys by The Alan Guttmacher Institute (hereinafter referred to as "AGI state health (or welfare) survey" for the respective year), and their results have been published periodically in *Family Planning/Population Reporter (FP/PR)*, and other periodicals. *FP/PR* also reports on all state legislation and court decisions affecting abortion services.

Information on the numerous relevant bureaus and agencies of the Department of Health, Education and Welfare have been obtained through continuous review of the *Federal Register*, in which all proposed or final regulations are published; internal DHEW memoranda; and extensive personal interviews with key DHEW officials.

2 1976 AGI national organization survey, unpublished data.

3 Resolution adopted Feb. 7, 1973, by American Hospital Association House of Delegates.

4 Policy Statement, American College Health Association, October 1973.

5 American Medical Association House of Delegates, June 1973.

6 D. Delmar, "Congress Asks Ob/Gyns When Abortion Needed," *Ob.Gyn. News*, Sept. 15, 1977.

7 B. L. Lindheim and M. A. Cotterill, "Training in Induced Abortion by Obstetrics and Gynecology Residency Programs," *Family Planning Perspectives*, 10:24, 1978.

8 "American Public Health Association Recommended Program Guide for Abortion Services," *American Journal of Public Health*, **63**:639, July 1973.

9 Policy Statement, American College of Obstetricians and Gynecologists (ACOG), Feb. 10, 1973.

10 Letter from E. E. Nichols, ACOG, to Sen. Edward W. Brooke, July 18, 1977.

11 Policy Statement, National Association of Social Workers, 1975.

12 1976 AGI state medical society survey.

13 1976 AGI state hospital association survey.

14 Institute of Medicine, *Legalized Abortion and the Public Health*, Washington, D.C.: National Academy of Sciences, 1975.

15 Ibid., p. 8.

16 Joint Commission on Accreditation of Hospitals, *Accreditation Manual for Hospitals*, Chicago, 1973, pp. 28, 22, 123.

17 The Alan Guttmacher Institute, "Hospitals and Abortion," Report by the AGI National Council Committee on Hospital Provision of Abortion Services (mimeo), Jan. 21, 1977.

18 Nancy Dixon Jacobs, associate director, Joint Commission on Accreditation of Hospitals, personal communication, Feb. 27, 1976.

19 Foundation Center Associate Service Data Bank, New York, N. Y.

20 Ibid.

21 Robert Wood Johnson Foundation, "Community Hospital–Medical Staff Sponsored Primary Care Group Practice Program of the Robert Wood Johnson Foundation" (mimeo), p. 7.

22 Robert Wood Johnson Foundation, "Special Report" (mimeo), February 1977, p 14.

23 Letter from David E. Rogers, M.D., president, Robert Wood Johnson Foundation, to Frederick S. Jaffe, Jan. 11, 1977.

24 Robert Wood Johnson Foundation, "Community Hospital . . .," p. 6.

25 C. F. Muller, "Insurance Coverage of Abortion, Contraception and Sterilization," *Family Planning Perspectives*, **10**:71, 1978.

26 B. L. Lindheim, "Services, Policies and Costs in U.S. Abortion Facilities, *Family Planning Perspectives*, **11**:283, 1979.

27 "The Abortion Profiteers," *Chicago Sun-Times*, Nov. 12–17, 1978.

28 P. Hodge, "8 Clinics Pass Abortion Tests," *Washington Post*, Apr. 4, 1976.

29 P. Williams, "Existing Policies Within the Federal Government Which Are in Conflict with the 1973 Supreme Court Decisions on Abortions," American Civil Liberties Union Reproductive Freedom Project (mimeo), May 5, 1975.

30 Ibid., p. 15.

31 Department of Health, Education and Welfare, "HEW News" (mimeo), Dec. 6, 1975.

32 Personal interviews between Barbara L. Lindheim and DHEW legislative and legal staff, January 1977.

33 "Students Are Asked View on Abortion," *New York Times*, Jan. 4, 1979.

34 Department of Health, Education and Welfare, Public Health Service, National Institutes of Health, *Inventory and Analysis of Federal Population Research*, Fiscal Years, 1972, 1973, 1974, 1975, 1976, 1977, 1978.

35 Ibid.

36 Center for Disease Control, *Morbidity and Mortality Weekly Report*, Nov. 4, 1977, p. 361.

37 U. S. Commission on Civil Rights, *Constitutional Aspects of the Right to Limit Childbearing*, Washington, D.C., April 1975.

38 Ibid., p. 31.

39 Personal interviews between Barbara L. Lindheim and DHEW legislative and legal staff, January 1977.

40 Bill Peterson, "Abortion Alternatives Cited in HEW Memo," *Washington Post*, Nov. 27, 1977.

41 "Give Abortion Advice, Task Force on Teens Recommends to HEW," *Washington Star*, Nov. 28, 1977.

42 Letter from Joseph A. Califano, Jr., to Rep. Daniel J. Flood, June 2, 1978.

CHAPTER FIVE

Explanations and Extrapolations

The health system's grudging response to the Supreme Court's 1973 abortion decisions is not hard to understand. Abortion is controversial. Health leaders—like the leaders of other professional establishments—try to avoid controversy when possible.

They easily could rationalize their inactivity: for hospitals, professional organizations, foundations, and government agencies to have dealt with abortion in ways that were appropriate to their leaders' professional roles and responsibilities could have jeopardized other important tasks. With so many unmet needs to address—and public support required to obtain the necessary resources—they understandably had little incentive to tackle the new and divisive abortion issue. So it is not surprising that the health system and the doctors who largely control it have denied their responsibility, assumed by the Court, to help women realize their new constitutional right—a right that is exercised through the use of specialized services over which doctors hold monopoly control.

Some health professionals, like many other Americans, bitterly oppose abortion on religious, moral, or philosophic grounds. True, the majority of doctors—the most influential of health professionals—long had favored abortion reform. In 1967, for example, 87 percent of physicians who responded to a *Modern Medicine* survey favored liberalizing the laws.[1] But this abstract proposition had been transformed by the Court into a very concrete one. The issue no longer was what the law *should* be but rather what roles individual professionals and institutions were to play in the delivery of abortion services—and the health system hesitated to respond.

A number of studies have examined the attitudes of physicians, nurses and other health personnel toward abortion.[2] The results are mixed: approval of abortion as a legitimate means of coping with the crisis of unwanted pregnancy coexists with negative attitudes—disapproval—particularly among older professionals who received their training when the procedure was illegal. This is understandable given that many professionals had been taught to believe that in treating reproductive-age women, virtually their only responsibilities were to insure the women's continuing fecundity and their babies' health. These attitudes persist to some degree and undoubtedly influence the response of physicians, particularly older physicians, to abortion.

The physician who declared, "A woman is a uterus surrounded by a supporting organism and a directing personality"[3] expressed a view shared by a number of his peers. For a person holding such a view, the responsibility of assisting patients in managing their fertility can be difficult, even when only contraceptive care is involved. Responding to healthy women's requests to terminate unwanted pregnancies must be far more difficult.

Doctors may feel threatened, too, by the degree to which birth control and abortion have contributed to changing roles and opportunities for women. A recent study found that physicians who believe roles other than motherhood should be open to women also are significantly more likely to offer a pregnant patient an alternative to childbirth.[4] The abortion option, finally, is symbolic of new—and for many Americans—profoundly disturbing developments in personal and sexual mores. Doctors, socialized to wield authority, now are asked to help implement women's emancipation—which may threaten them on personal, professional, and broadly social grounds. However, the fact that younger professionals are more likely to approve of abortion suggests that the health system's overall attitude will change in time.

Nurses generally are less supportive of abortion than physicians. They tend to be particularly negative when their professional role is restricted to the technical aspects of the abortion procedure, and they are not allowed to provide counseling and to deal with the complex human factors that lead women to choose abortion.

In hospitals that do not rotate abortion duty among their interns and residents, those who end up performing large numbers of abortions tend to regard them as a burden. What is more, since few hospitals provide abortion services, this inequality in meeting the need for abortion services has been exacerbated: a handful of staff members in hospitals that offer abortion services must compensate for the reluctance of their colleagues and the unwillingness of other institutions to perform abortions. On the positive side, several studies show that professionals become more favorably disposed to abortion as they come to understand their abortion patients' needs and gain experience in providing the service.[5]

The health-care providers' ambivalence could have been predicted. Before the abortion law changes of the last decade, abortionists were treated as pariahs. Reputable physicians would not be seen in their company.

This disdain was painfully clear at the 1955 Arden House Conference on Abortion, where the presence of a physician who performed clandestine abortions created much tension—even though the renowned obstetrician Alan Guttmacher introduced him to the group as a longtime colleague and personal friend. This abortionist reported to the conference that he had received 5,000 referrals from some 350 doctors in his state during his 35 years of abortion practice. But when he finally became enmeshed in legal difficulties, not one of them stepped forward to testify in his defense.[6]

It was the newly organized medical profession—not the churches—that in the last century led the crusade to make abortion a crime. Doctors ended the practice, derived from common law, that permitted abortion before "quickening," in the fifth month of pregnancy. The physician-activists who led this crusade had personal, professional, and political motives.[7]

Many regarded abortion as morally wrong, to be sure. But they also were intent on professionalizing the practice of medicine and restoring doctors to a respected position as leaders of society. The abortion issue gave them a means to highlight the dangers inherent in a practice that was carried out largely by "quacks" and "irregular doctors." By warning of these risks, they were able to persuade state legislatures to enact sanctions against these practitioners.

Doctors and law-makers shared a concern: abortion historian James C. Mohr recounts that abortion was more common among Protestants than among Catholic immigrants. This prompted fears that the native, Protestant population soon would be outbred by "the ignorant, the low-lived and the alien." These nativist fears about Catholic birth rates, Mohr says, "played a greater role in the drive for antiabortion laws in 19th-century America than did Catholic opposition to the procedure."[8]

Dislike for abortion persisted, and if anything was more openly expressed, as legal and safe illegal abortions became more common. Medical economist Victor Fuchs notes that peer approval is an important incentive for doctors, whose contempt for abortionists extended to colleagues who performed legal abortions under liberalized state laws or with hospital abortion committee approval.[9] A 1971 survey of North Carolina doctors found many were afraid of losing colleagues' and patients' respect if they performed too many abortions.[10]

After abortion was legalized in New York, the physician Robert Hall found that in most large hospitals a few doctors did most of the abortions. "The rest of the staff," he added, "regards these doctors with esteem not markedly higher than that previously reserved for the backstreet abortionist."[11] Given these attitudes, older physicians' reluctance to perform abortions is understandable.

Most U.S. physicians have had little difficulty shifting to a more affirmative position on abortion in the last decade.[12] But the older attitudes doubtless have left an imprint, which could easily be deepened by current realities. It is understandable that some doctors continue to feel stigmatized for participating in abortion services, after hearing a congressman declare: "Instead of being just a healer, he [the physician] now becomes an executioner as well. [The Supreme Court decision] provides him with a license to kill."[13]

There is little doubt expressed that abortion is effective in resolving the problem of an unwanted pregnancy. There is disagreement about how that resolution is to be understood. Abortion has some health effect. But it rarely is necessary to save a woman's life. Abortion also has important social and emotional effects—and these usually are uppermost in people's minds when they debate the subject.

A significant part of health professionals' resistance comes from those who believe it inappropriate—perhaps dangerous—for medicine to intervene except when physical health is at stake. "We are in danger of becoming the tools of social planners," warned Dr. Gregory White, of Illinois, when the American Medical Association (AMA) House of Delegates adopted a resolution in 1970 endorsing liberalized abortion laws.[14]

An obstetrician at Milwaukee County General Hospital similarly explained his unwillingness to perform abortions not by citing his religious beliefs but by his conviction that he "cannot approve of the use of a surgical approach for the solution of a social problem."[15] In the same vein, Eunice Shriver, of the Kennedy family, who opposes abortion on moral grounds, argues against Medicaid funding because she asserts that medicine's only proper role is to use "medical techniques to avert death, crippling, and physical incapacitation."[16] Even as experienced a medical educator and ethicist as the late André Hellegers, who was director of Georgetown University's Kennedy Institute, asked: "What is the disease for which we carry out this 'medical' procedure of abortion?"[17]

The double standard inherent in this argument against abortion can be seen most easily by addressing Hellegers' question not only to abortion but to all transactions between physicians and patients. About 80 percent of all ambulatory visits to physicians are for 60 common problems, including self-limiting illnesses like sore throats, colds, fatigue, and headaches, according to preventive medicine advocate Kerry L. White. But medicine has truly efficacious forms of beneficial intervention for only about 10 percent or 20 percent of all the problems that people bring to physicians.[18] If it is appropriate for doctors to deal only with those problems of physical disease for which medical care is effective—as Hellegers' logic suggests—then White is correct when he observes that "many physicians had better plan to get other jobs tending bar or driving cabs, because they are obviously superfluous."[19]

No one, of course, is seriously proposing that U.S. doctors stop providing the bulk of their services, which have little clear relationship to immediate somatic well-being—or that health-financing programs cease to pay for them. As White points out, "substantial benefits accrue to the patient even as a result of his visit to a doctor, but these are more due to the fact that the physician took an interest . . . than to the specific form of the intervention."[20] Rather, most of these critics seem to object only to abortion. The doctors invoke ostensibly "medical" criteria selectively to justify their unwillingness to perform this service.

The advent of legal abortion could have been viewed as giving health professionals another important means to assist patients in optimizing their own well-being and that of their families. Instead, it has been viewed by some as threatening their professional roles. At the AMA's 1970 meeting, a physician from Ohio put it this way: "Legal abortion makes the patient truly the physician: She makes the diagnosis and establishes the therapy."[21]

In these circumstances, it was charged, the physician becomes "merely" the technician, carrying out the patient's wishes—and this does not fit well with the profession's self-image as healer and teacher. Again it is curious that this charge is raised only when abortion is considered. It is not leveled at any of the myriad other transactions between patients and doctors in which the patient decides that he needs a medical visit, and the doctor uses his professional judgment to provide the reassurance (and often the placebo) he believes the patient really wants. In fact, the only real difference between the doctor's role in these examples of commonly sought care and that required in abortion is that in the former the patient is seeking the physician's wisdom and advice—as illusory as they may be—while in abortion the decision usually has been made by the patient beforehand. The doctor does not see himself as the decision-maker, which annoys him. Worse, the wide use of hospital abortion committees in the two decades prior to legalization cast doctors as members of tribunals, before which women quite literally had to plead their cases. The contrast between the absolute power enjoyed by these committees of doctors and doctors' new roles under the Supreme Court rulings may well have exacerbated the resentment of some of them toward women and their newly aquired right to choose abortion.

Abortion thus raises a number of issues that relate to the consumer's role in health care. It is in fact a precursor of other situations in which the traditional authoritarian relationship between doctor and patient is being challenged. Consumers increasingly are demanding more adequate information about their options in dealing with health problems and greater accountability on the part of physicians and health institutions. These changes are coming at a time when many forward-looking health leaders have begun to say that personal health can be most enhanced in the future if individuals will take greater responsibility for their own lives and well-being.

There is little doubt that in the last five years U.S. women with unwanted pregnancies have been willing to confront and resolve difficult problems with major implications for their well-being and that of their families. In so doing, they have created a need for abortion services that the mainstream health system has been unable or unwilling to meet.

The reasons that some doctors advance for opposing abortion as a medical service thus run counter to the major contemporary trend in thinking about health care that elevates the consumer's decision-making role and diminishes the doctor's. But the fact that these arguments typically are raised *only* against abortion leads one to suspect that they are advanced in lieu of religious or moral objections.

Health professionals have a right to their religious beliefs. But when they frame their contentions as professional arguments, the proper means of assessing their position is professional, not religious. In this context, their antiabortion views are biased. It would be more appropriate for a doctor who is opposed to abortion to state his religious view that abortion is "killing", rather than argue that it distorts the role and purpose of the medical profession.

Physicians' hostile reaction to consumers' increasing role in abortion decision-making is particularly interesting in light of the need to contain health care costs, which are rising much faster than costs of other goods and services. Health analysts and economists are nearly unanimous in explaining why: besides the increasing cost of specialized medical technology, in health care it is not the consumer but the provider who controls the total process of care.

The provider—the doctor—makes the decisions that determine how much or how little is spent. The consumer is said not to be concerned by the providers' role in escalating costs, because much of the direct cost for medical services is paid for by third parties like insurance plans. These factors, it is argued, lead to unnecessary services and expenditures.

The abortion market, ironically, more nearly fits economists' picture of an ideal medical market than any other health service. The basic decision on whether to use the service is made by the consumer, not the provider, and most of the cost is directly borne by consumers, in part because of the limited abortion coverage in most insurance plans. In terms of the premises of the economists' argument, the market already is restricting abortion services to those that in fact are needed—classic market conditions prevail. This suggests, in turn, that few of the abortions that are performed are truly "unnecessary" or chosen simply for convenience, as critics charge.

In the light of these contradictory themes, it is not difficult to see that significant underlying moral and religious attitudes largely explain the health system's failure to respond to the demand for abortion. That health professionals with a predisposition to regard abortion as a crime would have difficulty adapting to a situation in which it is legal—and is, indeed, the most frequently performed surgical procedure—should surprise no one.

Similar difficulties have arisen in other nations that have legalized abortion in the last decade. In these countries, too, a large proportion of abortions are performed outside mainstream health institutions. In England and Wales the established health system has not met the need; in 1977, for example, half of all abortions were performed outside National Health Service hospitals in nonsubsidized private-sector facilities.[22] In Canada only about one-fifth of nongovernmental hospitals provided abortions in 1976.[23] This congruence with the U.S. experience suggests the need for greater effort by health leaders everywhere to formulate an adequate approach to abortion as a health service and to facilitate the process of dealing with the philosophical and practical issues that abortion raises.

To attribute the medical system's failure to moral controversy, as some health professionals do, does not relieve the profession of its responsibility. The fact remains that a significant social change has occurred that involves the health system, but the system has refused to respond in ways commensurate with its social role. This denial of responsibility has had the following important effects:

It has resulted in unequal access to legal abortion services in various parts of the country and among different groups of American women. It has denied public officials objective information and professional advice on how to deal with a difficult and sensitive subject—advice they had every right to expect. It has deprived physicians, nurses, social workers, and other health professionals of adequate guidance about their proper roles. It has left a vacuum that has been filled by extremists—intensifying the controversy.

Perhaps most critical of all, it has meant that the professional leadership of the U.S. health system has not initiated a serious effort to develop a tenable public policy on a difficult issue that affects the system's ability to function. The health leaders thus have helped neither their patients who need and want abortion services, nor those of their colleagues who have deep moral objections to abortion, nor the many other doctors who simply want guidance as to what to do.

References

1 "Abortion: The Doctor's Dilemma," *Modern Medicine*, Apr. 24, 1967, p. 12.

2 See, for example, M. W. Harper, B. R. Marcom, and V. D. Wall, "Do Attitudes of Nursing Personnel Affect the Patient's Perception of Care?", *Nursing Research*, **21**:327, 1972; S. R. Wolf, T. T. Sasaki, and I. Cushner, "Assumption of Attitudes toward Abortion during Physician Education," *Obstetrics and Gynecology*, **37**:141, 1971; P. Mascovich, B. Behrstock, D. Minor, and A. Colman, "Attitudes of Obstetric and Gynecologic Residents toward Abortion," *California Medicine*, **119**:29, 1973; R. Hall, "Abortion: Physician and Hospital Attitudes," *American Journal of Public Health*, **61**:517, 1971; and G. Hendershot and J. W. Grimm, "Abortion Attitudes Among Nurses and Social Workers," *American Journal of Public Health*, **64**:438, 1974.

3 Dr. Iago Galdston, cited in M. S. Calderone (ed.), *Abortion in the United States*, New York: Hoeber-Harper, 1958, p. 118.

4 C. A. Nathanson and M. H. Becker, "Physician Behavior as a Determinant of Utilization Patterns: The Case of Abortion," *American Journal of Public Health*, **68**:1104, 1978.

5 P. Mascovich et. al., op. cit.

6 M. Calderone, op. cit., p. 171.

7 J. C. Mohr, *Abortion in America*, New York: Oxford University Press, 1978, pp. 160–170, 88–89.

8 Ibid., p. 167.

9 V. Fuchs, *Who Shall Live?*, New York: Basic Books, 1974, p. 60.

10 W. B. Walker and J. F. Hulka, "Attitudes and Practices of North Carolina Obstetricians—The Impact of the North Carolina Abortion Act of 1967," *Southern Medical Journal* **64**:441, 1971.

11 Cited in J. Saltman and S. Zimering, *Abortion Today*, Springfield, Ill.: Charles C. Thomas, 1973, p. 106.

12 J. C. Mohr, op. cit., p. 257.

13 Rep. Henry Hyde, *Congressional Record, House*, Nov. 13, 1977, p. H10969.

14 "Abortion, Training Policies Hold Spotlight at AMA, "*Hospital Practice*, Aug. 1970, p. 19.

15 U.S. District Court, Eastern District of Wisconsin, Deposition of Dr. Richard F. Mattingly, Dec. 2, 1974, p. 57.

16 Eunice Kennedy Shriver, letter to *New York Times*, Dec. 16, 1977.

17 A. Hellegers, "Biological Origins of Bioethical Problems," *Obstetrics and Gynecology Annual*, **6**:7, 1977.

18 K. L. White, "Health Problems and Priorities and the Health Professions," *Preventive Medicine*, **6**:565, 1977.

19 Ibid., p. 561.

20 Ibid., p. 565.

21 "Abortion, Training Policies Hold Spotlight at AMA," loc. cit.

22 C. Tietze, "Induced Abortion: *1979*, Third Edition, The Population Council, New York, 1979, table 2, p. 28.

23 R. F. Badgley, D. F. Caron, and M. G. Powell, *Report of the Committee on the Operation of the Abortion Law, Minister of Supply and Services*, Ottawa, 1977.

CHAPTER SIX

The Catholic Connection

The only reason we have a pro-life movement in this
country is because of the Catholic people and the Catholic
Church.[1]

Roy White, Executive Director,
National Right to Life Committee

Catholic spokesmen decry criticism of the Church's involvement in antiabortion political activities as thinly disguised anti-Catholicism. They
say this criticism is an attempt to limit religious institutions' right to
participate fully in the formulation of public policies.

Religious denominations *do* have the right—even the obligation—to
speak out on issues that are fundamental to their beliefs. They have the
right and the duty to seek to influence policy through moral education
and leadership. But opinions vary on the *extent* to which the separation
of church and state mandated by the Bill of Rights should limit religious
denominations' direct involvement in organized political activity.
Many political thinkers argue that it is inappropriate for religious
groups to try to enact their sectarian religious doctrines into law, particularly if those doctrines are not accepted by large segments of the
public.

As clearly stated in the *Pastoral Plan for Pro-Life Activities,* issued in
1975 by the National Conference of Catholic Bishops, the Roman
Catholic Church disagrees. It acknowledges that it intends to become
deeply involved in antiabortion political efforts. What has been
obscured, however, is the extent to which the Right-to-Life (RTL)

movement in the United States serves as a secular arm of the institutional Roman Catholic Church.

Both the Church and RTL groups proclaim that their convergent interests in abortion do not mean they are organizational and political bedfellows. National RTL organizations say their leadership and members include many non-Catholics, and national Church officials do in fact limit their public participation in secular antiabortion activities. But while many non-Catholic individuals and a few other religious groups are active in antiabortion efforts, there is convincing evidence that Catholics and the Catholic Church overwhelmingly dominate the RTL movement. Not only do Catholics comprise the bulk of RTL rank-and-file organizations, but the Church provides the movement's financial and institutional base.

This relationship differs on the national and local levels: the Church frequently is directly involved in local RTL activities. The Catholic hierarchy and national RTL organizations are more circumspect in their connections.

At the state and local level, Catholic churches provide organizational and material assistance, as well as symbolic authority, for RTL activities. In some states, there were well-established advocacy networks that now help the RTL cause. Local Catholic churches provide RTL groups with physical facilities, supplies, fund-raising help, and volunteer workers. In many states with effective RTL movements, seemingly distinct Church and RTL structures mask what in reality is a unified organizational effort.

The Church's antiabortion mobilization began during the abortion law liberalization battles of the late 1960s. It was furthered by the establishment, in November 1972, of the Bishops' Committee for Pro-Life Activities, to focus and coordinate the Church's antiabortion efforts. This committee distributes material on abortion to Catholic organizations throughout the nation and has the primary responsibility for disseminating the Catholic position on abortion to the nation as a whole.

In 1973, the bishops set up an independent lobbying group, the National Committee for a Human Life Amendment (NCHLA). Its charge is to secure a constitutional amendment to overturn the 1973 Supreme Court decisions. While NCHLA has actively represented the bishops' position on abortion-related legislation, the Church has had its greatest impact in recent years through the issuance and implementation of an extraordinary document, the *Pastoral Plan for Pro-Life Activities*.[2] This is a detailed, 13-page blueprint for political mobilization that was approved unanimously by the National Conference of Catholic Bishops.

The Pastoral Plan calls on all Church-sponsored and identifiably

Catholic organizations and agencies to undertake a comprehensive "prolife" legislative program. The main goal is to win passage of a constitutional amendment that would protect the unborn child to the maximum extent possible. Secondary goals include enactment of federal and state laws and the adoption of administrative policies to restrict abortion. These aims are to be realized by investing the resources and prestige of the Church in the development of grass-roots political organizations that would work for the interim measures while laying the educational and organizational groundwork for eventual constitutional victory.

The *Plan* notes that it is "absolutely necessary to encourage the development in each congressional district of an identifiable, tightly knit and well-organized pro-life unit."[3] Despite the disclaimer that its congressional district unit "is not an agency of the Church, nor is it operated, controlled or financed by the Church,"[4] the *Plan* stipulates that each of these seemingly independent units should have a chairperson to serve as liaison with church-sponsored prolife groups; "the task of these church-fostered pro-life groups," the bishops stipulate, "is essentially political, that is, to *organize people* to help persuade the elected representatives . . . [to] pass . . . a constitutional amendment" (emphasis added).[5]

The *Pastoral Plan* has received wide publicity. It has generated substantial dismay in both Catholic and non-Catholic circles, because it was unprecedented for a religious group to involve itself in the political process in so explicit and highly organized a manner. A critical editorial in the liberal *National Catholic Reporter* suggested, for example, that the bishops might be trying to create a "Catholic party."[6] Another retort came from the National Association of Women Religious, an organization of 3,000 nuns. They issued a statement in 1977 that affirmed their opposition to abortion but warned that a constitutional ban would be an "imposition of one [moral] view on the rest of society."[7]

Given the *Plan's* unprecedented and controversial character, why did the bishops adopt it? The main reason seems to be that despite all their vocal opposition to abortion, the bishops were under attack by right-wing elements in the Church who charged they were not doing enough. Randy Engel, of Export, Pennsylvania, the head of an RTL secular group called the U.S. Coalition for Life, complained in January 1975:

> By any measurement, financial or otherwise, abortion (and the whole population control program of the state) is not a top priority of the Catholic hierarchy. . . . As long as they stall, no one, including Congress and grass-roots pro-lifers, can or should accept rhetoric for action and a sincere commitment to life.[8]

Prominent RTL law professor Charles Rice wrote: "The pro-life movement will be capable of victory if the bishops will do their job. Therefore, to the bishops we ought to say, 'Fulfill thy ministry.'"[9]

A nurse who was active in a local RTL chapter in Iowa reiterated this point in a statement quoted in the Catholic journal *America:* "Some people seem to think the clergy is pushing us. That's backwards. We pressured the bishops to make a public stand."[10]

The repeated defeat of antiabortion constitutional amendments undoubtedly was viewed by the bishops' intramural critics as proof that the hierarchy had been lax. With no prospects for early achievement of an abortion ban in sight, RTL pressures on the hierarchy to do something visible intensified. As one activist noted, "If the bishops don't stand up on this issue, what can they ever stand up on?"[11]

Non-Catholics may be largely unaware that the bishops preside over a deeply divided church. There is a pervasive split between a minority that is theologically, socially, and politically progressive and the predominant conservative majority. Church commentators report that the willingness of "liberal" bishops—who have deep reservations about the Church's single-minded focus on abortion—to go along with the antiabortion mobilization was bought with conservative support for progressive domestic and foreign policy positions that the liberals sought.[12]

The bishops know that many of their flock do not follow them on abortion—although this rarely is publicly acknowledged. When questioned about polls that show that a majority of Catholics now support legal abortion, Archbishop Joseph Bernardin, then President of the National Conference of Catholic Bishops, conceded that winning a majority of Catholics to a proamendment attitude "is not something we can accomplish overnight."[13]

These factors all argued for a major antiabortion commitment by the bishops: deeply held religious values would be defended, conservative elements in the Church would be mollified; Catholic lay people could be educated and mobilized; and the RTL movement could be fortified with the community resources of thousands of Catholic churches.

Just who are the abortion opponents?

For many of the RTL troops, involvement in antiabortion work represents their first foray into organized politics. The majority are people of traditionalist orientation. Most are women. They typically are Catholic, older, blue-collar people. They bring ideological commitment and a single-minded zeal to their cause, which they have endowed with a crusading fervor.

This fervor has helped the RTL movement win political influence disproportionate to its actual numbers. As its leaders have acquired greater political maturity and sophistication, they have become more effective in representing their cause in the national political arena.

These political skills have been apparent in changing strategy and tactics. In the early years, the opponents had only one goal: A constitutional amendment to outlaw all abortions. Their strategy was to win public and political support through large, vocal demonstrations. They provoked emotional confrontation with legislators, often using preserved fetuses as props. It was several years before these methods were largely supplanted by more traditional lobbying and political-action techniques, in the hands of increasingly professional and effective representatives. "They stopped throwing fetuses and started acting like other responsible lobbies," one congressional aide observed.[14]

Like any political or social movement, the RTL forces include a number of factions, with different motives, ideologies, and strategic approaches to their common goal. Although some effective state RTL groups emerged very quickly in the years following the Supreme Court decisions, the national movement in Washington first was dominated by several small, highly vocal groups, with uncertain constituencies. One of the most visible was Nellie Gray's March for Life, a group whose most important undertaking had been to organize the mass demonstrations on Capitol Hill each January protesting the 1973 ruling. An estimated 28,000 to 45,000 people rallied for this occasion in 1980.

Another early group was the U.S. Coalition for Life, which calls itself a research and lobbying organization. But it seems to be primarily a vehicle for the energetic antiabortion campaign of Mrs. Engel.

Initially, the only RTL organization on the national scene that possessed demonstrable political power and expertise was NCHLA. Much of its funding continues to come from individual contributions from Catholic dioceses, which gave more than half of the $900,000 it reported receiving in 1976 and the first quarter of 1977.[15] The NCHLA employs a number of registered lobbyists to represent the Catholic Church's official position on abortion in Washington; its critical role in the passage of the 1976 amendment to the appropriations bill for the Department of Labor and HEW is detailed in Chapter 10.

The National Right to Life Committee (NRLC) started as a small group of committed volunteers who expended much effort trying to resolve the movement's incessant internecine battles. It forged a loose national coalition of the local RTL groups that are the backbone of the movement. The NRLC had its origins inside the Church. But it quickly moved to disassociate itself from the Church, both organizationally and in its public image. From its earliest days, NRLC has attempted to downplay the

Church-RTL movement connection by emphasizing that many of its national leaders are not Catholics. In 1974, a Catholic publication reported that NRLC "seemed to be moving in the direction of a lower Catholic profile for the antiabortion movement."[16] In 1978, incoming President Carolyn Gerster opened her first press conference by remarking: "I would like to note that I am a Protestant."[17]

This national RTL umbrella organization claims 3,000 affiliated chapters with 11 million members (although it has provided no evidence to support the figure). The group's leaders include physicians, lawyers, clergymen, and other professionals. But it mirrors its grass-roots constituency in its intransigence on abortion issues, which often bring it into conflict with the Church. Some factions are critical of the Catholic Church for not promoting hard-line RTL goals with adequate fervor.

There is also tension arising from the increasingly conservative political cast of the movement, which conflicts with a far more politically progressive Church hierarchy and membership.

Local RTL organizations have from the earliest days been dominated by antiabortion Catholic supporters, Catholic symbolism and imagery, and—most important—Catholic resources. Local newspaper reports show that this relationship operates in many parts of the U.S.

Catholic churches, schools, and service organizations often are cited as meeting places and sources of volunteers for RTL political activities and demonstrations. For example, a 1976 Pro-Life Council of Connecticut meeting to "make abortion an issue in the upcoming election" was held at St. Patrick's Cathedral in Norwich.[18] In Chicago, however, a cautious John Cardinal Cody felt compelled to limit the in-church preaching and fund-raising activities of Reverend Charles Fiore, founder of a political organization for electing antiabortion congressional candidates.[19]

During the struggle over state-Medicaid abortion funding, Massachusetts Citizens for Life distributed antifunding petitions on the steps of a Catholic church.[20] In Maryland, in 1978, an antiabortion group called Stop Taxes for Abortion collected signatures to win a statewide referendum on public funding. The group's director, George Yourishin, said that while the drive did not have official Catholic backing, many signatures were collected in front of individual churches; the petition drive was announced from the pulpits. Signs announcing the drive were observed in several churches.[21]

The Iowa Pro-Life Action Council distributed 300,000 brochures at Catholic churches before the 1978 election. They urged the defeat of Senator Dick Clark because of his opposition to a constitutional amendment banning abortion.[22]

One of the more visible signs of RTL's Catholic orientation is the degree to which antiabortion demonstrations are dominated by Catholic imagery and symbols. This is most obvious in the annual march on Washington in January. Large contingents of students, bused to the Capital from parochial schools, carry crosses, church banners, and statues of the Virgin Mary and patron saints.

A group called Shield of Roses regularly pickets abortion clinics. At a demonstration in Milwaukee, these avowedly nondenominational protesters prayed and carried rosaries, and their leader vowed to carry on "with the assistance of the Mother of God."[23]

The *Pastoral Plan* is designed to formalize and coordinate these activities. The archdiocesan implementation of the *Plan* in St. Louis has been cited as a model for the rest of the nation. Archbishop John Carberry has been very active in antiabortion efforts, and almost all of his 254 parishes have their own prolife committees, which sponsor educational and liturgical programs using material and speakers provided by the archdiocesan offices. According to Father Edward J. O'Donnell, coordinator of the archdiocesan prolife committee, these efforts have yielded important achievements. Missouri passed what O'Donnell calls "the most restrictive abortion law in the country" (although it subsequently was invalidated by the Supreme Court); and the Missouri legislature was the first officially to call for a constitutional convention to adopt an antiabortion amendment. The mayor and city of St. Louis refused and were ultimately upheld in their refusal to allow abortions in the public hospitals. A majority of congressmen from the archdiocese have supported antiabortion legislation.

Father O'Donnell credits this antiabortion success to "having the archdiocese behind it. When you have the backing of the Archbishop, the pastors will go along with you."[24]

What Father O'Donnell neglects to mention is that these victories were achieved in tandem with the highly organized Missouri Citizens for Life (MCL), the secular RTL organization. The archdiocese cosponsors educational events with MCL. During the 1976 primary campaigns, for example, the archdiocese's weekly parish bulletins ran the results of an MCL candidate poll on the abortion issue. These results were fortified by a message from Cardinal Carberry calling for opposition to candidates who fail to respect the "sanctity of human life."[25]

As these examples indicate, there were close financial and organizational ties between individual RTL groups and the local Church even before adoption of the *Pastoral Plan*. But this involvement only occasionally is visible, for antiabortion groups promote an image of broadbased support from citizens of all religions. The fear of suits challenging the Church's tax-exempt status increases the caution with which Church-affiliated political activities are publicized.

A comprehensive examination of the Church-RTL nexus on the state and local level would require a major investigative research effort. However, there are two existing sources of documentation for that relationship: investigative reports from Minnesota and New York that were published in two independent newspapers.

Interviews with leaders and members of Minnesota Concerned Citizens for Life (MCCL) and Catholic Church officials in Minnesota published in the *Minneapolis Tribune* provide insights into their connections. The director of the Minnesota Catholic Conference, John Markert, said: "If MCCL weren't there, we'd have to invent them."[26]

A review of the record shows, however, that the Minnesota Church in fact *did* invent MCCL—which has been cited as the model for the independent, congressional-district prolife groups in the *Pastoral Plan.*

The MCCL was founded in 1968 by a Minneapolis Newman Center priest and a Methodist physician. According to St. Cloud diocesan prolife director Reverend Paul Zylla, in 1969 or 1970 he and Bishop George Speltz decided "we should use MCCL as much as possible . . . . We decided to use their materials and urge Catholic people to get involved, setting up chapters where they didn't exist.[27]

The Church-MCCL relationship is expressed in close financial, strategic, and organizational cooperation. In 1977, Minnesota dioceses formally contributed $12,000 to MCCL. In addition, a Catholic official said that "a fair amount of money is contributed by parishes, social action committees, rosary societies and other church groups."[28]

The political bonds between the two entities are equally close. Minnesota Catholic Conference director Markert describes them as a "co-lobby" in the Minnesota Legislature. He says, "We strategize together, keep track of each other, divide up meeting assignments, coordinate as much as we can."[29]

The MCCL is beholden to the Church for membership, too. When speaking to Catholic groups, Markert urges them to join MCCL. The archdiocesan newspaper and the director of an annual Church fund-raising and educational event, the "Respect Life" campaign, frequently encourage Catholics to become involved in MCCL. Some parish churches distribute its literature; others regularly announce MCCL meetings and fund-raising activities.[30]

Before the February 1978 precinct caucuses, which are the first step in developing party platforms and selecting candidates in Minnesota, 100,000 copies of an MCCL newsletter carrying instructions on how to introduce antiabortion resolutions and elect RTL delegates were handed out, mostly at Catholic churches.[31]

The MCCL leaders and Church officials nevertheless averred the independence of the two organizations. Their reasons are not hard to surmise, for as the Reverend James Hahn, pastor of Holy Spirit Catholic Church, explained: "A lay person has more credibility. When people see a guy coming up in a clerical collar, they think he's just carrying the party line."[32]

In January 1978, the liberal independent *National Catholic Reporter (NCR)* published a cover story that revealed in exhaustive detail the fact that the secular New York State Right to Life Committee (NYRTL) and the state's Catholic bishops had maintained a "financial hand-in-glove relationship for a number of years."[33] According to the article, and files available to the authors, the bishops not only allowed NYRTL to solicit contributions at the annual "Respect Life" Sunday that they sponsored but also actively joined in planning the event. For example, a September 6, 1976, letter from Bishop Edward Head of Buffalo to his pastors requests them to "announce that this appeal will be conducted . . . . I ask that you cooperate with the Right-to-Life Committee which will be in contact with you."[34]

At about the same time, Marge Fitton, the NYRTL state treasurer, sent a letter to NYRTL officials outlining plans for the Respect Life fund-raising: "Because of the Catholic Committee's positive spirit of cooperation . . . we expect that our largest contributions will be from the Catholic community."

The letter lays down specific instructions for making arrangements with the churches. The parishioner designated by the local pastor to handle the Respect Life collection is to be contacted. Fitton notes:

> Every door at every service should be covered by a *parish* volunteer. . . . The *parish* representative will collect the donations and either send or deliver the money to the local chairman (emphasis added). The collections are not to be made during any service. However, unless the pastor objects, volunteers should stand in the vestibule or foyer of the Church.

The final instruction is to contact Charles Tobin at the New York State Catholic Conference in case of difficulty.[35]

When *NCR* interviewed Tobin, who is executive director of the Catholic Conference, he maintained that the relationship between the bishops and NYRTL was merely "informational." He denied that he acted as a liaison between the two groups, that the Catholic Conference received collection reports, or that it knew how the money was used. Yet a September 6, 1977, letter from Tobin to Helen Greene of NYRTL details plans for the collection:

"It is essential that local RTL people contact the diocesan pro-life director to follow up on the arrangements for the solicitation."[36]

In a letter to the bishops, Tobin says: "The money will be divided on a one-third basis among national, state and local RTL organizations. . . ."[37]

Despite the risks inherent in using Church solicitations for political-action groups, minutes from the December 6, 1975, NYRTL board of directors' meeting show that Tobin rejected a NYRTL suggestion that money from Respect Life collections go to a nonprofit educational RTL foundation—the only way the money permissibly could have been spent for RTL purposes under Internal Revenue Service rules. But minutes from the September 11, 1976, board meeting do indicate NYRTL concern about the source of the funding. They warn, "No church checks should be sent to the state office."[38]

The Church also was involved in strategic planning sessions. In her May 4, 1976, chairman's report, Helen Greene of NYRTL said she had "met with the pro-life chairmen and the bishops in Buffalo . . . . Ninety percent of the people present were former RTL'ers. Future meeting with Mr. Tobin of the Catholic Committee is being set up."[39] In New York as in Minnesota—and undoubtedly elsewhere as well—implementation of the *Pastoral Plan* generated an active partnership between secular and Church-sponsored antiabortion efforts.

The importance of church collections to RTL is apparent when the NYRTL financial statements are examined. Revenues from October 1, 1975, through September 30, 1976, were $102,835. The largest single item was $60,933 from the Respect Life collections, 59 percent of *all* revenues that year. Membership fees for the entire state brought in $832 and donations $471.[40] The 1977 statement indicates increasing dependence on Respect Life collections: now $77,657, or 68 percent of the total, came from these church collections.[41]

A tape recording obtained by *NCR* is even more disturbing in that it suggests that some RTL activists are aware of the impropriety and potential illegality of raising money in churches but are willing to condone it. The tape is from a February 1974 meeting of NYRTL leaders, who discuss a 1973 Rockville Centre, New York, diocesan collection. One NYRTL member says that "for all practical purposes it was a church collection and therefore could in no way be paid to NYRTL, Inc."[42] But the meeting chairman declares: "Now this was done because it is legal and not tainting of church funds if you take church collections and pay to the indebtedness of the unborn."[43]

Since the adoption and implementation of the *Pastoral Plan*, the bishops have continued, through their lobbying arm, the NCHLA, to oppose abortion and advocate the passage of a constitutional amendment. However, while maintaining their national posture, the bishops have indicated that they are backing away, however slightly, from the *Pastoral Plan's* premise that electoral decisions should be based almost exclusively on the basis of a candidate's position on abortion. In a statement issued on October 26, 1979, the administrative board of the U.S. Catholic Conference disclaimed the notion of a "religious voting bloc" and urged voters to "examine the positions of candidates on the full range of issues as well as the person's integrity, philosophy and performance." The statement, entitled "Political Responsibility: Choices for the 1980's," listed 12 issues, including abortion, on which candidates should be assessed. While this statement does not indicate a change in the position of the Church hierarchy on abortion, it does suggest that the Church is no longer willing to endorse single-issue politics with abortion as the paramount political issue.[44]

References

1 G. Plagenz, "Abortion Is Becoming 1976 Election Issue," *Cleveland Press,* Aug. 2, 1975.

2 National Conference of Catholic Bishops, *Pastoral Plan for Pro-Life Activities,* Nov. 20, 1975.

3 Ibid., p. 11.

4 Ibid., p. 12.

5 Ibid., p. 11.

6 *National Catholic Reporter,* Nov. 21, 1975.

7 "Bishop Rejects Abortion 'Compromise,' Calls for Constitutional Amendment," *Planned Parenthood Washington Memor,* Sept. 9, 1977.

8 "Right to Life: Time for a New Strategy?", *Triumph,* January 1975.

9 Ibid., p. 15.

10 P. J. Weber, "Bishops in Politics: The Big Plunge," *America,* Mar. 20, 1976.

11 Ibid.

12 T. Fleming, "Divided Shepherds of a Restive Flock," *New York Times Magazine,* Jan. 16, 1977.

13 K. A. Briggs, "Carter Campaign Moving to Mollify Catholics After Dispute Over Democratic Party's Abortion Stand," *New York Times,* Aug. 26, 1976.

14 W. Taylor, "Abortion Opponents Switch From Emotional Approach," *Washington Star,* Sept. 16, 1975.

15 M. Winiarski, "Abortion Fight: Crusade of Many Faces," *National Catholic Reporter,* Mar. 3, 1978.

16 "Right-to-Lifers Fail to Agree on Amendment," *National Catholic Reporter*, June 21, 1974.

17 B. Kenkelen, "Pro-Life Aim: Put God on Capitol Hill," *National Catholic Reporter*, July 14, 1978.

18 "Pro-Life Poll," *Norwich Bulletin*, Oct. 6, 1976.

19 E. S. Gilbreth and R. G. Schultz, "Cody v. Fiore: Standoff on Anti-Abortion Activity," *Chicago Daily News*, Jan. 3, 1978.

20 B. Peterson, "Politics of the Jugular," *Washington Post*, Dec. 10, 1977.

21 S. Saperstein, "Md. Abortion Fees Face Hurdle in Referendum Push," *Washington Post*, June 30, 1978.

22 W. Sinclair, "Anti-Abortion Activists Help Scuttle Clark in Iowa," *Washington Post*, Nov. 9, 1978.

23 "Abortion Argued," *Milwaukee Courier*, Aug. 7, 1976.

24 "Catholics Divided on Church's Political Role in Abortion Fight," *Planned Parenthood Washington Memo*, Apr. 8, 1976.

25 Archdiocese of St. Louis, "Pro-Life: Missouri Citizens for Life Survey, Information Provided for Parishioners" (mimeo), July 1976.

26 L. Sturdevant, "Catholic Church Closely Tied to State Pro-Life Group," *Minneapolis Tribune*, July 16, 1978.

27 Ibid.

28 Ibid.

29 Ibid.

30 Ibid.

31 L. Sturdevant and S. Dornfeld, "Antiabortion Group Strong Despite 'Little Guy' Claim," *Minneapolis Tribune*, July 18, 1978.

32 L. Sturdevant, "Anti-Abortion Activist in St. Cloud was 'Tested' with her 15th Child," *Minneapolis Tribune*, July 17, 1978.

33 M. Winiarski, "Bishops–Right to Life, 'Hand-in-Glove' in N. Y.," *National Catholic Reporter*, Jan. 27, 1978.

34 Ibid.

35 Ibid.

36 Ibid.

37 Ibid.

38 Ibid.

39 Helen M. Greene, chairman, New York State Right to Life Committee, chairman's report, May 4, 1976.

40 New York State Right to Life Committee, Inc., statement of revenues, Oct. 1, 1975, through Sept. 30, 1976.

41 New York State Right to Life Committee, Inc., statement of revenues, Oct. 1, 1976–July 31, 1977.

42   M. Winiarski, "Tape Tells Debt Paid, But How?", *National Catholic Reporter*, Feb. 21, 1978.

43   Ibid.

44   Administrative Board, U.S. Catholic Conference, "Political Responsibility: Choices for the 1980s," *Origins*, **9**:349, 1979.

CHAPTER SEVEN

Absolute Evil versus Sometimes Good

Organized religious groups hold radically different theological beliefs about the morality of abortion and the circumstances, if any, under which it is permissible. Discrepancies exist, to be sure, between religious doctrine and adherents' practices—as the long history of widespread use of illegal abortion in European and Latin American Catholic countries shows. It also is true that individual members of all religious groups, and nonbelievers, can be found on all sides of the abortion issue. Organized religions nevertheless remain the principal institutions that hold and preach moral doctrines on abortion. The conflict in their teachings presently is irreconcilable.

Organized religions may no longer command the same allegiance from their members that they did in the past. But they remain influential in the formation of laws and public policies, and political leaders usually are reluctant to offend them.

The irreconcilability of religious beliefs on abortion makes the task of formulating equitable laws and public policies extraordinarily difficult. Neither the Supreme Court nor the Senate Judiciary Subcommittee on Constitutional Amendments, after reviewing the abortion doctrines of the principal U.S. denominations, could find a way to resolve the conflict. They acted accordingly. Both declined to enact into law the doctrines of any one group or denomination.

Yet the conflict between religions over abortion continues and now transcends the abortion question. Thus, despite significant progress that has been made toward ecumenism in the last two decades, John C. Bennett, the distinguished Protestant leader and president emeritus of

Union Theological Seminary, says: "One of the most troublesome aspects" of the abortion conflict is that "it is the chief remaining public question on which there is a tendency for Catholics as Catholics to differ with many Protestants."[1]

A committee of Catholic and Protestant Episcopal officials, which has been working for 12 years to solidify ecumenical bonds, now cites "growing disagreement" between the two faiths in human sexuality, marriage, and the family. It proposes further study of "new and perplexing" questions in the role of women in the churches, abortion, mixed marriages, and homosexuality.[2]

In October 1977, more than 200 theologians and ethicists, representing for the most part Protestant and Jewish groups—but including six Catholic scholars—issued a statement decrying the Catholic bishops'

> campaign to enact religiously based antiabortion commitments into law
> . . . as a serious threat to religious liberty and freedom of conscience.
>   There may be some ecumenical risks in such candor, but those risks have already been assumed by those who have pressed the absolutist position [on abortion] on religious grounds. In the long run, the true test of ecumenical authenticity is the ability to sustain dialogue and friendship in spite of sharp disagreements on matters of substance.[3]

The theologians' fears have been confirmed. Several religious groups recently have felt compelled to respond, forcefully, to what many view as an escalating Catholic offensive on abortion rights.

An agency of the United Methodist Church was a plaintiff in a federal court suit that successfully challenged the Hyde amendment.[4] The suit alleged that the amendment impinges on the religious liberties of poor Methodist women who wish to obtain abortions in accordance with their religious beliefs.

In January 1979, leaders of 20 major Protestant and Jewish denominations, convened by the Religious Coalition for Abortion Rights, issued "A Religious Statement on Abortion: A Call to Commitment." It states that abortion rights are an "issue of major concern." The statement urges members to undertake an educational effort to inform the public of the theological basis for abortion rights and calls for the denominations to increase their commitments to political and pastoral "prochoice" activities, and to increase, too, their opposition to a prolife amendment.[5]

The same day, three dozen Jewish and Protestant clergy of the Religious Leaders for a Free Choice marched in full ecclesiastic regalia to St. Patrick's Cathedral in New York City. They presented Catholic officials with a proclamation expressing their alarm at "the growing escalation of violent language and acts that have the appearance of support of the leadership of the Church." The proclamation added the following:

"It is our belief that the continuation of this position not only threatens the peace of our ecumenical position but . . . the civil amity and political tolerance that make our democracy work."[6]

To gain perspective on the type of public abortion policy that is tenable in a society made up of adherents of many different faiths, it is necessary to examine what the principal religions actually teach and preach on abortion. This subject—and particularly the evolution of doctrinal positions—is a vast one.[7] Our aim here is not a comprehensive analysis, for which we are not qualified, but a sketch of some of the highlights. This effort is particularly necessary because the Roman Catholic position is reasonably well known, partly because it is clearcut, while the more nuanced beliefs of most Protestant and Jewish denominations are less well understood.

The Catholic Church teaches, in essence, that direct termination of pregnancy never is permissible. In his famous 1930 encyclical on marriage, *Casti Connubii*, Pope Pius XI described abortion as a "very serious crime . . . which attacks the life of the offspring while it is yet hidden in the womb of its mother." Dismissing the idea that serious medical, social, or eugenic reasons may justify abortion, he wrote:

> Can any reason ever avail to excuse the direct killing of the innocent? For this is what is at stake. The infliction of death whether upon mother or upon child is against the commandment of God and the voice of nature: "Thou shalt not kill."[8]

This condemnation was repeated by Pius' successors, Pius XII and John XXIII, and by the Second Vatican Council. It declared in 1965: "From the moment of its conception life must be guarded with the greatest care, while abortion and infanticide are unspeakable crimes."[9]

In 1968, in the encyclical *Humanae Vitae*, Pope Paul VI condemned both contraception and abortion. He declared that "the direct interruption of the generative process already begun, and above all willed and procured abortion, even if for therapeutic reasons, are to be absolutely excluded as licit means of regulating birth."[10] Pope Paul's position has been reaffirmed on several occasions by Pope John Paul II.

The only exceptions allowed under official Catholic doctrine are *indirect* abortions, as when a woman has an ectopic pregnancy or uterine cancer. In these cases, the indicated procedure to remove the fallopian tube or uterus has as its *direct* purpose the saving of the woman's life, and the death of the fetus is regarded as the *unintended* and *indirect* result.

This narrow exception is consistent with the principle of "double effect" in Catholic moral theology. Some Catholic writers cite this principle to suggest that Church doctrine on abortion is not as uncompromising as is commonly supposed.

In one remarkable recent essay, for example, Reverend Richard A. McCormick, S. J., of Georgetown University, suggests that the "official" formulation of Pius XI and Pius XII prohibiting direct abortion even to save a woman's life should be disregarded, in favor of an interpretation that "the Church's *substantial* conviction is that abortion is tolerable only when it is a life-saving, therefore also life-serving, intervention"[11] (Emphasis in the original). Legal scholar John Noonan cites this exception when he claims that the Catholic position does not encompass "an absolute valuation of fetal life," but rather establishes "a general rule of inviolability of the fetus."[12] Ethicist Daniel Callahan observes, however, that this is not a meaningful difference:

> The full weight of the "general rule" is such that, in the ordinary sense of the word (where the great run of even disastrous pregnancies are concerned), the force of the rule is absolutist, displaying no "balance" at all. The "weighing" in question is decisively one-sided [and] takes physical life alone as the only value at stake, leaving no real room for even investigating any other considerations which might come into play.[13]

The Church's absolute, or near-absolute, condemnation of abortion is accompanied by sweeping penalties for Catholics who participate in it. "To emphasize the special evil of abortion," the U.S. Catholic Bishops declared in a pastoral message issued after the Supreme Court's 1973 decisions: "Under Church law, those who undergo or perform an abortion place themselves in a state of excommunication."[14]

Several Jewish groups and Protestant denominations, including some fundamentalists, join the Catholic bishops in demanding a constitutional amendment banning abortion. But as a matter of doctrine, many of these groups in fact permit abortion in a much broader set of circumstances than the Catholic Church does. The Mormon Church, for example, denounces abortion as a "revolting and sinful practice" but permits it "in the rare cases where, in the opinion of competent medical counsel, the life or good health of the mother is seriously endangered or where the pregnancy was caused by rape and produces serious emotional trauma in the mother."[15]

An Orthodox rabbi who testified before the Senate Judiciary Subcommittee on Constitutional Amendments in support of an amendment "to guarantee the fetus protection under law" submitted a lengthy review of the decisions of rabbinic authorities on abortion, which states that "Judaism has always sanctioned therapeutic abortion in at least limited circumstances" because "the mother's life has priority over the fetus' life." The review showed that abortion also has been approved by some authorities to preserve the mother's health and sanity.

"The status of the embryo's claim to life during the first 40 days following conception is not entirely clear," Rabbi J. David Bleich declared. He went on to say that some rabbis have ruled that a married woman who is pregnant as a result of an adulterous relationship may abort the pregnancy.[16]

The Lutheran Church-Missouri Synod also gives precedence to the mother's life when it is threatened by the pregnancy but finds that psychiatric and economic grounds do not by themselves justify abortion. Rather: "Instances of rape and incest create very special problems." Although the Synod's position is almost as absolute as that of the Catholic Church, it treats those who transgress differently. Synod members are called on "to deal lovingly" with the offense of "sinful abortion."[17]

The uniformity of the Catholic Church's condemnation of abortion as homicide during this century in fact obscures an historical disagreement within the Church, not only on the morality of abortion but also on the penalties to be imposed for it. For hundreds of years a distinction was drawn between abortion of the "unformed" fetus—which was believed not to possess a soul until 40 days of gestation for males and 80 days for females—and the later, "formed" fetus, which did have a soul. "Excellent authors allowed for this first period more lenient case solutions which they rejected for following periods," the Vatican noted in 1974.[18]

It was not until 1869 that this distinction finally was eliminated and the penalty of excommunication meted out for abortion at *any* state of gestation. Indeed, not until a new Code of Canon Law was promulgated in 1971 was the woman undergoing the abortion included, for the first time, among those to be excommunicated.[19]

This position is predicated on the belief that a fetus becomes a "person" at the moment of conception, with a right to the protections that civil and moral law confer on all persons. This also is the core contention of those who seek to enact antiabortion laws like the Hyde amendment, since the claim that abortion is "murder" wholly depends on this belief.

While the U.S. Catholic bishops in testimony before Congress have asserted that "it is an accepted biological fact that human life begins at fertilization," the Vatican itself states: "It is not up to biological sciences to make a definitive judgment on questions which are properly philosophical and moral, such as the moment when a human person is constituted or the legitimacy of abortion."[20,21]

Reputable Catholic theologians, nevertheless, continue to debate when a fetus becomes "ensouled," as a key determinant of fetal "personhood." "It must be said," theologian Bernhard Haring states flatly, "that the question about the precise moment after which we are faced with a human being in the full sense is not yet settled and will probably not easily be determined."[22]

Ethicist Daniel Callahan has demonstrated that the question of when a fetus becomes a person is not scientific but religious or metaphysical.[23] Two legal scholars come to a similar conclusion: Guido Calabresi of Yale describes the question of whether life begins at conception or parturition as "purely religious,"[24] and Lawrence H. Tribe of Harvard finds that "the only bodies of thought that have purported in this century to locate the crucial line between potential and actual life have been those of organized religious doctrine."[25]

The theological issue of the beginning of personhood nevertheless has dominated the *political* debate on abortion, precluding serious examination of its other, more critical aspects. In a similar way, this framing of the issue tends to distort the *religious* debate as well. Callahan says:

> This makes it exceedingly difficult, within the Catholic problematic, to try and weigh other values—the mother's duty toward her children, her psychological state and freedom, her economic situation—or to raise or answer other kinds of questions; the first question asked tends to preempt the others . . . . No room is left for the integration of a full range of rights, personal and communal.[26]

It is precisely over these questions that the major Protestant denominations and Reform and Conservative Judaism part company with the Catholics. None regard abortion as anything less than a serious moral and human question. But for all of them, the central issue is not whether the fetus becomes a "person" at conception but the achievement of morally desirable goals for both the born and the unborn, and the responsibility of the individual to conscientiously weigh all factors and choose between competing rights in a way that will maximize human values.

These religious outlooks do not condemn abortion as "murder." They rather stress that to further responsible parenthood, termination of pregnancy in some circumstances may be a moral act. In the words of the theologians who signed "A Call to Concern," it may be "the most loving act possible."[27] A large number of Protestant and Jewish groups have consistently supported legal abortion. Many also have spoken out in support of public funding of abortion in recent years.[28]

Protestant thinking on the relativity of abortion is well summarized in a 1973 National Council of Churches report, which cites several central goals that have to be taken into account in any decision about abortion:

> They include affirmation of the sanctity of life and of the quality of life; women's ability to live with dignity and equality, and to be responsible participants in determining the course of their lives; the obtainment of a healthful and happy pregnancy; and provision of a supportive climate for children in their developing years.[29]

When a crisis produces a conflict between these goals, the moral responsibility is to balance the competing values—which can be done only by the individuals directly concerned. Different Protestant groups place varying emphases on these values in their denominational statements. In its 1972 Resolution on Responsible Parenthood, for example, the United Methodist Church declared:

> Because human life is distorted when it is unwanted and unloved, parents seriously violate their responsibility when they bring into the world children for whom they cannot provide love. . . . When, through contraceptive or human failure, an unacceptable pregnancy occurs, we believe that a profound regard for unborn human life must be weighed alongside an equally profound regard for fully formed personhood, particularly when the physical, mental and emotional health of the pregnant woman and her family show reason to be seriously threatened by the new life just forming. . . . Continuation of a pregnancy endangering the life of the mother is not a moral necessity. In such case, we believe the path of mature Christian judgment may indicate the advisability of abortion.[30]

The Lutheran Church in America, in a 1970 statement on Sex, Marriage and Family, characterized abortion as "always a serious matter." Nevertheless, "A woman or couple may decide responsibly to seek an abortion."[31]

The American Lutheran Church similarly has affirmed that "all pertinent factors responsibly considered, the developing life may need to be terminated in order to defend the health and wholeness of persons already present and already participating in the relationships and responsibilities of life."[32] Like concepts are expressed in a 1974 Statement of the Presbyterian Church in the United States. The United Presbyterian Church in the United States of America, in 1972, went further, to state that "women should have full freedom of personal choice concerning the completion or termination of their pregnancies, and . . . the artificial or induced termination of pregnancy, therefore, should not be restricted by law."[33]

Other Protestant denominations also advocate the removal of legal restrictions on abortion to permit, in the words of a 1973 Episcopal Church statement, "a free and responsible exercise of Christian conscience" in making abortion decisions.[34] Similar positions have been taken by the United Church of Christ and the Reformed Church in 1971[35] and the Christian Church (Disciples of Christ) in 1975.[36] In 1968, the American Baptist Churches in the United States of America expressed their belief that "abortion should be a matter of responsible personal decision," and called for legal abortion.[37] Even the Southern Baptist Convention, regarded as one of the more conservative Protestant groups, has reaffirmed the principle of freedom of conscience on abortion.[38]

A consensus thus has emerged among these major Protestant groups, for which the primary moral responsibility is responsible parenthood and the obligation of each individual to weigh the circumstances of pregnancy conscientiously and make a moral decision. Major Jewish groups agree. These religious beliefs differ sharply from Catholic doctrine both in substance and in the manner in which they are to be observed. In essence, the conflict in beliefs juxtaposes an absolute evil against an evil that may be necessary—and sometimes can be a positive good.

References

1   J. C. Bennett, "Avoid Oppressive Laws," *Christianity and Crisis*, **32**:287, 1973.

2   Anglican–Roman Catholic Consultation in the U.S.A., *Where We Are: A Challenge for the Future*, 1977, pp. 9, 11, 12.

3   "A Call to Concern," *Christianity and Crisis*, **37**:222, 1977 (advertisement).

4   *McRae et al. v. Secretary DHEW*, 421 F. Supp. 533 (E.D. 1976), *Vacated and remanded* 433 U.S. 916 (June 29, 1977).

5   "A Religious Statement on Abortion: A Call to Commitment," Religious Coalition for Abortion Rights, Washington, D.C., Jan. 22, 1979.

6   L. Oelsner, "New York Clergymen Protest Catholic Stand," *New York Times*, Jan. 23, 1979.

7   For a comprehensive discussion of the Roman Catholic doctrine and its evolution, see D. Callahan, *Abortion: Law, Choice and Morality*, New York: Macmillan, 1970, Chapter 12. The best brief discussion of the range of Protestant beliefs is found in National Council of Churches, *Abortion: A Paper for Study*, New York, 1973. The evolution of the Jewish position is presented in D. M. Feldman, *Marital Relations, Birth Control and Abortion in Jewish Law*, New York: Schocken, 1975.

8   *Casti Connubii, Acta Apostolica Sedis*, **22**:562, 1930.

9   Pastoral Constitution on "The Church in the Modern World," in W. A. Ab-

bott, S. J. (ed.), *The Documents of Vatican II*, New York: America Press, Association Press, 1966, p. 256.

10 *Acta Apostolica Sedis*, **60**:481, 1968.

11 R. A. McCormick, "Abortion: Rules for Debate," *America*, July 22, 1978.

12 J. T. Noonan, Jr., "Abortion and the Catholic Church: A Summary History," *Natural Law Forum* **12**:85, 1967, cited in Callahan, op. cit., pp. 414–15, 430.

13 Callahan, op. cit., pp. 430–31, 424.

14 Pastoral Message of the Administrative Committee of the National Conference of Catholic Bishops, Feb. 13, 1973, reprinted in *Abortion–Part I, Hearings before Subcommittee on Constitutional Amendments of the Committee on the Judiciary*, U.S. Senate, 93d Cong., 1974, p. 239.

15 Testimony of David L. McKay, president, Eastern State Mission, The Church of Jesus Christ of Latter-Day Saints, in *Abortion–Part I*, op. cit., p. 318.

16 Testimony of Rabbi J. David Bleich, Rabbinical Council of America, in *Abortion—Part I*, op. cit., pp. 287, 289, 293, 296, 299, 302, 303.

17 Testimony of Jean Garton, National Board for Social Concern, Lutheran Church–Missouri Synod, in *Abortion–Part I*, op. cit., pp. 321, 322, 323.

18 Sacred Congregation for the Doctrine of the Faith, *Declaration on Abortion*, Nov. 18, 1974, published by U.S. Catholic Conference, Washington, D.C., 1975, p. 3.

19 Callahan, op. cit., p. 413.

20 Testimony of U.S. Catholic Conference on Constitutional Amendment Protecting Unborn Human Life, in *Abortion–Part I*, op. cit., p. 187.

21 Sacred Congregation for the Doctrine of the Faith, op. cit., p. 6.

22 B. Haring, "A Theological Evaluation," in J. T. Noonan, Jr. (ed.), *The Morality of Abortion*, Cambridge: Harvard University Press, 1970, p. 129.

23 Callahan, op. cit., Chap. 11.

24 G. Calabresi, "Birth, Death and the Law," *The Pharos*, April 1974, p. 10.

25 L. H. Tribe, "The Supreme Court, 1972 Term—Foreword," Harvard Law Review, **87**:20, 1973.

26 Callahan, op. cit., p. 419–20.

27 "A Call to Concern," loc. cit.

28 See Chap. 9, reference 10, for a list of religious organizations supporting legal abortion. Religious groups supporting public funding of abortion include:
American Friends Service Committee
American Jewish Congress
American Protestant Hospital Association
Baptist Joint Committee on Public Affairs
Central Conference of American Rabbis
Church of the Bretheren
Clergy Consultation on Abortion
Episcopal Church

Episcopal Churchwomen
Federation of Protestant Welfare Agencies
National Council of the Churches of Christ in the U.S.A.
Reform Church in America
Reorganized Church of Jesus Christ of Latter-Day Saints
United Methodist Church

Members of the Religious Coalition for Abortion Rights include:

American Baptist Church, National Ministries
American Ethical Union
American Ethical Union, National Women's Conference
American Humanist Association
American Jewish Congress, Women's Division
B'Nai B'rith Women
Catholics for Free Choice
Christian Church (Disciples of Christ), Division of Homeland Ministries
Episcopal Women's Caucus
Lutheran Church in America, Division for Mission in North America
National Council of Jewish Women
National Federation of Temple Sisterhoods
Planned Parenthood Federation of America, Religious Affairs Committee
Presbyterian Church in the U.S., Committee on Women's Concerns
Presbyterian Church in the U.S., General Executive Board
Union of American Hebrew Congregations
Unitarian Universalist Association
Unitarian Universalist Association, Women's Federation
United Church of Christ, Board of Homeland Ministries
United Church of Christ, Office for Church in Society
United Methodist Church, Board of Church and Society
United Methodist Church, Women's Division, Board of Global Ministries
United Presbyterian Church, U.S.A., Church and Society Unit
United Presbyterian Church, U.S.A., Washington Office
United Presbyterian Church, U.S.A., Women's Program Unit
Woman's League for Conservative Judaism
Young Women's Christian Association

29   National Council of Churches, op. cit., p. 3.

30   Reprinted in ibid., p. 17.

31   Reprinted in ibid., p. 12.

32   Reprinted in National Council of Churches, *A Synoptic of Recent Denominational Statements on Sexuality*, 2d Ed. New York, 1975, p. 24.

33   Reprinted in National Council of Churches, *Abortion: A Paper for Study*, op. cit., p. 19.

34   Reprinted in ibid., p. 10.

35   Reprinted in ibid., pp. 16, 17.

36 Reprinted in National Council of Churches, *A Synoptic . . . op. cit., p. 26.*

37 Reprinted in National Council of Churches, *Abortion: A Paper for Study,* op. cit., p. 9.

38 K. A. Briggs, "Baptists Dilute Abortion Backing," *New York Times,* June 18, 1976.

CHAPTER EIGHT
Vox Populi

Measuring public opinion is difficult, particularly when the subject is complex and has moral and religious overtones. Opinion polls typically are limited to a few oversimplified questions—crude instruments for making subtle distinctions or tapping attitudinal nuances. The answers frequently depend on the way the questions are worded and the order in which they are presented. Polls thus are least useful in measuring small differences in attitudes and most useful in identifying gross trends in opinion on easily understandable questions.

Polling organizations in the United States began asking about abortion in the 1960s. The polls since then support five general conclusions: the *first*, not surprisingly, is that few Americans have extremist or absolutist abortion views. The majority neither unquestioningly support nor automatically condemn abortion. *Second*, a major increase in approval of abortion has occurred since the 1960s, with the result that most Americans now approve of legal abortion under at least some circumstances. A sizable minority approve of abortion under most circumstances, while a smaller group remains opposed for any reason, as is clear from Table 1.

The *third* general conclusion that can be drawn from the polls is that the abortion issue's complexity, the ambivalence it generates, and the correspondingly complicated attitudes people bring to it are reflected in marked changes in measures of opinion that depend on the way the issues are presented and on societal events at the time the poll is taken. The *fourth* conclusion is that increasing approval of abortion has been paralleled by a marked narrowing of the historical religious, educational,

TABLE 1.   NORC Surveys 1965–1980

"Should it be possible for a pregnant woman to obtain a legal abortion?"

Percent believing it should be legal for reasons of	1965	1972	1973	1974	1975	1976	1977	1978	1980	Change 1965–80
Mother's health	73	87	92	92	91	91	90	91	90	+17
Rape	59	79	83	86	84	84	84	83	83	+24
Defect in child	57	79	84	85	83	84	85	82	83	+26
Mother unmarried	18	43	49	50	48	50	50	41	48	+30
Family poor	22	49	53	55	53	53	53	47	52	+30
No more children wanted	16	40	48	47	46	46	46	40	47	+31
Approval for no reason	22	10	6	5	7	6	6	7	7	−15
Approval for all 6	11	36	43	42	41	42	40	34	43	+32

NOTE: Percentages exclude those who did not answer or said they didn't know.

SOURCE: NORC, *National Data Program for the Social Sciences, Cumulative Codebook for the 1972 –1977 General Social Surveys,* October 1977.
D. Granberg, "A Multifaceted Analysis of Attitudes Toward Abortion in the U.S.A. 1965–1978," Final Report to National Institute of Child Health and Human Development, DHEW, November 1979, updated by NORC, June, 1980.

and regional differences in attitudes toward it: by 1980, most population subgroups were essentially alike in their support for legal abortion. And *fifth*, the polls have shown that legalized abortion is an intense political issue only for a small minority of people—and they are about evenly split between proponents and opponents.

The most detailed trend data on attitudes toward legal abortion have been gathered and reported by the National Opinion Research Center (NORC), which has been polling on abortion since 1965. Respondents have been asked whether it should be possible for a pregnant woman to obtain a legal abortion for each of six different reasons, ranging from presumably clearcut situations—"hard" reasons—to those that are more ambiguous, or "soft." As can be seen in Table 1, abortion for the three "hard" reasons—pregnancy that is a threat to the woman's health, pregnancy resulting from rape, or the risk of a seriously defective fetus—has had high levels of support since the end of the 1960s. Abortion for the "soft" reasons—low income, pregnancy outside marriage, and when no more children are desired—has had lower levels of support.

By 1980, between 82 and 91 percent of respondents approved of legal abortion for "hard" reasons, between 47 and 52 percent approved for "soft" ones. Between 1965 and 1980, there had been increases of 24 to 31 percentage points in approval of both the "hard" and the "soft" reasons, except for health endangerment, where the increase was smaller but the proportion approving in 1965 had been higher.

Although there was a small decline in approval of abortion for the "soft" reasons in 1978, compared to 1977, the overall upward trend brought the level of approval for the "soft" reasons from about one-fifth of the population in 1965 to around 50 percent or more in 1980. For each item, the proportion approving has more than doubled in this period. In the years covered by these surveys, the proportion of Americans not approving of legal abortion for any reason has declined from 22 percent to 7 percent and the proportion approving it for all six reasons has increased from 11 percent to 43 percent.

These figures suggest the degree to which professed feelings about abortion are subject to what people perceive as the attitudes of the larger society. The greatest increases in approval occurred between 1965 and 1972, when there were drives in many states to reform restrictive abortion laws; this was particularly true for the "soft" reasons. After 1973, the levels of approval for each of the six items jumped six to eight percentage points, as people apparently responded to the legitimizing influence of the Supreme Court decisions.

There then was almost no change through 1977, despite the fact that over five million American women had legal abortions in the interim—an experience that might have been expected to positively influence the attitudes of the far-larger group of their parents, spouses, partners, and friends. But the attitudes people express about abortion seem to be keyed more to events and the climate of opinion in the society at large than to personal experience or willingness to use abortion.

The one other marked change in the opinion indices came in 1978, when for the first time approval dropped for almost all items. For the "hard" reasons the dip was minimal; but approval for the "soft" reasons decreased between five and eight points. However, by 1980, approval had gone up again to 1977 levels.

It appears that the impact of the restrictive actions in 1977 of the U.S. Supreme Court, President Carter, the Congress, and the Department of Health, Education and Welfare; the overt and implicit antiabortion sentiments they expressed; and the controversy they generated have influenced the degree to which Americans voice support of abortion for the less-compelling reasons. To a significant extent, however, these declines seem to signify ambivalence, rather than rejection of legal abortion. The number of women obtaining abortions has continued to increase since 1977, as it has each year since the Supreme Court decisions. In addition, polls that do not allow respondents to differentiate between conditions for abortion showed no decrease in general levels of support for legal abortion in this period.

The Gallup organization has asked a series of questions similar to the NORC items, prepared by sociologist Judith Blake. Respondents have been asked if abortion should be legal when the mother's health is in danger, when the child may be born deformed, when "the family does not have enough money to support another child," and when "the parents simply have all the children they want although there would be no major health or financial problems involved in having another child."

The reported results, like the NORC series, confirm significant increases in support for legal abortion in the late 1960s and early 1970s. By 1972, support for abortion when the mother's health is at stake was voiced by 87 percent of whites and 63 percent of nonwhites, while three-fourths of whites and 63 percent of nonwhites approved abortion for possible congenital deformity.[1] The proportion disapproving of abortion when the family lacks money to support another child declined from 72 percent of respondents in 1968 to 47 percent in 1974,[2] which appears to be roughly comparable to the NORC results on approval of abortion in poverty cases.

The proportion approving of abortion when no more children are wanted increased from 11 percent in 1968 to 30 percent in 1977.[3] Like the NORC findings, this represented a tripling of approval for the "softest" reason in less than a decade, although the level of approval in response to Blake's question is below that for the NORC question. Blake has acknowledged that the wording of her question, as well as its place in the order in which questions were asked, "may have engendered a negative bias in respondents."[4]

The complexity and ambivalence of people's feelings about abortion are shown by the sensitivity of responses to changes in the way the issues are framed. These pitfalls are illustrated by a test that Blake conducted in 1973 on the effect on the responses of the order in which questions are asked. (It should be noted that in the NORC survey, the "hard" and "soft" questions are intermixed.) Instead of asking all questions of all respondents in the usual hard-to-soft order, she gave half the respondents the same questions in the reverse order, asking first if abortion should be legal when no more children are wanted, and last if it should be when the mother's health is in danger. The result of reversing the order of the items was that approval of abortion when no more children were wanted jumped from 28 percent of men and 32 percent of women to 41 percent of both. A less spectacular, but still significant, increase in approval was registered for the poverty question, asked second in the reverse order series.[5]

The Harris Survey has used a different sort of question since 1972. Respondents had been asked if they approved legalization of abortion in the first trimester of pregnancy, and, after 1973, if they approved the Supreme Court decisions. As indicated in Table 2, the proportion favoring legal abortion in the first three months increased from 42 percent in 1972 to 52 percent in 1973 and to 60 percent in 1979. Aside from an

TABLE 2. Harris Survey, 1972–1978

"Do you favor or oppose the Supreme Court decisions making abortions up to three months of pregnancy legal?"

Percent who:	1972*	Feb. 1973	Apr. 1975	Apr. 1976	Aug. 1976	July 1977	Feb. 1979
Favor	42	52	54	54	59	53	60
Oppose	46	41	38	39	28	40	37
Not sure	12	7	8	7	13	7	3

*In 1972, the survey asked whether or not the respondent favored legalizing abortion.

SOURCE: Louis Harris, Harris Survey News Releases, May 26, 1975; April 18, 1977; and March 6, 1979.

unusually low level of disapproval recorded in 1976, however, there has been little change in opposition since 1973—about 40 percent.

The NORC, Gallup, and Harris series suggest that while approval of abortion has increased substantially since the 1960s, and the majority of Americans generally support the availability of legal abortion, many continue to have some reservations, especially when the reasons for terminating a pregnancy seem less than compelling. These series also all show that very few people disapprove of legal abortion under all circumstances and that a substantial minority approve of it for most of the specified indications. By 1975, in the NORC series, only 7 percent of respondents stated that legal abortion should not be available for any reasons, while 41 percent supported it for all of the reasons cited.

A somewhat-higher level of support is indicated by polls that have asked more general questions—especially those involving a medical decision or the strict legality of abortion. For example, in the November 1979 CBS News/*New York Times* Poll, 68 percent agreed that the "right of a woman to get an abortion should be left entirely up to the woman and her doctor."[6] And 73 percent in the 1979 Harris Survey agreed that "any woman who is three months or less pregnant, should have the right to decide, with her doctor's advice, whether or not she wants to have an abortion."[7] In a July 1977 Yankelovich, Skelly and White Survey, 64 percent said that "abortion should be legal."[8] However, the October 1979 NBC News—Associated Press Poll recorded only 53 percent agreeing that "every woman who wants an abortion should be able to have one."[9] The element of permissiveness implicit in the latter question apparently reduced the level of approval.

Only a minority of respondents support the unrestricted availability of late abortions and the unrestricted right of a woman to choose abortion without her husband's approval. Thus, 75 percent of Gallup respondents in 1975 agreed that abortion should be legal under all or some circumstances. But this proportion drops to 70 percent approving first-trimester abortions for these circumstances, 46 percent approving in the second trimester, and only 37 percent approving in the third trimester.[10] In the 1979 Harris Survey, 60 percent favored the Supreme Court decisions legalizing abortion in the first trimester of pregnancy, but approval dropped to 46 percent for second-trimester abortions, while 66 percent favored the Court's "decision . . . that the states have a right to ban all abortions in the final three months of pregnancy except in those cases where the woman's life is endangered."[11] (Actually, the Court ruled that such late abortions could be banned only when such prohibition did not endanger the life or *health* of the pregnant woman. The wording of the question may have prejudiced the answer.) Similarly, a poll by RL Associates for the Planned Parenthood Federation showed that while 78 percent of Americans opposed government interference "in a woman's decision about whether to have an abortion or not," 65 percent favored government regulation "to make sure that abortions are performed during the first three months before the baby is well-developed."[12] The fact that approval levels tend to fall when the question is broken down into greater detail also suggests that many persons who generally support the availability of legal abortion are ambivalent about its use.

This ambivalence is clear in polls that examine feelings about a constitutional amendment outlawing abortion; they indicate weaker support for abortion than polls that directly query respondents' support for legal abortion. In March 1976, Gallup found 49 percent of its sample opposed to and 45 percent in favor of an amendment that would ban all abortions except when a woman's life would be in danger.[13] The September Yankelovich and CBS News/*New York Times* polls the same year reported 56 percent opposed to an amendment,[14] compared to 66 percent opposed in the NBC Poll in February of the same year.[15] In contrast, support for the availability of legal abortion for the "hard" reasons of health, rape, and serious fetal defects—which would be outlawed under most proposed constitutional amendments—is expressed by 80 to 90 percent of the public in this same period.

While there have been few major changes in public opinion about abortion since 1973, there has been a significant narrowing of attitudinal differences among some social and demographic subgroups. Traditionally, larger proportions of women, blacks, Catholics, less-well-educated, and older people have opposed abortion than have men, whites, non-Catholics, better-educated, and younger people. Midwesterners and Southerners have been less supportive than have people from other regions. Some of these differences continue, but now they are much smaller.

After 1972, attitudinal differences between people of varying educational levels decreased rapidly, largely because of increased approval among persons who did not graduate from high school. The white-nonwhite differences were almost completely eliminated.[16] The 1975 National Fertility Survey found that since 1965, approval of abortion among married women had increased rapidly in all regions of the country. The remaining regional differences were much smaller than they had been a decade before. The increase in approval was most striking in the South, which had been the most conservative region in 1965; by 1975, the South registered a greater degree of approval of abortion than the West and was second only to the Northeast in this regard.[17] Recent polls also show only small differences remaining in the attitudes of men and women.

Nowhere is the change in attitude more dramatic than among Roman Catholics. Virtually every survey shows rapid increases in approval of legal abortion among Catholics. By 1978, the remaining differences between Catholics and non-Catholics were small. In the November 1979 CBS News/New York Times Poll, 64 percent of Catholics agreed that the right of a woman to have an abortion should be left entirely to the woman and her doctor, only five perentage points lower than Protestants.[18] The April 1979 Gallup Poll indicated that 69 percent of Catholics favored legal abortion under some or all circumstances, compared to 79 percent of Protestants. Twenty percent of Catholics compared to 17 percent of Protestants said that abortions should be legal under all circumstances. Only 25 percent of Catholics thought they should be *illegal* under all circumstances, compared to 32 percent in 1975, as indicated in Table 3.

TABLE 3. Gallup Poll, 1975–1978

"Do you think abortions should be legal under any circumstances, legal under only certain circumstances, or illegal under all circumstances?"

Percent who believe abortion should be:	1979		1978		1975	
	Protestants	Catholics	Protestants	Catholics	Protestants	Catholics
Legal under all circumstances	20	17	18	20	18	17
Legal under certain circumstances	59	52	58	53	58	50
Illegal under all circumstances	17	25	19	23	21	32
No opinion	4	6	5	4	3	1

SOURCE: The Gallup Poll, News Releases, January 22, 1978; April 22, 1979.

Half of all Catholic respondents to the February 1979 Harris Survey reported that they favored the 1973 Supreme Court decisions,[19] and 50 percent of Catholics, compared to 54 percent of the non-Catholics, told the October 1979 NBC News-Associated Press Poll that they agreed that every woman who wants an abortion should be able to have one.[20]

Social researcher and priest Andrew Greeley finds "most striking"[21] the detailed evidence of the convergence of Catholic and non-Catholic attitudes in the NORC surveys: between 73 percent and 84 percent of Catholic respondents in 1976 approved of legal abortion for the three "hard" reasons and between 38 percent and 45 percent approved of it for the "soft." These percentages are only slightly lower than the national totals shown in Table 1. The absolute increase between 1975 and 1976 in the proportions of Catholics approving abortion for each reason ranged from 23 to 30 percentage points.

Not only do large numbers of Catholics support the legality of abortion, but 66 percent reported in the 1977 NORC survey that they would have an abortion or urge their wives to have one if there were a "serious threat of a defective child"; 76 percent said they would do so if pregnancy threatened the mother's health. The comparable figures for Protestants were 76 percent and 83 percent, respectively. Almost half of Catholics who are religious enough to attend mass weekly said they would abort a defective child.[22]

These figures strongly suggest that despite the uncompromising Catholic doctrine on abortion and the prominence of the institutional Church in the Right-to-Life movement, the majority of Catholics increasingly both support the availability of legal abortion and voice a willingness—under certain conditions—to avail themselves of that option.

What does appear to be the case is that more observant Catholics—and more observant adherents of all religious faiths—are more likely to oppose abortion than those who are less strongly committed to religious beliefs. Thus, 40 percent of those described by the 1979 NBC News-Associated Press Poll as "strong religious adherents" said they agreed that every woman who wants to have an abortion should be able to have one, compared to 65 percent of those categorized as weak religious adherents.[23] Analyses of the NORC surveys also found that opposition to abortion increased with increased religious commitment. This relationship was strongest among Catholics, but it is true of all religious groups except Episcopalians, though only barely discernible among Presbyterians and Jews.[24]

The convergence of abortion attitudes among different religious, educational, and socioeconomic subgroups may indicate a maturation in the way people are able to view abortion. As the rhetoric that has characterized the abortion debate gradually is replaced by the realization of the benefits accompanying the legalization of abortion and an appreciation of the human dimensions of the issue, people have been able to regard it more thoughtfully—despite a great deal of emotional and moral ambivalence.

It has been argued that much legislative and administrative effort to restrict abortion is attributable to politicians' fear of electoral retaliation from large numbers of antiabortion constituents. But we have seen that the minority fundamentally opposed to abortion under any circumstances is offset by a greater number who support legal abortion under all circumstances. What is more, every survey that has examined the political salience of abortions has concluded that Americans by and large do not consider it a critical national issue.

When Roper pollsters asked a sample of voters in May 1976 to rank 15 policy issues in order of their importance, passing a constitutional amendment prohibiting abortion placed fifteenth and was chosen by only 4 percent of the sample.[25] Similarly, candidate Jimmy Carter's own polls reportedly found that voters presented with a list of 25 issues ranked abortion last in importance.[26]

In most surveys, only about 15 percent of respondents say they would choose a candidate on the basis of his or her abortion position. A survey commissioned by the Committee for Pro-Life Activities of the National Conference of Catholic Bishops found in 1974 that 13 percent of all respondents—and 18 percent of Catholic respondents—said they would vote against a candidate *supporting* abortion. However, 15 percent of the entire sample—and 13 percent of Catholics—also said they would vote against a candidate *opposing* legal abortion.[27]

A number of polls taken in the election year of 1976 suggest similar results. Harris reported that 18 percent of his April sample were opposed to legal abortion and that 15 percent of those who supported it would vote against a candidate solely on the basis of his or her abortion views.[28] Yankelovich in October found 13 percent of the electorate would use a candidate's abortion position as a litmus test, but these respondents again were evenly split between abortion supporters and opponents. Only 15 percent of Catholics questioned in this survey reported they would vote for or against a candidate because of his or her abortion views.[29] The June 1976 Roper Survey also found only 13 percent of respondents choosing a candidate on this issue.[30]

The lack of salience of the abortion issue was reconfirmed in the 1978 elections, when, in spite of considerable attention given to antiabortion sentiment and political activities, just 7 percent of those questioned by the CBS News/*New York Times* Poll reported they would change their vote on the basis of a candidate's position on abortion. However, three-quarters of this group were abortion opponents.[31]

The 1979 Harris Survey suggests that this issue may have taken on some increased political prominence. Thirty-nine percent of respondents declared that they would vote against a candidate they otherwise agreed with if they disagreed with him on the abortion issue. Notably, 53 percent of those who opposed the Supreme Court abortion decisions would switch votes on the abortion issue alone compared to just 30 percent of those who favored the decisions.[32]

If measuring public attitudes about abortion is fraught with difficulty, attempting to assess feelings about public funding of abortion services is even more complex, for the abortion issues here become entwined with many Americans' strong feelings about welfare and public spending. The ambivalence about welfare and the poor has been well documented: Americans appear to favor public assistance for the "deserving poor"—those who are trying to help themselves but are trapped by circumstances outside their control—but they are inclined to deny aid to people they regard as "indifferent, wasteful, or somehow abusive of values held by the majority."[33]

The elderly and infirm traditionally have been regarded as "deserving," and have received relatively generous support. Younger women and their children—recipients of Aid to Families with Dependent Children (AFDC)—have been viewed as less deserving and have received considerably lower levels of financial assistance.

The preponderance of single-parent families in the AFDC case load has added the stigma of implied moral looseness, and the disproportionate number of blacks and Hispanics in this group has injected a strong dose of racism into the mix. Abortion is held to allow the irresponsible to avoid "paying the price" for sexual license. There is, at the same time, a justifiable concern among taxpayers about the rapidly rising costs of assistance programs.

Given that these fundamentally negative views about welfare recipients and welfare affect responses to questions about the funding of abortions for Medicaid-eligible women, it is difficult to extract what it is that is being disapproved in polls. This ambiguity is seen most clearly in the CBS News/*New York Times* Poll of July 1977. Thirty-eight percent of the sample agreed and 55 percent disagreed that "the Government should help a poor woman with her medical bills if she wants an abortion.[34] But 26 percent did not support public funding of maternity services either. If, as is likely, all of these respondents also opposed public funding of abortions, only 29 percent of the sample would be left who supported the provision of maternity services but opposed subsidized abortions. Curiously, when the almost identical question on abortion funding was asked three months later, but without the maternity care item, 47 percent supported public funding of abortion and 44 percent opposed it. Although in most opinion polls blacks have been somewhat less supportive of legal abortion than have whites, two-thirds of the black respondents in the sample supported public funding of abortion.[35]

In August 1977, in the middle of congressional debate on the Hyde amendment to ban most Medicaid-funded abortions, the Harris Survey asked a series of questions that highlight the paradoxical structure of attitudes toward public funding of abortion: the proposed ban was supported by 47 percent and opposed by 44 percent. But respondents also agreed, by a 55 to 34 percent margin, that "the U.S. Supreme Court in its original decision was right to say whether a woman has an abortion is a decision she and her doctor should make, and the new ban interferes with the right of a pregnant woman to make that decision."

Even more to the point, 51 percent agreed with statements that "the ban is wrong because poor women who cannot afford legal abortions will be forced to have unwanted children or to have dangerous illegal abortions." They agreed, too, that "such a ban is unfair, because it means that rich women, who can afford abortions, will have them, while poor women, who can't afford them, will not."[36]

Abortion until recently was a crime, and it is still condemned by several religious groups. The fact that many persons remain opposed to it therefore is hardly surprising. What *is* surprising is the rapid increase in approval of abortion over the last decade among *all* segments of the population. "While it is no doubt true . . . that public support for unrestricted abortion still falls considerably short of consensus," sociologists Elise F. Jones and Charles F. Westoff note, "movement in that direction has been continuous—and the momentum appears to have shifted in favor of the least restrictive circumstances."[37]

References

1 J. Blake, "Elective Abortion and Our Reluctant Citizenry: Research on Public Opinion in the United States," in H. and J. Osofsky (eds.), *The Abortion Experience: Psychological and Medical Impact*, New York: Harper and Row, 1973, pp. 449, 460.

2 J. Blake, "The Abortion Decisions: Judicial Review and Public Opinion," in E. Manier, W. Liu, and D. Solomon (eds.), *Abortion: New Directions for Policy Studies*, Notre Dame: University of Notre Dame Press, 1977, table 1.

3 J. Blake, "The Supreme Court's Abortion Decisions and Public Opinion in

the United States," *Population and Development Review,* **3:**112, March/June 1977, table 1.

4   J. Blake, "The Supreme Court's Abortion Decisions . . ." op. cit., p. 48.

5   J. Blake, "The Abortion Decisions . . ." op. cit., p. 59 and table 3.

6   CBS/*New York Times* Poll, release, Nov. 10, 1979.

7   L. Harris, ABC News—Harris Survey News Release, Mar. 6, 1979.

8   Yankelovich, Skelly and White, Inc., poll for *Time,* August 1977.

9   NBC News—Associated Press Poll, #122, Oct. 12, 1979.

10   The Gallup Poll, "Stage of Pregnancy Key to Public Approval of Abortion," release, Apr. 7, 1975.

11   L. Harris, 1979, op. cit.

12   RL Associates, "Abortion as a National Issue," a report prepared for Planned Parenthood Federation of America, Inc., October 1979.

13   The Gallup Poll, "Abortion," *The Gallup Opinion Index,* no. 128, March 1976.

14   Yankelovich, Skelly and White, Inc., poll for *Time,* September 1976, and CBS News/*New York Times* Poll, October 1976.

15   NBC News Poll, February 1976.

16   W. R. Arney and W. H. Trescher, "Trends in Attitudes Toward Abortion, 1972-1975," *Family Planning Perspectives,* **8:**117, 1976, tables 3 and 7.

17   E. F. Jones and C. F. Westoff, "How Attitudes Toward Abortion Are Changing," *Journal of Population,* **1:**5, 1978, table 3.

18   CBS News/*New York Times* Poll, 1979, op. cit.

19   L. Harris, ABC News–Harris Survey News Release, 1979, op. cit.

20   NBC News–A.P. Poll, 1979, op. cit.

21   A. Greeley, "Catholic Attendance Still Falling," *Chicago Tribune,* Jan. 10, 1978.

22   "Acceptance of Abortion on Increase, New Poll Says," National Catholic News Service, Washington, D.C., and A. Greeley, "Findings on Catholic Abortion Views Shattering, "*The Fall River Anchor,* Jan. 26, 1978.

23   NBC News–A.P. Poll, 1979, op. cit.

24   D. Granberg, "A Multifaceted Analysis of Attitudes Toward Abortion in the U.S.A., 1965–1978," Final Report to the National Institute of Child Health and Human Development, DHEW, November 1979.

25   The Roper Poll, May 1976.

26   "Courting the Catholics," *Newsweek,* Sept. 20, 1976.

27   Committee for Pro-Life Activities, National Conference of Catholic Bishops, "Abortion, Attitudes and the Law" (mimeo), March 1975.

28   L. Harris, "Poll: Abortion is a Safe Issue," *New York Post,* Apr. 12, 1976.

29   Yankelovich, Skelly and White, Inc., poll for *Time,* October 1976.

30 The Roper Poll, June 1976.

31 A. Clymer, "Nation Votes Today in Skeptical Mood," *New York Times*, Nov. 7, 1978.

32 L. Harris, 1979, op. cit.

33 See G. W. Carter, L. H. Fifield, and H. Shields, "Public Attitudes Toward Welfare—An Opinion Poll," Regional Research Institute in Social Welfare, University of Southern California, December 1973.

34 "Public Likes Carter, Survey Finds, More for His Style Than Programs," *New York Times*, July 29, 1977.

35 CBS News/*New York Times* Poll, release, Nov. 1, 1977.

36 The Harris Survey, "Abortion Debate Continues," release, Aug. 18, 1977.

37 E. F. Jones and C. F. Westoff, 1978, op. cit., p. 7.

CHAPTER NINE

Heating Up the Controversy

On March 7, 1974, John Cardinal Krol of Philadelphia, president of the United States Catholic Conference, and three other cardinals appeared before the Senate Judiciary Subcommittee on Constitutional Amendments. They testified in favor of an amendment reversing the Supreme Court's 1973 abortion rulings. The hearings were being held, Subcommittee Chairman Birch Bayh of Indiana explained, because "we have a moral obligation . . . not to dispose of this particular issue by silence . . . . One of the basic strengths of our country is our right to respectfully disagree and yet to pursue the truth."[1]

This appearance by the four cardinals was unprecedented in the annals of Congress. The prelates acknowledged that it demonstrated the importance the Church attaches to the abortion issue.

Decrying legalization as "the worst mistake in the Court's history," the Cardinals said their intent was not "to advocate sectarian doctrine but to defend human rights."[2] Although they did not endorse any of the proposed amendments before the subcommittee, they set forth principles that the Church favored for drawing up such an amendment: it would convey legal personhood to the unborn child from conception onward and allow no exception to the ban on abortion.[3]

Asked their view of a less-sweeping amendment, Humberto Cardinal Medeiros of Boston said flatly: "We are unwilling to compromise in principle."[4]

The Catholic prelates' dramatic testimony far overshadowed the appearance, on the same day, of leaders of the Methodist, Presbyterian, United Church of Christ, and Reformed Jewish denominations to *op-*

pose a constitutional amendment. These witnesses stressed their substantially different beliefs as to the morality of abortion and the question of when meaningful human life begins. To enact an amendment that satisfied the Catholic Church, they emphasized, would enshrine in the Constitution "the most extreme position of one group of religious persons," and overrule the views held with equal integrity by many others.[5] The opponents' views were summarized by Bishop A. James Armstrong of the United Methodist Church:

> Our belief in the sanctity of unborn human life makes us reluctant to approve abortion. But we are equally bound to respect the sacredness of the life and well-being of the mother, for whom devastating damage may result from an unacceptable pregnancy. In continuity with past Christian teaching, we recognize tragic conflicts of life with life that may justify abortion.[6]

In the next 16 months, the subcommittee heard 84 witnesses, representing many segments of the scientific, religious, professional, and political communities. The proposed amendments fell basically into two categories: "human-life" or "right-to-life" amendments that would entirely prohibit or severely restrict abortion by granting legal "personhood" to the fetus at conception, and "states'-rights" amendments that purported to return the power to legislate on abortion to the states.

The subcommittee, in September 1975, voted seven times on four different proposed amendments—and declined to report out any of them. The reasons were explained by Senator Bayh:

> At the time my Subcommittee began its hearings on the proposed amendments, I stated that I was personally opposed to abortion. My views have not changed [but] I feel that we cannot and must not use the Constitution as an instrument for moral preference . . . . It is precisely in areas that are so intimate, where public attitudes are so deeply divided, both morally and religiously, that private choice can be defended as our Constitution's way of reconciling the irreconcilable without dangerously embroiling church and state in one another's affairs.[7]

The Bayh hearings were the culmination of the first phase of the antiabortion campaign in Congress that had begun immediately after the Supreme Court decisions of January 22, 1973. Within weeks of the ruling, several "human-life" and "states'-rights" constitutional amendments had been introduced in the House of Representatives. Within four months, Congress had been presented with amendment proposals backed by a total of 41 sponsors.

Important legislative initatives rarely are dealt with quickly. Amending the Constitution, if anything, would be expected to be even slower.

It therefore was a sign of the extraordinary haste and impatience of congressional antiabortion leaders that Representative Lawrence J. Hogan, the sponsor of the House "human-life" amendment, started a discharge petition in July to bypass the normal procedure of subcommittee and committee hearings and approval before a vote by the House. This tactic usually is employed only when legislation that sponsors believe has strong support has been bottled up for months or years in a hostile committee.

A successful discharge petition requires 218 signatures. A constitutional amendment needs a two-thirds vote of approval in both houses before being submitted to the state legislatures. It is indicative of antiabortion leaders' serious miscalculation of their own strength that Hogan never was able to muster even 100 of his colleagues to sign the petition,[8] although by this time there were 19 proposed amendments in the House, with 36 sponsors. The antiabortion Congressional leaders failed to recognize that there was serious disagreement over the form and wording of the amendment.

By the time the Senate Subcommittee on Constitutional Amendments began its hearings, in early 1974, there were 58 proposed amendments. Of these, 18 were "human-life" amendments like Representative Hogan's in the House; six others were modeled on a modified "human-life" amendment proposed by Senator James L. Buckley of New York, which might have allowed some exceptions to the abortion ban. The remaining 34 were "states'-rights" proposals to return to the states the right to regulate abortion.

The latter clearly were the most popular among members of Congress. Without actually moving to outlaw abortion, the legislators could demonstrate their concern about it, while at the same time disposing of this troublesome issue by throwing it back to the states. However, this approach—the only one that had any chance of congressional approval—was unacceptable to abortion opponents.

Antiabortion leaders in Congress demanded a universal "human-life" amendment, incorporating the principles outlined by the bishops, who, while refusing to endorse a specific amendment, rejected all but the strictest proposals. The National Right to Life Committee (NRLC), for example, which was established "to work for the restoration of restrictive laws against abortion," stated it would support only a strict "human-life" amendment.

Both Church theologians and factions of the secular RTL movement, however, were divided about such questions as whether "conception" refers to fertilization or to the implantation of the fertilized egg in the uterus—which occurs several days later. They also disagreed about whether intrauterine devices were abortifacients, and whether emerging scientific knowledge on embryonic development might have theological implications that would permit abortion very early in pregnancy. The antiabortion groups' inability to settle these issues has been suggested as one reason for the bishops' failure to propose or endorse a specific constitutional amendment. These problems, and the complex legal ramifications of any amendment, undoubtedly also contributed to the bishops' failure to submit to Congress the detailed memorandum on abortion that they promised to prepare.

The irreconcilability of positions on the abortion issue cited by Senator Bayh, made an impasse inevitable. The only constitutional remedy capable of winning any support in a nation in which the majority supported legal abortion would have had to be flexible and allow for exceptions. But the supporters of actions to restrict abortion would accept nothing less than a total ban. Senate minority leader Hugh Scott, who had hoped to defuse this obstructive and divisive issue by fashioning a compromise solution, explained in a 1975 letter to his constituents why he had abandoned the effort:

> [It] has met with great opposition from both sides. The "right to life" movement considers my proposal too liberal; the feminists consider it restrictive and discriminatory . . . . It is both useless and unrealistic to pursue this avenue any further."[9]

The RTL forces did not go unopposed in their early attempts to overturn the 1973 decisions. Initially, in fact, the abortion-rights activists were more experienced politically, although they, too, were better organized in the states than they were nationally.

The abortion-rights advocates included civil-rights, professional, religious, and civil-libertarian organizations, many of which had participated in earlier drives to reform restrictive state abortion laws.[10] A partial list of major national organizations that support legal abortions includes four legal and civil-liberties organizations, 16 health and medical societies, 12 social service organizations, 12 women's groups, and some 50 religious associations. Individual supporters included representatives of the Jewish, Baptist, Lutheran, Moravian, Presbyterian, Unitarian Universalist, United Church of Christ, Methodist and Episcopalian faiths.

Organizations like the American Bar Association, American Association of University Women, and the major environmental, labor, religious, and welfare groups for the most part limited their abortion involvement to the issuance of supportive public statements. A few worked actively in defense of legal abortion and public funding for it.

The most prominent advocates of legal abortion are organizations with a particular interest in reproductive rights. They include the National Abortion Rights Action League (NARAL), Planned Parenthood Federation of America, the Religious Coalition for Abortion Rights (RCAR), the American Civil Liberties Union (ACLU), Zero Population Growth, the Center for Constitutional Rights, and the major women's political groups like National Organization for Women (NOW), the National Women's Political Caucus, and the National Council of Negro Women. Of all these groups, NARAL and RCAR are the only national-membership lobbying organizations whose sole purpose is abortion rights.

The 1973 Supreme Court decisions—which served to rouse the opposition—would have an opposite effect on most supporters of legal abortion. Suddenly, abortion was legal *throughout* the nation. Many felt the battle was won. The diverse organizations of the abortion-rights coalition turned back to their other, primary concerns.

It thus fell to a handful of political-action and legal-defense organizations to cope with the attempt to enact abortion restrictions after 1973. Among these groups, the media prominently featured the radical feminists. Just as RTL supporters brought an absolutist theological fervor to their crusade (which made good copy), so these feminists imbued their support of legal abortion with an equally quotable ideologic rhetoric and fervor. This further polarized the abortion debate by pitting the radical feminist demands against the religious absolutism of the antiabortionists.

The more broadly based organizations began to speak up again only after abortion rights had begun to be eroded by restrictions on public funding and antiabortion efforts to block the availability of abortion for all women.

The Bayh subcommittee's refusal to report out a constitutional amendment was a crushing blow to antiabortion activists, who had expected quick congressional action to reverse the 1973 decisions. But they rallied, renewing their efforts to prod Congress into taking regressive steps.

Responding to RTL pressure, Representative Don Edwards, in 1976, held brief hearings on antiabortion amendments in his Judiciary Subcommittee on Civil and Constitutional Rights, but no amendment was reported out. Meanwhile, using an obscure parliamentary maneuver, Senators Jesse Helms and James Buckley managed to bypass the Senate Judiciary Committee and to place the strict Helms "human-life" amendment directly on the Senate calendar. Despite heavy RTL lobbying, however, the full Senate, after debate, affirmed the subcommittee's decision by voting to table the amendment.

In the face of these repeated defeats, a reassessment of RTL strategy and tactics was not long in coming. As discussed in Chapter 6, in November 1975, the National Conference of Catholic Bishops released the *Pastoral Plan for Pro-Life Activities*, a blueprint for political mobilization. The RTL movement's need to redirect its efforts toward interim goals and to create a political base apparently was perceived by antiabortion leaders. Some also must have sensed that the Catholic hierarchy's stated intention to throw its resources into grass-roots political activities enhanced their political credibility.

The new strategy was outlined by RTL leader Randy Engel, who urged restrictive riders on "any and all federal legislation related directly or indirectly to health," in order to keep the abortion issue visible and build support. She argued that the efforts to win interim legislation would provide antiabortion workers with political experience, would educate the public, and would force members of Congress to go on record one way or the other. Not least important, she added, this strategy would require the forces supporting abortion rights to expend time, effort, and resources in opposing the riders.[11]

This shift in RTL strategy came just before the opening of the 1976 presidential campaign. Initially, antiabortion activists again were frustrated in their attempts to convince the Democratic Platform Committee to support a constitutional amendment. Instead, the plank on abortion declared that an amendment was "undesirable."[12] While President Gerald Ford gave only a half-hearted endorsement—saying he would "support but not seek" a "states'-rights" amendment—the Republican Party Platform was more forceful: it called for an amendment "to restore the protection of the right to life for unborn children."[13]

The first nominating decisions, several months before the conventions, were in Iowa. It was widely reported in the local and national press that the Church was very involved. It coached parishioners to participate in nominating caucuses in support of antiabortion candidates and resolutions.[14]

This primary marked abortion's emergence as an important issue in the presidential campaign. It also was the occasion of Jimmy Carter's first expressed opposition to abortion. And the entry of Ellen McCormack as an antiabortion candidate in the Democratic primary race sealed the special status that the media accorded abortion during the campaign year.

Candidates in primaries are particularly susceptible to antiabortion pressure because of the typically small voter turnout. Low turnouts give special-interest groups more impact than they have in general elections. And in this primary, the persistence of RTL demonstrators in harassing candidates they opposed put many contenders on the defensive.

As a Catholic presidential candidate who supported the legality of abortion, Sargent Shriver drew great wrath form antiabortion activists. Senator Bayh, also a contender for the presidency, was another favorite target of these demonstrators because his subcommittee had failed to report out a constitutional amendment. In New Hampshire, one of his speeches was drowned out by a bugle player sounding "taps." Tacks were thrown on the ground outside halls where he was scheduled to speak to flatten the tires of vehicles in his motorcade. Senator Bayh declared, sadly, that this was "hardly the way that reasonable men and women should discuss the issues." A Catholic aide of antiabortion candidate Ronald Reagan, who had endorsed a "human-life" amendment, was even more pessimistic: "This issue will demean politics."[15]

Although RTL candidate McCormack won only three of the more than 3,000 delegates to the Democratic Convention, abortion reemerged as a major issue in the fall campaign. This was largely because of the perception that Carter, as a fundamentalist Southerner, had a "Catholic problem." This problem was assumed to be exacerbated by President Ford's support of a states'-rights constitutional amendment, compared to Carter's opposition to any amendment.

Candidate Carter's problems with urban Catholic voters frequently were attributed to his position on abortion. His staffers felt that if he was not sensitive to the abortion issue, "a lot of Catholics are going to see it as a sign that we don't give a damn about them, whether they agree with the demonstrators or not."[16] However, Catholic social scientist Father Andrew Greely advanced a more accurate and compelling explanation when he observed:

"Carter represents the old tradition of Southern populism which was fundamentally and often viciously anti-Catholic."[17]

Every survey taken during this period showed that voters, including Catholic voters, placed abortion at or near the bottom of lists of campaign issues (as was detailed in Chapter 8).

The Catholic bishops, however, had a different priority. "The central issue in our nation and our world today is the sanctity and dignity of human life, [which] are directly, massively violated by legalized abortion in our country," Archbishop Joseph L. Bernardin wrote to President Ford.[18]

Both Carter and Ford took the extraordinary step of meeting with the bishops, who voiced their "disappointment" at Carter's abortion stand and said they were "encouraged" by Ford's endorsement of a states'-rights amendment. This episode generated such widespread dismay that the bishops quickly affirmed that the Church was "absolutely neutral" in the presidential contest. The criticism came from women's groups, non-Catholics, and Catholic religious bodies like the National Federation of Priests Councils, which said it feared that abortion had been stressed by the hierarchy "to the neglect of other important social issues."[19]

Defeat of the proposed amendments probably was the decisive factor in redirecting the antiabortion forces toward passage of narrower restrictive legislation like the Hyde amendment (as discussed in Chapter 10). But the RTL movement and the Church have by no means abandoned their primary goal, a "human-life" constitutional amendment. Their shift in strategy has produced tactical changes that tend to obscure the essential fact that the final aim continues to be to stop all abortions.

In August 1977, for example, Archbishop Bernardin reminded the Knights of Columbus that restricting public funding of abortion is not "an acceptable social compromise." He called for "early enactment" of a constitutional amendment.[20]

By 1977, the old RTL internal debate over acceptable wording for an amendment largely had been resolved. The resulting consensus was a strict "human-life" amendment that might possibly permit abortion only to prevent the pregnant women's death.

The question then became how best to achieve this end. Led by supporters of the McCormack campaign, some abortion opponents began a drive to bypass the Congress and convene a constitutional convention for the purpose of amending the U.S. Constitution to outlaw abortion. Thirty-four states must ask Congress to call such a convention, and in 200 years this amendment method has never been used.

The prospect of such a convention has in the past generated deep concern from scholars, legal experts, and public officials, since there are no guidelines on how it would operate. Of particular concern is whether it would or could be limited to the subject for which it was called. The American Bar Association, in 1973, warned that a convention carried great potential for a "grave constitutional crisis."[21] President Carter spoke out against a constitutional convention on a balanced budget in 1979, characterizing it as "extremely dangerous" and "completely uncontrollable."[22]

A decision by the New York State Catholic leadership to withhold support from the New York RTL faction that is working for a constitutional convention reflects the attitude of the national Church hierarchy—which has not endorsed this approach. Mildred Jefferson, former head of NRLC, adamantly opposes the convention route. She said:

"Not under any threat, bribe or blandishment will I lead or follow the pro-life movement into the constitutional convention wilderness."[23]

But Dr. Jefferson has been replaced as NRLC president by Carolyn Gerster, a convention advocate. This signals an organizational commitment to a convention campaign—a position generally identified with the extremist element of the RTL movement.

The NRLC meanwhile is increasingly articulating its goals in political terms. At its 1978 annual convention, it announced it would step up its campaign for a human-life amendment by actively enlisting voters, establishing a "citizens' lobbying arm" in Washington, and campaigning in state and congressional elections against its enemies.[24]

This development has been accompanied by a hardening of positions, leadership changes, and the increasingly prominent identification of NRLC with conservative special-interest and lobbying groups. Thus, while the organization takes no official position on contraception, Dr. Gerster has attacked Planned Parenthood, the oldest and largest provider of birth-control services and a favorite target of the ultraconservative RTL faction. Despite its official condemnation of violence—and its offer of $5,000 rewards for information on perpetrators of violence against abortion facilities—the NRLC convention for the first time endorsed picketing and sit-ins at abortion clinics, saying, "Abortion represents the epitome of violence to our unborn . . . ."[25]

The NRLC's longtime Washington lobbyist, Thea Rossi Barron, was fired, reportedly because of her "liberal" leanings, and replaced by Judie Brown, whose political mentor, Paul Weyrich, is a well-known "new-right" political organizer.[26] Weyrich, along with right-wing direct-mail fundraiser Richard Viguerie, established the Committee for the Survival of a Free Congress in 1974. More important, NRLC has established a political action arm called LAPAC—standing for Life Amendment Political Action Committee—which may legally engage in partisan political activity.

In the opening days of the 1980 election campaign, LAPAC targeted for defeat 12 liberal and moderate senators and members of Congress. This "hit list" included several legislators already targeted for defeat by other "new-right" organizations for their support of labor-law reform, civil rights, and passage of the Equal-Rights Amendment and human services legislation. The conjunction of "new-right" and RTL interests can clearly be seen by LAPAC's pursuit of Senator Frank Church of Idaho. Church supported restricting the use of federal funds for abortions and was the author of the congressional conscience clause giving medical personnel who object to abortions on moral, ethical, or religious grounds the right to refuse to participate in the procedures. Regardless of his conservative record on abortion, Church, along with numerous senators not on the "hit list," refused to endorse a human-life amendment to the constitution. Church was placed on the LAPAC list not only because of his refusal to endorse a human-life amendment but also because of "new-right" opposition to his advocacy of civil rights and labor-law reform.

One other conjunction of the RTL movement with the "new right" was the 1978 defeat of Iowa's outspokenly prochoice Senator Dick Clark. RTL activists worked hard for his defeat in Iowa, and LAPAC contributed $5,000 to his opponent.[27] However, Clark had also been vocally opposed by opponents of gun control and the Panama Canal treaty. In addition, Clark's opponent had received support from the government of South Africa because of Clark's opposition, as a member of the Senate Foreign Relations Committee, to apartheid.[28] Regardless of the numerous forces opposing Clark, the RTL movement claimed credit for his defeat.[29]

The growing right-wing political orientation of the national RTL movement and public officials' perception that, at the local electoral level, its supporters are a force not to be ignored, threaten to escalate the abortion dispute. The movement is flexing its muscles, preparing to take on issues affecting more vocal, better-organized, middle-class women. It is moving beyond the easier target of the powerless poor. The state-based constitutional convention campaign accordingly is more than a symbolic threat to legal abortion—and also to political order and stability in the nation.

By the end of 1978, antiabortion activists had succeeded in getting 13 states to pass convention resolutions, although this effort had flagged by the end of that year. During 1979, only two more states were added to this list. The most serious dangers were either that enough states would join this effort to pressure Congress itself into approving a constitutional amendment or that the far-more-popular campaign for a convention to enact a balanced-budget amendment would be co-opted by RTL supporters. The attempt in 1978 by Senator William Scott to piggyback a "states'-rights" abortion amendment onto a constitutional amendment giving voting rights to District of Columbia residents, although easily defeated in the Senate, is warning that this method may be tried again.

The new leadership of NRLC has announced its commitment to the constitutional-convention drive. Its emerging emphasis on state political activity and on partnership with sophisticated conservative political-action groups indicate that it might win the support of other state legslatures. How far RTL zealotry in pursuit of a constitutional ban on abortion will take us along this dangerous road remains to be seen.

References

1 *Hearings Before the Subcommittee on Constitutional Amendments of the Committee on the Judiciary of the U.S. Senate* on S.J. Res. 119 and S.J. Res. 130, Part 1,

93d Cong., 2d Sess. 1974, pp. 159–160.

2   Ibid., p. 154.

3   Ibid., pp. 157–158.

4   Ibid., p. 168.

5   Ibid., pp. 154, 185, 168, 364.

6   Ibid., pp. 225–256.

7   *Congressional Record, Senate,* **121**:S16093, Sept. 17, 1975.

8   "Discharge Petition for 'Right to Life' Constitutional Amendment," *Planned Parenthood Washington Memo,* July 11, 1973, p. 2.

9   Letter of Sen. Hugh Scott to constituents, *Planned Parenthood Washington Memo,* Apr. 7, 1975.

10   Religious organizations supporting legal abortion include:

American Baptist Churches
American Ethical Union
American Ethical Union, National Women's Conference
American Friends Service Committee
American Humanist Association
American Jewish Congress
American Lutheran Church
Baptist Joint Committee on Public Affairs
B'nai B'rith Women
Board of Church and Society, United Methodist Church
Board of Homeland Ministries, United Church of Christ
Catholics For a Free Choice
Center for Social Action, United Church of Christ
Central Conference of American Rabbis
Christian Church (Disciples of Christ)
Church of the Brethren
Church and Society Unit, Women's Program Unit, and Washington Office, United Presbyterian Church, U.S.A.
Church Women United
Clergy Consultation Service on Abortion
Commission on Social Action of Reform Judaism
Episcopalian Church
Federation of Protestant Welfare Agencies
Friends Committee on National Legislation
Lutheran Baptist Convention
Lutheran Church in America
Moravian Church in America, Northern Province
National Association of Laity
National Council of Jewish Women
National Federation of Temple Sisterhoods
Presbyterian Church in the U.S., Committee on Women's Concerns and General Assembly
Religious Coalition for Abortion Rights
Reformed Church in America

Reorganized Church of Jesus Christ of Latter-Day Saints
Union of American Hebrew Congregations
Unitarian Universalist Association and Unitarian Universalist Women's
  Federation
United Church of Canada General Council
United Methodist Church, General Conference
United Methodist Church, Women's Division and Board of Global Ministries
United Synagogue of America
Women of the Episcopal Church
Woman's League for Conservative Judaism
Young Woman's Christian Association

Professional, service and public-interest organizations supporting legal
abortion include:

American Academy of Child Psychiatry
American Association of University Women
American Bar Association
American Civil Liberties Union
American College Health Association
American College of Obstetricians and Gynecologists
American College of Nurse-Midwives
American Home Economics Association
American Medical Association
American Medical Women's Association, Inc.
American Parents' Committee
American Protestant Hospital Association
American Psychiatric Association
American Psychoanalytic Association
American Psychological Association
American Public Health Association
American Veterans' Committee
Americans for Democratic Action
Americans United for Separation of Church and State
Association of Planned Parenthood Physicians
Center for Constitutional Rights
Center for Law and Social Policy
Center for Women's Policy Studies
Child Welfare League of America
Community Service Society
Environmental Action
Environmental Policy Center
Friends of the Earth
Group for the Advancement of Psychiatry
League of Women Voters
Medical Committee for Human Rights
National Association of Social Workers
National Association of Women Deans, Administrators and Counselors–
  Intercollegiate Association of Women Students

National Commission on the Observance of International Women's Year, 1975
National Council of Women of the United States
National Council on Family Relations
National Council of Negro Women.
National Education Association
National Emergency Civil Liberties Committee
National Organization for Women
National Urban League
National Women's Political Caucus
Physicians' Forum
Planned Parenthood Federation of America, Inc.
Sierra Club
United Auto Workers
Women's Equity Action League
Women's Legal Defense Fund
Women's Lobby
Workmen's Circle
Young Women's Christian Association of the U.S.A.
Zero Population Growth

11 "Abortion Foes Differ on Strategy in Wake of Defeat of Constitutional Amendment," *Planned Parenthood Washington Memo*, Oct. 17, 1975.

12 R. Walters, "Mixing Politics and Religion," *The National Journal*, Jan. 24, 1976.

13 *The New York Times*, excerpt, Sept. 29, 1975, p. 21.

14 R. Steele and J. Doyle, "1976's Sleeper Issue," *Newsweek*, Feb. 9, 1976.

15 Ibid.

16 D. M. Alpern, E. Clift, J. Doyle, T. M. DeFrank and H. Bruno, "Courting the Catholics," *Newsweek*, Sept. 20, 1976.

17 Ibid., p. 16.

18 "Candidates Genuflect to Bishops," *Planned Parenthood Washington Memo*, Sept. 16. 1976.

19 P. Shabecoff, "Archbishop Asserts Church Is Neutral in White House Race," *The New York Times*, Sept. 17, 1976.

20 "Bishop Rejects Abortion 'Compromise,' Calls for Constitutional Amendment," *Planned Parenthood Washington Memo*, Sept. 9, 1977.

21 "Calls for Constitutional Convention on Antiabortion Amendment Increasing," *Planned Parenthood Washington Memo*, Mar. 11, 1977.

22 M. Tolchin, "Carter Faults Plan to Balance Budget," *New York Times*, Jan. 18, 1979.

23 "National Right-to-Life News," April 1977, cited in *Planned Parenthood Washington Memo*, May 27, 1977.

24 N. Sheppard, Jr., "Group Fighting Abortion Planning to Step Up Its Drive," *New York Times*, July 3, 1978.

25 B. Kenkelen, "Pro-life Aim: Put God on Capitol Hill," *National Catholic Reporter*, July 14, 1978.

26 M. Winiarski, "National Right to Life, Political Right Interlink," *National Catholic Reporter*, Nov. 10, 1978.

27 *National Catholic Reporter*, Nov. 10, 1978.

28 *Washington Post*, Mar. 25, 1979.

29 "Single Issue Politics," *Washington Post*, Dec. 12, 1978.

CHAPTER TEN
The Unfairness of Life

By sharply limiting the ways that states can interfere in a woman's decision, with her doctor, to terminate her pregnancy, the 1973 Supreme Court rulings left opponents of abortion few means to restrict its availability. The primary goal—an antiabortion constitutional amendment—has proven elusive. In the interim, antiabortion legislators at all levels of government have scrambled to find ways to enact regressive laws that would circumvent the Court's intent. Some of these efforts have failed of enactment and others have been struck down as unconstitutional. But abortion opponents have had more success with one target—public funding of abortion.

On the national scene, antiabortion members of Congress had two major avenues for restrictive action against the 1973 Supreme Court rulings: approval of a constitutional amendment to reverse the Court and curtailment of federal funding of abortion. The first failed. The focus of restrictive activities then shifted to the Medicaid program, the major source of federal funds for abortions.

Medicaid is the major health-assistance program for the poor. Congressman Henry J. Hyde of Illinois explained why he and his colleagues focused their antiabortion efforts on this program:

> I would certainly like to prevent, if I could legally, anybody having an abortion, a rich woman, a middle class woman, or a poor woman. Unfortunately, the only vehicle available is the HEW [Department of Health, Education and Welfare] Medicaid bill. A life is a life.[1]

Medicaid is administered by the states under federal guidelines. They share the costs. The federal government pays 50 to 90 percent of necessary medical costs for people who meet eligibility criteria set by the states within federal guidelines.

To participate in Medicaid, a state must offer basic health benefits, including medical and surgical care, and hospitalization for all welfare recipients in federally aided programs. If it chooses, a state may also offer a wider range of medical services and cover poor people not on welfare.

Abortions were covered routinely, like other basic surgical care, in most Medicaid programs in the years immediately after abortion became legal. By 1977, about 295,000 women were obtaining Medicaid-funded abortions annually, at a total cost of about $87 million.[2] These women accounted for almost one-quarter of all abortions performed in the United States that year. A Medicaid ban that denied them this service thus would be a highly visible victory for the RTL forces. If followed by similar state action, it could sharply reduce the number of abortions performed for poor women.

Committed antiabortion congressmen launched several major attacks on Medicaid funding after 1973. Although some were passed in one house, all ultimately were defeated. By 1976, however, the situation had changed. Issuance of the *Pastoral Plan* and the role of abortion in the presidential campaign had made abortion a far more salient issue. As the campaign reached a climax, without warning, freshman Congressman Hyde proposed an amendment to the HEW-Labor Department's appropriations bill banning federal funds "to pay for abortion or to promote or encourage abortion."

The brief debate that followed was highlighted by vigorous objections from Representative Daniel J. Flood of Pennsylvania, the then-powerful chairman of the Labor-HEW Appropriations Subcommittee, who was himself soon to be a leading proponent of restrictive abortion legislation. After stating his belief that abortion is "wrong, with a capital 'W,'" Flood denounced Hyde's proposal as "blatantly" discriminatory:

> It does not prohibit abortion. It prohibits abortion for poor people. . . .
> To accept the right of this country to impose on its poor citizens . . . a morality which it is not willing to impose on the rich as well—we would not dare do that. This is what this amendment does. . . . It is a vote against the poor people.[3]

Despite Flood's impassioned plea, the amendment was adopted by a vote of 207-167 in the House. The Senate just as decisively rejected it, 57-28.

Both houses then reaffirmed their original positions. The resulting impasse over abortion funding continued until late in September. With elections looming, agreement finally was reached on language that banned HEW funds for abortion "except where the life of the mother would be clearly endangered if the fetus were carried to term."

It is noteworthy that 72 representatives who had voted against a comparable amendment in 1974—the last time that the House had had a roll-call vote on this issue—now voted *for* the Hyde amendment, in the heat of the election campaign. Observers have suggested that the Senate's similar willingness to go along with the amendment also reflected a well-calculated political gamble, since there was widespread belief that the Supreme Court, in forthcoming decisions on two Medicaid cases, would agree with the six lower federal courts that had already ruled such funding restrictions for abortion to be unconstitutional.

These expectations initially were confirmed, when implementation of the 1976 Hyde amendment was blocked on the first day of the new fiscal year: U.S. District Court Judge John F. Dooling issued a temporary restraining order, followed by a preliminary injunction, barring enforcement of the ban on funding of abortions. This injunction remained in effect for most of the next year.

The following year, on June 17, 1977, Representative Hyde introduced a similar amendment to the new, 1978 HEW-Labor appropriations bill. This one called for a total ban on abortion funding for the purpose of preventing "the slaughter of innocent, inconvenient unborn children."[4]

The following week, in *Beal v. Doe* and *Maber v. Roe*, the Supreme Court ruled that states could deny Medicaid funding for "nontherapeutic" abortions.

The House adopted the new Hyde amendment by a 201-155 vote. Perhaps because the Senate now realized that the Supreme Court might not bail it out, it was more firmly opposed than in 1976 to the new amendment. The Senate held that Medicaid should pay for "medically necessary" abortions, as it pays for other necessary medical services. The phrase "medically necessary" then became the focus of a debate that continued for six months, holding up passage of the $60-billion appropriation bill until well into the new fiscal year.

This congressional battle was extraordinary in several respects. In a debate that filled 228 pages of small type in the *Congressional Record*, amendment supporters advanced only two supporting arguments: the amendment would prevent the killing of unborn children and it would preclude payment for abortions with public funds derived in part from taxpayers who regard abortion as murder. The debate mostly was rhetoric; much of it was bombast.

"Why should taxpayers be forced to pay for any woman's abortion?" demanded Representative Eldon Rudd in June, as the House opened its debate.[5] Rudd then was a freshman Republican congressman from Scottsdale, Arizona, the fashionable suburb of Phoenix. His state has the distinction of being the only one not participating in the Medicaid program. It relies instead on a limited, local medical-assistance effort, which suggests that Arizona taxpayers in general do not believe in paying for much medical care for the poor. Arizona's record on abortion thus is part and parcel of its dismal record on public medical care.

In 1976, Arizona's abortion rate had been 16 per 1,000 women of reproductive age, 29th in the nation. Only one in six of the state's public and private non-Catholic hospitals provided any abortions at all.[6] The congressman, answering his own question, above, declared:

> We are told that prohibiting the use of taxpayer dollars for abortions is discrimination against the poor, because without such abortion subsidies poor people could not afford to have abortions. By that logic, taxpayers could be forced by Congress to pay for poor people to have face lifts, hair transplants, expensive cars and tickets to the Kennedy Center—since without such support indigent citizens could not afford these amenities.
>
> Abortion is no more an individual right than these luxuries . . . . We are told by those who oppose this amendment that women should have freedom of choice. The cliche we hear most often is, "A woman has the right to control her own body." I agree. Let her exercise control—before she gets pregnant. But do not ask the taxpayers of America to pay the price when there is a failure to exercise control by forcing taxpayers to subsidize the ending of lives of unborn children as a convenience to adult women.[7]

In a few paragraphs, Representative Rudd thus neatly summarized several of the major themes propounded by congressmen who sought to bar subsidized abortions for the poor. They argued, to be sure, that their principal purpose was to stop the murder of innocent unborn children. But this crime became even less excusable if the woman was on welfare.

"We don't want a woman who wakes up with a hangnail to be able to get an abortion," said another House member, in opposing a clause that would have allowed Medicaid abortions for health reasons.[8]

Representative Hyde agreed: "The pregnant woman would not even have to claim she had a headache or athlete's foot to get an abortion."[9] A Massachusetts congressman, Silvo Conte, was willing to allow paid abortions only in cases of *forced* rape. Without that stipulation, he said, "any woman who wants an abortion under Medicaid could go in and say, 'I'm raped,' and there could be a lot of perjury."[10] Even in the edited version of this debate that appears in the *Congressional Record*, it is evident that many congressmen concur that abortion is a luxury and a convenience that is used by untrustworthy, promiscuous welfare women for trivial reasons, so they can avoid paying the price for their irresponsible behavior.

Irony abounds in this argument. For nearly three decades, the federal welfare program has been continually attacked by fiscal conservatives, who repeatedly have accused women recipients of being "brood mares" who intentionally had babies to increase their welfare allotments. But now, in 1977, these same welfare women, who account for 90 percent of adult Medicaid recipients, again were under congressional attack—this time because they used abortion to avoid bearing unwanted children.

Between June and December of 1977, a total of 25 roll-call votes were taken in the House in the attempt to reach a compromise. Innumerable sessions were held by conferees representing the two houses, and endless hours were consumed with arguments over the relative merits of terms like "serious" versus "severe," "permanent" versus "long-lasting," and "forced rape" versus "rape."

Despite the time it consumed, and the effort, this debate was the antithesis of deliberative, legislative decision-making:

None of the substantive committees responsible for the basic legislation held even a day of hearings on the ban. Not a single witness was heard. Virtually no factual evidence was adduced. No medical testimony was considered. Some of the 27 conferees—all males—revealed their underlying attitudes through the use of terms like "hardware" for intrauterine devices and "quick scrapes" for dilatation and curettage. They showed considerable ignorance on such serious topics as genetic counseling and birth defects.[11]

Catholic and allied antiabortion groups actively lobbied Congress during this period. In August, Archbishop Joseph L. Bernardin, president of the National Conference of Catholic Bishops, called for vigorous opposition to the expenditure of funds for abortion.[12] The most visible outside participant, however, was Mark Gallagher, lobbyist for the Bishops' National Committee for a Human Life Amendment. As The New York Times reported:

> Every time the Senate conferees make a compromise offer, Mr. Gallagher quietly walks to the conference table to tell a staff aide to the 11 House conferees whether the proposal is acceptable to the bishops. His recommendations invariably are followed.[13]

Finally, with funding for major social programs repeatedly held up and HEW employees facing a payless Christmas, a "compromise" amendment was adopted on December 7th. It barred federal funds for abortions except

> where the life of the mother would be endangered if the fetus were carried to term . . . for victims of rape and incest, when such rape or incest has been reported promptly to a law enforcement agency or public health service; or except in those instances where severe and long-lasting physical health damage to the mother would result if the pregnancy were carried to term when so determined by two physicians.

This compromise satisfied no one, least of all Representative Hyde. He voted against it because, he said, he was "unwilling to trade unborn life for a health condition or for any other circumstances, except to save another human life."[14]

In its June 1977 decisions on the two Medicaid cases, the Supreme Court had ruled—over unusually bitter dissents—that neither the Constitution nor the federal Medicaid statute prevented a state from refusing to pay for "elective" abortions.[15] It was implied that the Court might, however, overrule a ban on the funding of abortions that were judged to be medically necessary.

When President Carter, three weeks later, was asked his opinion of the new Court ruling, he achieved some notoriety when he replied:

> As you know there are many things in life that are not fair, that wealthy people can afford and poor people can't. But I don't believe that the federal government should take action to try to make those opportunities exactly equal, particularly when there is a moral factor involved.[16]

When Judge Dooling subsequently lifted his temporary injunction blocking implementation of the 1977 Hyde amendment, he thus joined the Supreme Court, the President, and Congress in signaling to abortion opponents that they now had a constitutionally valid means to restrict abortions by limiting Medicaid funding.

Many states already had shown their willingness to follow this restrictive route. Between 1973 and 1975, 13 states had adopted laws or administrative policies limiting Medicaid abortion funding, almost all of which had been thrown out by the federal courts. The newly restrictive federal posture toward abortion funding now reinforced the strong antifunding forces in the states.

By the end of 1979, 40 states had moved to restrict Medicaid reimbursement for abortion. In 23 states, legislative initiative was not even necessary; funding was restricted by executive or administrative decree. The other 17 states enacted laws to limit abortion coverage.[17]

In some states, major legislative battles occurred. In Massachusetts, which has the second-largest proportion of Catholic residents of any state, legislators were subjected to intense lobbying efforts. One Catholic state senator was denounced from the pulpit and publicly condemned by the Knights of Columbus; his office was inundated with more than 5,000 letters and phone calls from abortion opponents. A local priest told his parish, "Your Irish-Catholic senator is voting with the baby-murderers."[18]

A Worcester, Massachusetts, legislator, Jerry D'Amico, observed: "I'm used to political pressure—but it's a different kind of pressure when God is involved."[19]

Abortion-rights forces used "equally fierce, gut-level tactics, bordering at times on political blackmail," according to state Senator Chester Atkins, one of the chief targets of this lobbying. He said: "I was subjected to the most vicious, ugly lobbying effort that I've ever seen. It shocked and disappointed me."[20]

The "prochoice" coalition contacted several of his financial backers urging them to threaten to withhold future support if he voted to restrict abortion funding. The head of the prochoice coalition reported that another senator, Carol Amick, had come under even more pressure:

"At one point a group from NOW [National Organization for Women] marched into her office and told her that they were going to go out and look for another candidate to run against her during the next election."[20]

As this emotional process unfolded, Governor Michael Dukakis promised to veto restrictive legislation—then did so repeatedly. Each veto generated yet another round of fiercely emotional lobbying. Finally, after almost a year of turmoil and near-paralysis of the government, the legislature was able in July 1978 to override the governor's veto and to enact a law cutting off Medicaid funding for all abortions except to save the woman's life or in cases of rape and incest. The state legislature acted again in September 1979, this time with the support of a newly elected governor, Edward King, to further restrict state funds to permit *only* those abortions necessary to save the life of the woman.

In Illinois, after a similarly bruising battle, the governor's veto proved insufficient; it was overridden by both houses of the legislature. But Michigan Governor William Milliken's unbending stand led to the eventual defeat of restrictions, after a prolonged impasse. The courageous determination of Governor Hugh Carey, a staunch Catholic, to maintain funding in New York contributed significantly to the defeat of antiabortion efforts there. In Maryland, a politically sophisticated and broadly based coalition of abortion-funding supporters was able to defeat the antiabortion forces, who described the conflict as their "last chance" to end the state's liberal abortion policy.[21] But even in these few states where attempts to limit public abortion funding were fore-stalled, the legacy of divisiveness and bitterness generated by the legislative debates will long remain.

Since 1973, all states have considered and most have passed some legis-lation dealing with abortion. The majority tried to restrict availability—and would have succeeded had the courts not consistently invalidated these statutes as unconstitutional. A Louisiana law, for example, restricted abortions to licensed hospitals—although the Su-preme Court had barred such a limitation for the first trimester. A Mis-souri law prohibited saline abortions, the most common second-trimester technique. In direct defiance of the Supreme Court, a Rhode Island statute limited abortions to life-threatening conditions.

With their relatively small electoral districts, state legislators—even more than congressmen—feel themselves vulnerable to organized pres-sure groups among their constituents. Many fear that antiabortion groups represent a large body of like-minded voters. The *Pastoral Plan* mobilization has strengthened this perception, and local Catholic cler-gy's involvement has sometimes lent credence to these fears.

In several states, major legal battles also ensued. By the end of 1979, 12 states were ordered by the court to pay for "medically necessary" abortions for Medicaid recipients. The most commonly used definition of a medically necessary abortion is the one articulated by the Supreme Court in *Doe v. Bolton:*

|w|hether an abortion is necessary is a professional judgment that . . . may be exercised in light of all factors—physical, emotional, psychologi-cal, familial, and the woman's age—relevant to the well-being of the pa-tient. All these factors may relate to health. This allows the attending physician the room he needs to make his best medical judgment.

An additional three states were ordered in court to provide state funds at least for those abortions for which federal reimbursement is availa-ble.[22]

Not all states, however, complied with the court orders. On January 26, 1979, the Federal District Court for the Western District of Missouri permanently enjoined enforcement of a 1977 state policy that would have permitted reimbursement only in cases in which the life of the woman is endangered. A full eight months later, according to the Mis-souri Department of Social Services, "Medicaid will not pay for any abortions or abortion-related procedures."[23]

A Catholic legislator in Maine, for one, charged that Portland parishes were lobbying strongly against a proposed regulatory statute on abortion that conformed to the 1973 guidelines. They "had implied that the Church would work to defeat in the next election lawmakers" who supported it.[24] When the Maryland legislature debated a similar bill in 1973, a spokesman for the archdiocese declared that "Catholic legislators who vote for the bill . . . might be subject to automatic excommunication."[25]

Adverse court rulings slowed the momentum of early efforts to get around the Supreme Court decisions. Then, in 1975 and 1976, the focus of legislative activity shifted to more narrowly drawn proposals involving reporting requirements and regulations. Other measures are intended to limit the provision of abortion services by making it too costly or difficult to establish and operate abortion facilities. It seems probable that this new generation of restrictive measures will be modified and limited by court challenges that already are under way.

Local government has many areas of responsibility that directly affect—and can be used to limit—community-based abortion services, including public health and safety codes and enforcement practices, building codes, and zoning regulations. While most of the 2,500 health facilities that offer abortions have been able to proceed without incident, some local controversies have arisen. Most involve attempts by RTL forces to discourage or shut down these services.

Although most of these local roadblocks have been thrown out by the courts, they confront—and discourage—potential providers with the prospect of long delays, high legal costs, and community controversy. One hotly contested case started in 1975, in Southboro, Massachusetts, when organizers of a proposed clinic obtained the necessary assurance from state health officials that they would not be in violation of any applicable zoning ordinances. But the town then voted to amend its zoning bylaws to make abortion clinics a flatly prohibited use, along with trailer camps, race tracks, junk yards, piggeries, and fur farms. This change followed two lengthy, bitter town meetings attended by hundreds of people, at which proponents and opponents clashed angrily.[26]

Three years later, the Massachusetts Supreme Court unanimously ruled the zoning change invalid. The court said public sentiment was not relevant to the issue, since conditioning rights on public opinion would lead to "the extinction of many liberties which are constitutionally guaranteed against invasion by a majority."[27]

Efforts to start abortion clinics have run afoul of local health-planning agencies, which have the authority to approve new facilities and services, in the context of detailed community-health plans. For example, the Scranton, Pennsylvania, planning council proposed to state in its regional health plan:

Abortions and sterilizations are currently legal in the land and are in demand in Lackawanna County. Insofar as possible all legal medical procedures ought to be made available to the public at the greatest safety and least possible inconvenience.[28]

This is a statement that any health plan could—and should—include. But it created an uproar. At the council's first hearing, speakers were divided into hostile camps. A representative of Pennsylvanians for Human Life presented an antiabortion slide show. Abortion-rights speakers argued for inclusion of the statement.

The council was flooded with letters opposing the statement; they came from antiabortion organizations, the area's hospital council, the Catholic diocese, and many Catholic groups. On a motion by Monsignor Kenneth Horan, director of social services for the Scranton Catholic diocese and a planning-council member, the statement was deleted from the plan.[29]

Local authorities also have enacted stringent regulations governing many facets of abortion clinics' operations. But the courts have consistently interpreted the 1973 Supreme Court ruling as precluding regulatory requirements that are more demanding than those for other medical procedures of similar risk—and accordingly have thrown out many of the restrictive regulations.

These attempts nevertheless continue to generate publicity for the antiabortion cause. One well-publicized attempt was the restrictive abortion ordinance enacted in Akron, Ohio. This measure attracted national attention and has spawned not only similar local ordinances elsewhere in other communities but also legislation in several states. The Akron case began when an Orthodox Jewish law student, Marvin Weinberger, formed a group called Citizens for Informed Consent, which sponsored the ordinance. Weinberger set out to get national publicity for his effort. Recruiting allies from Christian fundamentalist and Catholic congregations, he also soon won support in the city countil. A "prochoice" coalition of health professionals and women's and civil liberties groups was organized against the ordinance.

Unlike previous local ordinances, Akron's intruded directly into the decision-making process of both the patient and her physician. Its intent was to discourage women from obtaining abortions by setting up emotional as well as procedural obstacles. This is inherent in an "informed consent" provision, which requires that the doctor tell prospective abortion patients that "the unborn child is a human life from the moment of conception." The ordinance also requires the doctor to describe, in detail, the physical characteristics of a fetus at each week of its development, explain its "appearance, mobility, tactile sensitivity, including pain perception or response, brain and heart function," and warn that abortion may cause the mother "severe emotional disturbances."

With Akron city hall surrounded by demonstrators and TV cameras rolling, the ordinance was passed 7-6 in February 1978. One courageous Catholic council member who opposed it, explained, "It's pretty hard to go against my own religion, but I have a duty as a councilman . . . to uphold the laws of the land."[30] But the mayor, who also opposed the ordinance, decided not to veto it since he felt the controversy would continue and that a legal ruling therefore was needed to resolve the matter.

A year and a half later, the Federal District Court for the Northern District of Ohio struck down the parts of the ordinance that required the "detailed consent" of the woman as well as the notification of the parents of a minor seeking an abortion. The court, however, upheld those sections of the ordinance that require a 24-hour waiting period between the time that a woman gives her informed consent and the abortion is performed, as well as the ordinance's requirement that all abortions after the first trimester of pregnancy be performed in hospitals.[31]

Although the court invalidated the "detailed consent" and parental notification sections of the Akron ordinance, several states adopted similar legislation, both before and after the district court ruling.[32] In several states where such legislation has been attempted, the courts have enjoined enforcement of the requirements for parental notification and a waiting period.[33]

Local governments like the one in Akron clearly have tried to subvert the Supreme Court's abortion decisions, sometimes using methods that their leaders must know will ultimately fail legal review. This disregard of the law cannot help but be perceived as encouragement by a new breed of RTL activists, who recently have escalated the abortion conflict. These protesters have forced their way into abortion clinics, harassed patients, and refused to leave. In one case they invaded an operating room, frightening and conceivably even endangering a patient.[34] The activists claim to be imitating the civil-disobedience tactics of the civil-rights and anti-Vietnam War movements.[35]

These protesters are not limited to adults. "In Portland, Oregon," *Newsweek* reports, "two van-loads of parochial school children pulled up to the Lovejoy Specialty Hospital . . . . The students chased women leaving the clinic, shouting 'Murderers, murderers.'"[36]

The hatred that is implicit in much of the antiabortion rhetoric and actions cannot always be controlled. There was almost no violence around the abortion issue from 1973 to 1976. But since 1977, at least 15 abortion and contraceptive clinics sustained serious physical attacks, arson, and vandalism.[37]

The events that led up to the firebombing of a St. Paul, Minnesota, abortion clinic illustrate the process clearly. The local Planned Parenthood affiliate proposed to open a new headquarters that would provide early abortions. A citywide controversy ensued. The battle included rallies, picketing, litigation, harassment of individual and corporate supporters of Planned Parenthood, intimidation of clinic patients and staff, and ultimately violence. The son of a Planned Parenthood board member found a note in his junior-high-school locker that said: "To the baby-killer's son. If your mom doesn't arrange to stop killing babies, we'll arrange for something to happen to you."[38]

While the building was being remodeled, it was vandalized several times. A month after it opened, on Ash Wednesday 1977, a fire set by arsonists extensively damaged the structure. The leader of the citizens group that opposed the facility denounced the arson. But newsman Bill Moyers, in a TV documentary report, assessed the situation in more cogent terms:

"The politics of abortion has grown ugly. Passionate feelings stir extremist acts. Fierce rhetoric yields to firebombs."[39]

References

1 *Congressional Record, House,* June 17, 1977, p. H6083.

2 The Alan Guttmacher Institute, *Abortions and the Poor: Private Morality, Public Responsibility,* New York, 1979.

3 *Congressional Record, House,* June 24, 1976, p. H6647.

4 *Congressional Record, House,* June 17, 1977, p. H6083.

5 Ibid., p. H6088.

6 J. D. Forrest, C. Tietze, and E. Sullivan, "Abortion in the United States, 1976–1977," *Family Planning Perspectives,* **10**:271, 1978.

7 *Congressional Record, House,* June 17, 1977, p. H6088.

8 L. Wertheimer, "27 Men and Abortion," *Washington Post,* Nov. 25, 1977.

9 *Congressional Record, House,* Sept. 27, 1977, p. H10132.

10 *Congressional Record, House,* Nov. 13, 1977, p. H10969.

11 M. Tolchin, "Accord on Abortion Seems to be Distant," *New York Times,* Oct. 6, 1977.

12 "Bishop Rejects Abortion 'Compromise,' Calls for Constitutional Amendment," *Planned Parenthood Washington Memo*, Sept. 9, 1977.

13 M. Tolchin, "On Abortion, the Houses Still Remain Miles Apart," *The New York Times*, Nov. 27, 1977.

14 *Congressional Record, House*, Dec. 7, 1977, p. H12773.

15 *Beal v. Doe*, 45, U.S. Law Week 4781, June 21, 1977, and *Maher v. Roe*, 45, U.S. Law Week 4787, June 21, 1977.

16 Office of the White House Press Secretary, press conference no. 11, July 12, 1977, pp. 8–9.

17 The Alan Guttmacher Institute, op. cit., p. 23.

18 B. Peterson, "Politics of the Jugular," *Washington Post*, Dec. 10, 1977.

19 M. MacPherson, "Abortion Opponents Focus on States Still Funding Them," *Washington Post*, Nov. 17, 1977.

20 B. Peterson, op. cit.

21 Ibid.

22 P. P. Kalivada, "Abortion and Medicaid: Courts Reject Limits on Funding Necessary Medical Procedures," *Family Planning/Population Reporter*, **8**:80, 1979.

23 H. D. Smith, assistant medical claims payment supervisor, medical claims section, Missouri Department of Social Services, division of family services, personal communication, Aug. 30, 1979.

24 J. S. Day, "Abortion Regulation Bill Gets Initial House Approval," *Bangor News*, June 6, 1973.

25 S. S. Taylor, Jr., "House Hears Abortion Bill to Enact High Court Ruling," *Baltimore Sun*, Mar. 21, 1973.

26 See D. McDaniel, "State to Decide on Approving Abortion Clinic," *Framingham News*, June 8, 1976; C. Dunphy, "Abortion Clinic Ban Could Prove Costly," *Worcester Gazette*, July 29, 1976; and C. Graves, "Abortion Clinic Ban Approved," *Hudson Sun*, Aug. 13, 1976.

27 "Local Efforts to Block Abortion Clinics Rebuffed," *Family Planning/Population Reporter*, **6**:67, October 1977.

28 "HHPC Votes to Shun Abortion Issue," *Scranton Times*, Dec. 2, 1975.

29 Ibid.

30 J. Petosa, "Anti-Abortion Forces See Akron's 'Consent' Law as Exploding Myths," *National Catholic Reporter*, Mar. 17, 1978.

31 *Akron Center for Reproductive Health v. City of Akron* C78-155A (N. D. Ohio, Aug. 22, 1979).

32 Nebraska, L316, enacted Mar. 22, 1979; Maine, S484, enacted June 4, 1979; Louisiana, H1185, enacted July 10, 1978; Florida, H1814, enacted June 29, 1979; Missouri H523, H626, and H902, enacted June 29, 1979; North Dakota, H1581, enacted Apr. 8, 1979; Tennessee, H2415, enacted Apr. 12, 1979, and Illinois, S47, enacted Oct. 30, 1979.

33 *Women's Services, P.C. et al. v. Thone et al.,* Case No. CV78-L-289 (D. C. Neb., Nov. 9, 1979); *Women's Community Health Center v. Cohen,* Civ. No. 79-162p (D. Me., Sept. 13, 1979); and *Margaret S. v. Edwards et al.,* 8-2765 Sec. C. (E. D. La., filed August 1978).

34 "Abortion Under Attack," *Newsweek,* June 5, 1978.

35 L. Darling, "Small Group Keeps Dispute Alive," *Washington Post,* Nov. 29, 1977.

36 "Abortion under Attack," op. cit.

37 S. Rich, "Abortion Advocates Say Violence is Worsening," *Washington Post,* Mar. 7, 1978.

38 "Don't Blame a Person," *Duluth News-Tribune,* May 9, 1977.

39 CBS Reports, *The Politics of Abortion* (transcript), Apr. 22, 1978.

CHAPTER ELEVEN
Paying the Price

There are enough data to venture a first approximation of what were the probable consequences of the Hyde amendment and of the continuing failure of most public hospitals to provide abortions. They slowed—and very likely reversed—the earlier trend toward more equitable availability of abortion and its greater utilization by poor, young, and nonwhite women.

Previous chapters documented that serious inequities in the availability of abortion services existed before enactment of the Hyde amendment. The barriers to use of abortion created by distance, cost, and lack of information impact most strongly on poor, adolescent, and minority women. The effect of Medicaid in reducing the financial obstacles for poor women is shown by the fact that the abortion rate of Medicaid recipients in 1977 was three times higher than that of more affluent women. Nevertheless, inequities persisted. In 1977 the proportion of women obtaining abortions financed by Medicaid was three times greater in Illinois than in neighboring Iowa and Missouri, four times greater in Virginia than in North Carolina, and more than two times greater in New York than Connecticut.[1] There were also large differentials in the proportions of Medicaid-eligible women estimated to need abortion services who were able to obtain publicly financed abortions. In only eight states and the District of Columbia did Medicaid pay for abortions for as many as three-quarters of the Medicaid women in need. Nine states paid for fewer than one-quarter of the needed abortions, and six states paid for none.[2] These differences in the use of abortion by Medicaid-eligible women coming from geographically and culturally similar backgrounds were primarily the result of varying availability of abortion in the different states as well as differences in the scope of each state's Medicaid program. The restriction of Medicaid funding for abortion by many states certainly increased these inequities.

In states where Medicaid funding was cut off, some pregnant welfare recipients scraped together the money required for a legal abortion or obtained the procedure as charity. Some may have returned to the pre-1973 patterns of illegal and self-induced abortions. Many undoubtedly have borne unwanted children.

It is highly likely that the number of poor woman eligible for Medicaid who wanted abortions but were unable to obtain them was considerably higher than the 133,000 who were unable to do so in the year prior to enforcement of the Hyde amendment in 1977.[3]

Some insight into the impact of the abortion funding ban is provided by preliminary data collected by the Department of Health, Education and Welfare (HEW) for a 19-month period after the restrictive federal regulations went in effect. The data show that in states that adopted the restrictive language, the number of publicly funded abortions obtained by poor women fell by about 99 percent.[4] It made virtually no difference whether the restrictions allowed reimbursement for abortion only when the woman's life was endangered, or if rape and incest were added as reasons, or if the "compromise" 1977 Hyde amendment was employed as a model for the state law.[5] The protracted congressional debates over the Hyde language thus turn out to have been quite meaningless.

The HEW data indicate that of the few abortions reimbursed by the federal government under Hyde, at least eight out of 10 were for "life endangerment" and only the remaining handful were for rape, incest, or "severe and long-lasting physical health damage."[6] This is hardly surprising in light of doctors' and health facilities' understandable reluctance to provide abortions that in the end might be denied reimbursement by government auditors. For their part, women, even if aware of the intricacies of the law, are hesitant to endure the fear and shame of reporting sexual abuse or of undergoing a complex certification procedure to qualify for a reimbursed abortion.

By applying information from states that restricted funding, it is possible to project the likely potential impact of such restrictions.

If all restrictions were upheld in the states that by the end of 1978 had limited abortion funding, the annual total number of Medicaid-financed abortions would have declined by 70 percent. Over 200,000 fewer abortions would be paid for by public programs.

The unmet need for abortion services among poor women would increase 2.5 times. This means that unless they could pay for an abortion on their own, eight out of every 10 Medicaid-eligible women who are estimated to need and want abortions would be unable to get them.[7] If *all* states adopted the Hyde restrictions, the number of government-financed abortions for the poor would fall to fewer than 3,000 a year.

These results are important because the concept that the cutoff of Medicaid funding would *not* seriously interfere with a welfare-woman's right to choose abortion—presumably because she could pay for the operation herself—was a major point in Supreme Court Justice Lewis F. Powell's June 1977 ruling that states do not have to pay for "elective" abortions.[8] Comparable arguments were advanced in the congressional debates over the Hyde amendment. Yet, the average cost of an abortion is about $285, $44 more than the average total monthly welfare payment for *an entire family* for food, clothing and other necessities. In Mississippi, the average abortion cost is more than four times higher than the monthly welfare payment, and in Texas it is close to three times higher. Only in 13 states is the average abortion cost less than the monthly allotment.[9] Even these figures understate the difficulties facing pregnant Medicaid recipients, because the average abortion cost is heavily weighted by the lower costs charged in the free-standing clinics. Yet, as we have seen, Medicaid recipients are used to going to hospitals to obtain abortions, and the average hospital cost is $500 compared to $175 in the clinics.

The impact of restrictions on public funding undoubtedly also is reflected in some places in decreased availability of abortions in public hospitals. While fewer than one-fourth of the nation's public hospitals with maternity services performed any abortions, those that did were often important providers for the indigent women in their communities. But public hospitals are financially beleaguered, and many are reluctant to perform abortions if no Medicaid reimbursement is forthcoming. The 1977 Supreme Court abortion decisions allow public hospitals to refuse to pay for most abortions and many no doubt are using the ruling to justify service cutbacks. In the first quarter of 1978, public hospitals performed 20 percent fewer abortions than they had during the same period in 1977 when the Hyde amendment was not in force.[10]

Private philanthropy has played a declining role in financing personal health services generally. According to HEW figures, the proportion of these expenditures paid for by charity declined from 2.9 percent in 1960 to 1.1 percent in 1975.[11] Clinics and hospitals already subsidize some abortions for the poor, but it is virtually impossible for them to subsidize them all. At Hartford Hospital in Connecticut, for example, three or four reduced-rate or free abortions are provided each week, but a larger number of women are turned away. "The sad fact is that there is not enough money to take care of all patients who might want it," says Joseph D. Millerich, the hospital's assistant director of obstetrics and gynecology.[12]

Before the Hyde amendment, the health facilities that performed abortions provided about 85,000 of them at reduced fees or at no cost for women unable to pay. This already substantial number would have to be *tripled* if all Medicaid-eligible women were denied publicly funded abortions, and even then some women still would have to find money for the reduced charge.[13]

Some pregnant women who cannot obtain legal abortions will obtain illegal abortions or try to abort themselves. All of these choices lead to higher morbidity and mortality, since the complication rates are higher than those associated with legal abortion. Experts point out that even before the Hyde amendment, young, poor, and black women were at higher risk of abortion complications, partly because they obtained abortion disproportionately later in pregnancy than other women.[14] Many factors contribute to this situation, including the lower accessibility of abortion services—and of information about where to obtain them—for these women, a pattern that can only be made worse by the Hyde amendment.

HEW's Center for Disease Control (CDC) has been monitoring abortion complications in states that continue to fund abortions for Medicaid-eligible women and comparing them to states that have restricted payments. This surveillance effort found that, at least in the early period after the restriction of funding, there was no evidence that large numbers of Medicaid women were turning to illegal or self-induced abortion. However, the findings suggest that welfare women in cutoff states who obtain abortions, whether paid for by Medicaid or by themselves, are getting them later in gestation than more affluent women. In states that continue to fund abortions, there is no apparent change in the gestational stages at which Medicaid recipients obtain abortions.[15]

Early legal abortion is an extremely safe medical procedure. But each week of delay in obtaining an abortion increases the risk of medical complications by approximately 20 percent and the risk of death by 50 percent.[16] Even if all Medicaid-recipient women who obtained abortions in restrictive states prior to cutoff continue to get them, the number of complications, including grave complications and deaths, could be expected to rise considerably. In the year following the funding restrictions, CDC in fact did verify four abortion-related deaths that were attributed directly or indirectly to the Medicaid-abortion ban.[17]

The final—and most likely—consequence of the Medicaid cutoff is that more poor and adolescent women have borne unwanted children. A recent study of the impact of the Hyde amendment in two states, Ohio and Georgia, where the unmet need for abortion service among Medicaid-eligible woman was higher before the Hyde amendment, indicates that more than one-fifth the number of Medicaid-eligible women who obtained abortions funded by Medicaid in the year prior to the Hyde amendment were unable to obtain abortions in the year following its enforcement—an estimate the authors deem conservative, since a major Georgia public hospital continued to fund abortions for poor women, and the number of conceptions in Ohio was believed to be underestimated.[18] If only one-fifth of all abortions previously funded by Medicaid were denied and these unwanted pregnancies resulted in births, there would be some 60 thousand more unwanted babies born each year to welfare recipients.

The Hyde amendment thus has exacted a heavy price from poor, young, and minority women who were denied access to a safe, legal Medicaid-funded abortion, regardless of which course of action they followed. They faced greater risks of morbidity and mortality if they chose clandestine abortions, greater poverty and dependency if they carried their pregnancies to term.

Many younger women denied Medicaid abortions were unable to complete school or take a job. Most of their children were born out of wedlock, into already overburdened homes that were unprepared to give them the nurture that should be any child's birthright. Beyond the obvious economic and social disadvantages, these children also face the adverse emotional and developmental consequences that are the proven lot of unwanted children.[19]

The Medicaid cutoff also has exacted a heavy price from taxpayers in the form of greater medical-care expenditures for the delivery of unwanted babies and for their welfare assistance and social services. Antiabortion congressmen have sought to foreclose all talk of this consequence by saying that even to *think* about the costs and benefits of the Medicaid cutoff is to "elevate dollar values above life values."[20] This argument is obviously based on the belief that a fetus is a person and that the well-being of poor women is not itself a "life-value."

Nevertheless, estimates of the aggregate costs of the funding bans have been made for the nation as a whole and for individual states and localities. When the first congressional effort to cut off Medicaid funding was made in 1974, HEW submitted to the Senate-House Conference Committee an impact statement indicating that Medicaid was funding between 222,000 and 278,000 abortions annually, at a cost of $40 million to $50 million. The department estimated that for each pregnant Medicaid recipient who is forced to carry her unwanted pregnancy to term, the *additional* costs to federal, state, and local government of maternity and pediatric care and public assistance for the first year of the child's life alone would be approximately $2,200.[21] This implies that the added first-year costs to government could go as high as $450 – $565 million if all Medicaid abortions were halted and all the women carried their pregnancies to term.

In 1977, the head of HEW's Health Care Financing Administration, Robert A. Derzon, sent Secretary Joseph A. Califano, Jr., a memo estimating that each birth to a welfare woman denied a publicly funded abortion would result in $1,100 of additional governmental expenditures.[22] This calculation—which omitted most of the medical and social-service costs associated with welfare births—implied additional government costs of $100 million if only one-third of Medicaid women obtaining abortions had to carry their pregnancies to term. When the delivery-related costs are included, this estimate rises to about $200 million.[23]

Estimates in different states and cities, carried out with varying methodologies and assumptions, have produced similar predictions. A study by the state of Washington's Department of Social and Health Services showed that the additional costs of public assistance and medical care would be $3.4 to $7.2 million per year, if all of the state's 1,920 Medicaid abortions were denied and the women delivered the babies; the cost of the abortions was estimated at $384,000.[24] A study at the New School for Social Research showed that the additional first-year government costs of eliminating Medicaid funding of abortions in New York City would be $80 million if half the city's 44,000 Medicaid abortion patients carried their pregnancies to term. The 44,000 abortions would cost the city $10 million.[25]

These studies document the obvious: maternity and pediatric care and public assistance are considerably more expensive than abortion—and these are only the short-term costs. The added social-welfare costs of forcing poor women to bear babies they do not want eventually will be paid for either by taxpayers, in the form of higher social welfare outlays, or by the poor, for whom there will be fewer available funds for other urgent health and social needs.

It is ironic that the Hyde amendment was adopted by a Congress and supported by an administration whose principal stated national-welfare goal is to increase opportunities for self-sufficiency and self-support among welfare recipients, presumably for the benefit of the individuals concerned and all other taxpayers. In this light, the inequity of the Hyde amendment is matched by its irrationality.

References

1   The Alan Guttmacher Institute, *Abortions and the Poor: Private Morality, Public Responsibility*, New York, 1979, p. 19.

2   Ibid., p. 14.

3   Ibid., p. 13.

4   S. Rich, "New Curbs Cut Medicaid-Funded Abortions 99%, HEW Reports," *Washington Post*, Mar. 8, 1979, and unpublished data, Medicaid Bureau, Division of Analysis and Evaluation, Health Care Financing Administration: DHEW.

5   Ibid.

6   Ibid.

7   The Alan Guttmacher Institute, op. cit., p. 25.

8   *Maher v. Roe*, 45, U.S. Law Week 4787, June 21, 1977, p. 9.

9   The Alan Guttmacher Institute, op. cit., p. 27.

10   Ibid., p. 29.

11   Derived from A. M. Skolnik and S. R. Dales, "Social Welfare Expenditures, 1950-75," *Social Security Bulletin*, Vol. 39, no. 1., 1975, table 5, p. 15.

12   L. Oelsner, "Cutoffs on Medicaid Prompt Shift in Thinking on Abortion," *New York Times*, Dec. 11, 1977.

13   The Alan Guttmacher Institute, op. cit., p. 28.

14   M. B. Bracken and S. V. Kash, "Delay in Seeking Induced Abortion: A Review and Theoretical Analysis," *American Journal of Obstetrics and Gynecology*, **121**:1008, 1978.

15   Center for Disease Control, "Epidemiologic Notes and Reports: Health Effects of Restricting Federal Funds for Abortion—United States," *Morbidity and Mortality Weekly Report*, **28**:37, 1979.

16   W. Cates, Jr., K. F. Schulz, D. A. Grimes, and C. W. Tyler, Jr., "The Effect of Delay and Method Choice on the Risk of Abortion Morbidity," *Family Planning Perspectives*, **9**:266, 1977.

17   Center for Disease Control, op. cit., and personal communication, W. Cotes, CDC, April, 1980.

18   J. Trussell, J. Menken, B. Lindheim, and B. Vaughn, "The Impact of Restriction of Medicaid Funds for Abortion," *Family Planning Perspectives*, **12**:120, 1980.

19   H. Forssman and I. Thuwe, "One Hundred and Twenty Children Born After Application for Therapeutic Abortion Refused," *Acta Psychiatrica Scan-*

dinavia, **43**:71, 1966; Z. Matejcek, Z. Dytrych, and V. Schuller, "Children from Unwanted Pregnancies," *Acta Psychiatrica Scandinavia,* **57**:67, 1978; and Z. Dytrych, Z. Matejcek, V. Schuller, H. P. David, and H. L. Friedman, "Children Born to Women Denied Abortion," *Family Planning Perspectives,* **7**:165, 1975.

20   Rep. Jim Santini, *Congressional Record, House,* Sept. 20, 1976, p. H5171.

21   "DHEW Sees Far-Reaching Implications of Bartlett-Type Amendment for States and Poor," *Family Planning/Population Reporter,* **3**:114, 1974.

22   Robert A. Derzon, Memorandum to DHEW Secretary Joseph A. Califano, Jr., June 4, 1977.

23   R. Lincoln, B. Doring-Bradley, B. L. Lindheim, and M. A. Cotterill, "The Court, the Congress and the President: Turning Back the Clock on the Pregnant Poor," *Family Planning Perspectives,* **9**:207, 1977.

24   State of Washington, Department of Social and Health Services, "Estimated Impact of Eliminating Federal Funds for Non-Therapeutic Abortions, 1977 – 70—A Working Paper" (mimeo), Aug. 17, 1977.

25   New School for Social Research, Department of Urban Affairs and Policy Analysis, "Funding of Medicaid Abortions in New York City" (mimeo), Dec. 5, 1977.

CHAPTER TWELVE
The Holy Wars

Five years after the 1973 Supreme Court decisions, abortion seemed to have become an unavoidable issue in Congress. Contemplating yet another antiabortion rider in the spring of 1978, Representative William Clay of Missouri called abortion "an albatross on all legislation. This amendment is history repeating itself," he complained. "It's the Holy Wars all over again."[1]

A colleague, Frank Thompson of New Jersey, feared the amendment would imperil passage of a bill intended to end discrimination against pregnant working women. He said the tactic of attaching antiabortion amendments to pending bills was "causing a serious disruption of the legislative process."[2] House Speaker Thomas O'Neill of Massachusetts bluntly called the abortion issue a "plague on the House."[3]

Discounting the rhetoric of political discourse, these statements warrant serious attention because of the congressmen who made them: all are liberal Democrats; O'Neill and Thompson are part of the House establishment, while Clay is a member of the Black Caucus. They are also all Roman Catholics, a fact that normally is irrelevant—or even offensive—in political analysis. It became relevant because the amendment to which they referred had been demanded by the National Conference of Catholic Bishops.

Their warnings also merit attention because, unlike the Hyde amendments of 1976 and 1977, the legislative proposal in question did not affect only poor women on welfare. In fact it did not affect them at all. The bill rather concerned the 25 million American working women of child-bearing age. For the first time since the futile attempts of 1973 and 1975 to enact a constitutional amendment, the bishops again were seeking passage of an antiabortion provision that would affect people in all socioeconomic groups—and as such it was a harbinger of things to come.

The bill under debate was designed to mandate inclusion of pregnancy-related conditions in employee fringe-benefit programs like health insurance, sick leave, and temporary-disability plans. It would have amended the Civil Rights Act of 1964 to state explicitly that "women affected by pregnancy, childbirth or related medical conditions shall be treated the same for all employment-related purposes, including receipt of benefits under fringe benefit programs, as other persons not so affected." The bill was supported by both the Catholic hierarchy and a broad, formally organized coalition of national labor, health, civil-rights, and women's organizations, including both the Planned Parenthood Federation of America and an antiabortion organization, American Citizens Concerned for Life.

The National Conference of Catholic Bishops objected, however, that the bill would raise abortion "to the level of a civil right" and force Church-related institutions, such as hospitals, schools and social-service agencies, "to provide abortion disability benefits, a requirement with which we cannot comply."[4] Nothing in the bill, or course, required anyone to obtain an abortion or any institution to provide one. It merely mandated that benefit plans treat abortion the same way that they treat other covered conditions.

The bishops argued, however, that the religious principles of Church agencies would be violated simply by virtue of having to share the cost of benefit plans covering abortion. They therefore offered an amendment excluding "nontherapeutic abortions" from the bill's definition of mandated coverage. This demand was rejected by the Senate in September 1977. The House Education and Labor Committee, however, accepted the amendment in March 1978, forcing the bill into conference. The bishops' amendment thus jeopardized the prospect for the bill's passage, since it created the first serious split in the broad coalition that supported the measure.[5]

After a long, divisive conference, a "compromise" was struck whereby employers would have discretion, except when the woman's health was endangered by the pregnancy, as to whether or not they would pay for the actual abortion under their health-insurance plans, but they could not refuse to cover medical payments and earned sick leave or disability benefits for the treatment of abortion complications. Since the bill's whole point had been to divest employers of the *choice* of whether to cover female employees for pregnancy-related health conditions, women's and abortion-rights groups were extremely distressed by the inclusion of this discriminatory amendment—which largely negated the bill's impact for women terminating their pregnancies. However, they had no choice but to accept it, as Catholic Church and RTL lobbyists made clear that they would jettison the bill rather than allow coverage of abortion. As Representative Theodore Weiss observed, the bishops' amendment could mean "full-scale civil war [since] we are pushing the burden on employers and labor unions, who will be subjected to all kinds of boycotts and demonstrations."[6]

Even the restrictive abortion "compromise" included in the final bill, however, proved unpalatable for the bishops. On June 21, 1979, the U.S. Catholic Conference filed a class-action suit against the Justice Department to halt implementation of the abortion provisions of the measure.[7] As an employer, the USCC contends that requiring abortion coverage even in these limited instances constitutes an infringement of its free exercise of religion. However, the Federal District Court for the District of Columbia dismissed the suit on January 15, 1980, on technical grounds.

Pregnancy benefits affect women workers. A national health-insurance program would affect all Americans. As the Carter administration began to plan the comprehensive health-insurance program that the president had promised to voters, it soon became clear that the Church and RTL movement were prepared to insist that it exclude abortion. When Health, Education and Welfare (HEW) Secretary Joseph A. Califano, Jr., held a public hearing on national health insurance in October 1977, the official Catholic position was presented by Monsignor Lawrence J. Corcoran of the National Conference of Catholic Charities and lay lobbyist Francis J. Butler of the USCC. The Church favors comprehensive health insurance, they said; but, they added:

"We are opposed to provisions for contraceptive services and sterilization for contraceptive purposes. We are also opposed to the inclusion of abortion services as 'benefits' in any National Health Insurance plan."[8]

Contraception, sterilization, and abortion are, of course, the three health services proscribed by Catholic doctrine. This position therefore is virtually a demand that Congress enact into federal law the Catholic doctrine on impermissible medical care. In effect, the bishops are insisting that federal law help the Church impose its doctrine on everyone—whether they are believers or not. In addition to the enormous political obstacles that a comprehensive health-insurance proposal will necessarily face, an acrimonious debate over abortion and other fertility-control services cannot help but jeopardize any future plan's chance for passage.

The priority of fighting inflation may delay enactment of national health insurance in favor of controlling health costs. HEW might be expected, therefore, to be facilitating the difficult job of facing up to the new health-planning mechanisms that are central to this national effort. The heart of the health-planning program is the power of local, regional, and state health systems agencies (HSAs) to end duplicative and unnecessary health services, primarily through a "certificate of need" program. Decisions on hospitals' proposals to expand or modify their services or facilities are to be made by HSA boards composed of local service providers and "consumers," on the basis of detailed assessments of need.

Efforts to consolidate local obstetrical services have been a focus in the critical early phase of HSA activity. In 1978, HEW issued its "National Guidelines for Health Planning," that contained no guidance for the HSAs on how to incorporate hospital-based sterilization and abortion services into the planning process. There already was evidence that this omission would lead to confrontations between community residents who wanted access to these services, and denominational hospitals with doctrinal objections to providing them. Conflicts of this nature have since arisen in Baltimore; Westchester County, New York; Davenport, Iowa; and Cleveland, Ohio.[9]

The only HEW guidelines on hospital-based fertility facilities offered to local planners are numerical standards for births: hospitals with fewer than the annual requisite number of births annually are to close their obstetric units. But HEW chose to ignore the fact that applying this standard would mean limiting obstetrical services in many communities to Catholic hospitals. Women in these communities in need of sterilization and abortion services would not be able to get them in hospitals. The alternative—requiring denominational hospitals to deliver services that they regard as immoral—is equally unsatisfactory.

The Guidelines' one apparent (although oblique) reference to abortion and sterilization, and their potential for conflict, is an ambiguous statement that "special moral and ethical preferences" may necessitate an adjustment to the obstetrical standard, and that HSAs may include a "special adjustment" when application of the standard would result in "the denial of care to persons with special needs resulting from moral and ethical values."[10] For every two births in the United States, there is approximately one female sterilization or abortion procedure performed in hospitals. Thus, to classify these procedures as "special needs" is inexplicable and certainly serves to suggest to agencies that they ought not be integral to their decision-making.

In the absence of useful criteria, HSA decisions on whether area residents will have access to hospital-based abortions and sterilizations frequently reflect the personal beliefs of the HSA members. Disputes that arise often produce acrimonious community struggles—the antithesis of the cooperative process that is required if these planning bodies are to be effective.

One solution proposed was for the *Guidelines* to include abortions and sterilizations in the obstetrical criteria, but to exempt religious institutions whose tenets forbid these services—provided that other accessible health facilities would offer them, and that adequate referral arrangements were ensured.[11] This recommendation was ignored. In its desire to avoid dealing directly with this abortion issue, HEW once again endangered other important policy goals.

In the first year of the Carter administration, it became clear that the abortion controversy was hindering the administration's professed interest in helping to curb teenage pregnancies. A 1976 publication by The Alan Guttmacher Institute highlighted the parameters of the problem: There are 11 million sexually active teenagers, and sexual activity is beginning at increasingly younger ages. Ten percent of all 15-to-19-year-old women become pregnant each year. These 1 million pregnancies result in some 600,000 teenage births.

The great majority of teenage pregnancies and births are unintended, and teenage parents face substantially higher risks of sickness and death, incomplete education, poverty, and divorce. The programs available to prevent the pregnancies in the first place, or help pregnant teenagers cope with them, for the most part are woefully inadequate.[12]

When HEW Secretary Califano "saw those numbers," according to one of his assistants, "they just dazzled him."[13] The Secretary already had stated his personal opposition to public funding of abortion, and had set up an internal task group to examine "alternatives to abortion."

After that effort collapsed, a new task force was established with the mission of developing an HEW initiative on teenage pregnancy. The group met with professionals in the relevant fields and representatives of constituency groups, and prepared a report for Califano.[14] They recommended a balanced program of services to help teenagers prevent unwanted pregnancies, along with improved social services for those who chose to deliver their babies. Precluded by Califano's mandate from even considering abortion, the task force nonetheless stated that "abortion information, counseling services and research (are) essential to reduce the numbers of high-risk adolescent births, particularly for younger adolescents." It forcefully recommended that pregnant teenagers be provided with the option of abortion information, counseling, and referral.[15]

When the much-heralded "teenage initiative" emerged in the president's budget message in January 1978, even the balanced emphasis on family planning to prevent unwanted teenage pregnancies was gone. Instead there was a proposed new program to "coordinate" maternity, social, and educational services for pregnant teenagers—despite the fact that the HEW's own health journal recently had published a study documenting the scarcity of the very services that its new program was now to "coordinate."[16]

During congressional deliberations, according to a report in the *Washington Star*, the administration "quietly" decided once again to pass the buck to state and local-level groups on whether programs should include abortion. When asked about the likelihood of local controversies arising over the abortion issue, Peter Schuck, the HEW deputy assistant secretary for planning and evaluation, responded: "We realize that's going to happen."[17]

The administration thus once again demonstrated its willingness to barter access to abortion for RTL support.

Passed during the closing days of the 95th Congress, the Adolescent Health, Services and Pregnancy Prevention and Care Act of 1978 has as one of its major stated purposes the prevention of "initial and repeat pregnancies." According to the legislation, however, the primary emphasis of the program is "on adolescents who are 17 years of age and under and are pregnant or who are parents." Agencies receiving program grants are required to provide maternity and adoption counseling but only to inform adolescents of the availability of abortion.

The wider good to be gained from research and services that would enable women to deliver healthier babies is insufficient to deter antiabortion crusaders from attacking the benefit if it includes—or even suggests—any connection with abortion. Because scientists sometimes use aborted fetal tissue in their research, RTL activists succeeded, in 1974, in forcing a 13-month moratorium on all federal funding for fetal studies. It is ironic that most of this research is intended to benefit the health of pregnant women and their developing offspring!

Concern over protection of human participants in biomedical research began to grow during the late 1960s and led to congressional efforts to safeguard research subjects.[18] In 1971, the National Institutes of Health (NIH), which fund most federally supported biomedical research, set up a study group to review human research practices and policies. The Senate held extensive hearings on the subject early in 1973. During the considerable discussion of ethical issues that these efforts provoked, fetal research was never singled out for special treatment.

But in April 1973, Representative Angelo Roncallo of New York, the sponsor of several early antiabortion resolutions and bills, introduced a measure in the House to ban fetal research. Criminal penalties of up to 20 years' imprisonment were stipulated for persons carrying out research on a human fetus. The use of federal money for fetal research would be halted.

Despite opponents' pleas to wait for the outcome of the Senate hearings, the House overwhelmingly approved the Roncallo measure. Most who spoke in favor of it tied their support to their antiabortion beliefs. One speaker declared: "This measure may well be the first breakthrough in this Congress for the most important RTL principle."

New York Senator James Buckley offered provisions like Roncallo's as amendments to a Senate proposal to establish a commission to set rules and guidelines to protect human-research subjects. Although the chief sponsor of the commission proposal, Senator Edward Kennedy, opposed the amendments, he agreed to a compromise that placed a temporary moratorium on fetal research "before or after induced abortion" until the proposed commission developed policies to govern such research.

The newly formed National Commission for the Protection of Human Subjects quickly appointed a special study group to investigate fetal research. This panel reported that the past benefits of fetal studies had been great; the need for future research was greater still. Infant-health benefits included development of a vaccine against Rh hemolytic disease and transfusion techniques to save afflicted Rh incompatible fetuses *in utero*. Fetal research also had produced major advances in treating hyaline membrane disease, significant progress in the prevention and management of premature birth and brain injury during labor, the development of amniocentesis, and other experimental methods to identify and treat threatened fetuses before birth.

Research using human embryonic tissue earlier had led to landmark discoveries in child health, including vaccines against polio, measles, and, most recently, rubella. It made possible safety testing of various drugs for developing fetuses, infants, and young children.

The group concluded, finally, that, in the past, the number of ethically questionable studies that had been done had been "minuscule." Warning of the dangers to research that could result from political pressures, it advised the commission to recommend a "review process rather than specific restrictions" on fetal research.

These warnings were well justified: antiabortion forces succeeded in passing fetal-research restrictions, modeled on the Roncallo proposals, in 15 states. Although these statutes tended to be ambiguous, they had a chilling effect on fetal studies. Uncertainty about the definition of terms like "living" forestalled even the culture of fetal cells and the examination of tissue from dead fetuses. In Massachusetts, after four physicians were indicted for performing fetal research, a cancer-research project that used dead fetal tissue was disbanded.

Antiabortion groups nevertheless saw their position as the logical extension of their view that the fetus is a "person." They were willing to forego the very substantial benefits to mothers and their existing and future children that could result from research using tissue from aborted fetuses. The U. S. Catholic Conference, in testimony before the new federal commission in February 1975, sought to prohibit research using material from *any* fetus that had been intentionally aborted, regardless of the stringency of safeguards to protect fetal survival or the value of the research to society.

After the 13-month hiatus in fetal research, HEW, in August 1975, following commission recommendations, issued regulations lifting the ban on funding for most fetal studies. Women were given the right to consent to the use of their aborted fetal material for research. The regulations also established safeguards to prevent research on potentially viable fetuses.[19]

Less visible than the battle over fetal research has been abortion opponents' efforts to keep doctors and medical institutions from using new knowledge and techniques of genetic screening, diagnosis, and counseling, including methods to determine early in gestation whether the fetus is defective. Their opposition reflects the fact that these services inevitably involve the greater probability of abortion for women who believe it to be more moral to terminate a pregnancy than to deliver a seriously defective infant. Only in the spring of 1978, when the difficulties that the National Foundation-March of Dimes (MOD) was encountering in maintaining its genetics-services programs were described in the press, did the RTL forces' behind-the-scenes pressure to stop these programs come to light.

The procedures under attack by abortion opponents permit prenatal evaluation of fetuses for chromosomal abnormalities, metabolic disorders, and structural malformations of the brain and spinal cord. The key technique is amniocentesis, in which a few drops of the amniotic fluid that surrounds the fetus in the womb are aspirated through a needle passed through the abdominal wall. The fluid then is tested for genetic-disease markers. As with any developing health technology, the full range of applications for these new methods still is unknown. But they already are widely used and may have enormous potential benefit for pregnant women, their babies, and society in general.

The National Genetics Foundation says doctors now have identified more than 2,000 genetic diseases.[20] About 80 can be diagnosed prenatally, including Down's syndrome (mongolism), sickle-cell anemia, spina bifida or open-spine defect, and anencephaly, which is the absence of a brain.

The incidence of these conditions varies. Mongolism is estimated to occur in approximately one out of 280 infants born to women between age 30 and 35, soaring to one out of 65 in 45-year-old mothers.[21] Tay-Sachs disease, which inevitably—and painfully—kills its victims by age four, is rare in the general population but is relatively common among Eastern European Jews. The incidence of spina bifida and anencephaly together is estimated at two per 1,000 births.[22] Over all, it is estimated that a quarter of a million babies are born in the United States each year with serious genetic conditions.[23]

The human tragedy involved in the birth of a seriously abnormal baby needs no elaboration. Less well understood is the fact that massive health, social, and educational resources are required to help these babies survive and to assist them in the effort to become competent adults.

The development in recent years of perinatal intensive-care units at major medical centers, and their staffs' heroic efforts to save abnormal and low-birth-weight infants, is but one indicator of this societal commitment.[24] Another is the rapid development of human-genetics research. Harvard Medical School genetics expert Aubrey Milunsky has estimated that the United States could prevent a third of all genetically caused mental retardation by the year 2000 if it moved faster to diagnose fetal defects during pregnancy.[25] Of the 150,000 pregnant women over age 35 who each year are at high risk of bearing a child with mongolism, he said, only 20,000 now get amniocentesis, indicating an "astonishingly slow" implementation rate. He attributes the lag in part to antiabortion groups' growing opposition to amniocentesis and notes:[26]

> Amniocentesis is really a life-saving, not a life-destroying technology. Far more babies have been born because of amniocentesis, to women who otherwise would never have dared become pregnant for fear of some defect that ran in their families, than those not born because of abortion.[27]

The MOD, concurring, reports that 97 percent of all amniocenteses performed result in a finding that the fetus is normal; only 3 percent end in abortion of a defective fetus. The MOD's view is that many older women, and women with family histories of genetic disorders, might well choose abortion *a priori*, because of their statistical probability of bearing a defective baby, if they could not confirm, through amniocentesis, that their fetuses probably were normal.[28]

Beginning in 1971, the MOD, as part of its comprehensive birth-defects program, began making grants for genetics-services programs, including amniocentesis. It has been the principal financial support for these services and undoubtedly has done more than any other public or private agency to make them available. By 1978, MOD was providing $2.5 million for 82 genetics-services programs, 55 of which offered amniocentesis.[29]

This effort should have won gratitude and praise for MOD from all who seek to improve the outcome of pregnancy. Instead, its programs were branded "search-and-destroy missions" by some RTL leaders. They urged their followers, and Catholic dioceses and schools that long have participated in MOD's annual fund-raising Mothers' Marches, to boycott this fund drive.[30] The boycott threat apparently was effective in some areas, including Visalia, California; Richmond, Virginia; Toledo and Cincinnati, Ohio; Covington, Kentucky; and Grand Rapids, Michigan.[31]

Many meetings were held between MOD representatives, the objecting RTL groups, and the U.S. Catholic Conference in an attempt to resolve the dispute. In 1972, MOD adopted a policy forbidding the use of any of its funds to pay for abortion.[32]

One year later, Monsignor James T. McHugh of the Catholic Conference reported that senior MOD officials had pledged to "carefully scrutinize and monitor all its research proposals to insure that they are not directed toward encouraging abortion," and to cooperate with the conference on moral and ethical issues. Father McHugh now approved MOD, saying that "cooperation of Catholic groups and schools with the National Foundation is morally permissible because [it] does not fund, sponsor or directly encourage abortion."[33]

These reassurances failed to settle the issue. Right-to-Life leaders like John C. Willke of the National Right to Life Committee, and Randy Engel, executive director of the U.S. Coalition for Life, continued to attack MOD. In March 1975, in apparent response to continuing RTL calls for Catholics to boycott the foundation's fund drive, McHugh sent a confidential memo to all Catholic bishops reiterating the Catholic Conference's approving view and reporting that MOD had consulted with the conference and had taken steps to manifest "a more visible pro-life image."[34]

In May 1976, MOD's board of directors issued an accommodating formal statement stressing that its grantees could give amniocentesis patients scientific information on their pregnancies but not direct advice on abortions. But abortion opponents continued to criticize amniocentesis and MOD, which had refused to publish a booklet on the "pro-life" viewpoint that the National Right to Life Committee wanted to distribute to prospective parents of defective children.[35]

Then, in December 1977, at a meeting of HEW's Genetics Coordinating Committee, a high MOD official announced that his organization would virtually end its funding of genetics-services programs over the next several years. The MOD insisted its decision was not based on RTL pressure but on its long-standing belief that a voluntary health agency's role is to provide initial seed money to demonstrate the need for new services.[36] But RTL spokesmen claimed credit for the decision. They also complained that MOD was phasing out funding, not dropping it cold.

"This is hardly the type of basic change in attitude, policy or spending of their money that would encourage prolife groups to reverse their previous opposition to MOD," Dr. Willke wrote to RTL directors. "It seems obvious that . . . their ethic has not changed one bit."[37]

Abortion opponents' efforts to block MOD programs raised the question of whether the moral opposition of a determined minority will be permitted to deny other Americans access to beneficial new medical techniques. It also raises the question of why it was left to a private agency, with limited resources, to introduce an important new technology. While private agencies do often pioneer new health programs, funding and implementation typically are assumed by government, once a program's safety and effectiveness have been proved.

With amniocentesis, that point was reached in October 1975, when an NIH report found it to be safe and ready for mass application. HEW Assistant Secretary for Health Theodore Cooper declared:

> Few advances compare with amniocentesis in their capability for prevention of disability. It is most appropriate for the Public Health Service, as a matter of policy, to foster use of amniocentesis by those women for whom it is indicated, by educating both physicians and the public as to availability and applicability of the technique and . . . its safety.[38]

Congress, the same year, adopted the National Genetic Disease Act, which authorized funding of $30 million a year to pay for amniocentesis and other genetic screening, counseling, and treatment programs. But HEW did not request an appropriation under this act until 1978—and that request, for only $4 million, was barely more than MOD had been spending.

The next year, in a report to Congress, the Comptroller General recommended that HEW encourage and support the expansion of newborn screening programs.[39] HEW said it would do this through implementation of the Genetic Disease Act. Yet while Congress authorized expenditures of over $17 million for genetics programs in the 1979 budget, the administration again requested only $4 million annually in appropriations for 1979 and 1980. Given the inflation rate in these years, the administration's request represents a large *decrease* in already-inadequate funding levels, during a period when private funding was slated to drop. (Congress, however, appropriated $8 million for genetic services in its 1980 budget—twice the amount requested by the administration.)

The MOD's difficulties over abortion were widely known among health professionals. It seems likely therefore that HEW officials decided it would be wise to go slow in carrying out the new legislation. The resulting delay denied needed services not only to pregnant older women, who are prime candidates for amniocentesis, but also to many thousands of babies who could have benefited from newly developed diagnostic techniques for treatable metabolic disorders.

The highest state courts in New York and New Jersey have held that a physician can be found liable for failing to advise pregnant women who face an increased risk of bearing children with birth defects of the availability of genetic testing and counseling.[40] The New York court held that the physician could be held liable for the cost of lifetime care needed by a child afflicted with severe birth defects, while the New Jersey court awarded damages only for the emotional hardship endured by the parents. By placing the obligation on the physician to inform high-risk women of the availability of prenatal diagnostic techniques, these decisions are likely to dramatically increase the demand for genetic-screening services.[41]

Extremist RTL activitists also have displayed willingness to deny American families the potential benefits of research on *in vitro* fertilization, the "test-tube baby" technique. Current HEW biomedical research regulations do not contain specific standards for research with early fertilized human ova but require such projects funded by HEW to be approved by an Ethics Advisory Board. In effect, this requirement has resulted in a moratorium on HEW support for *in vitro* fertilization research.

Beyond the practical implications for couples who cannot otherwise have children, *in vitro* fertilization studies could lead to better means for controlling fertility and minimizing the risk of congenital disease. Yet at public hearings held under a directive from HEW secretary Joseph A. Califano, Jr., late in 1978, antiabortion witnesses testified against allowing funding for this work because it involved "aborting" the embryos that were used in the research or were unsuitable for implantation in a human uterus.[42]

The American public, as in most of the health and policy issues involving abortion, apparently does not agree. A Harris Poll late in 1978 showed that 85 percent of respondents agreed that *in vitro* techniques should be available to married couples who would otherwise be unable to have children, and 58 percent of respondents of childbearing age said they would personally consider using *in vitro* fertilization or similar techniques if they could not otherwise conceive.[43]

Flexibility on this issue was voiced by one renowned Catholic moral theologian, the Reverend Richard McCormick of Georgetown University's Center for Bioethics. He agrees that the federal government ought to permit *in vitro* research, even though he opposes the creation of living embryos for study. He believes, however, that the government should not fund such research.[44] Scientists on the advisory board noted that in practice most major research hospitals would be reluctant to undertake programs that the government itself was unwilling to support.[45]

While childless couples requested that HEW relax its ban, Catholic theologians continued to oppose the research. The Reverend Paul J. Murphy, S.J., a retired theology professor from Boston College, explained to HEW's advisory board:

> In place of that noble act of human generation, complete in its self-giving and loving union, we have laparoscopes sucking at ovaries, cannulae invading and traumatizing the privacy of the womb, masturbated spermatozoa lurking in the glass dish, chemically stimulated oocytes snatched before ovulation.
>
> The process may strike some as startlingly intricate and successful, but it is really crassly manipulative and coldly engineered, with nothing of love's embrace and self-communication. That, I submit, is dehumanizing, and reduces human generation to the level of animal husbandry.[46]

After nearly a year of hearings and deliberations, the 13-member Ethics Advisory Board concluded in June 1979 that *in vitro* fertilization is "ethically acceptable" if the final goal is to produce children for couples who are otherwise unable to have them, provided certain ethical and procedural safeguards are met. The board recommended that HEW end its moratorium on funding *in vitro* research. However, at the beginning of 1980, the secretary of HEW had neither formally accepted the board's report nor authorized the use of any HEW funds for research.[47] Regardless of the continued lack of HEW research funds, construction of the nation's first *in vitro* laboratory was approved by the Virginia state health commissioner in early 1980. Since it will not use any public funds, the laboratory, to be built at the Eastern Virginia Medical School, does not require HEW approval.[48]

References

1 M. Russell, "New Abortion Fight Seen Over Rider to House Bill," *Washington Post*, Mar. 2, 1978.

2 Ibid.

3 "The Capitol," *Washington Post*, Mar. 4, 1978.

4 "Will Church Institutions Be Forced to Make Medical Payments for Abortion?" *Origins—NC Documentary Service*, 7:37, Mar. 23, 1978.

5 "Pregnancy Disability Bill Passed by Senate Committee, Antiabortion Amendment Fails," *Planned Parenthood Washington Memo*, July 15, 1977; "Notes," Ibid., Sept. 30, 1977; and "Disability Benefits for Pregnancy Threatened by Antiabortion Rider," Ibid., Apr. 7, 1978.

6 M. Russell, op. cit.

7 *United States Catholic Conference v. Bell*, C.A. 17-1609, filed June 21, 1979.

8 Joint Testimony of Msgr. Lawrence J. Corcoran, National Conference of Catholic Charities, and Francis J. Butler, U. S. Catholic Conference, *Hearings on National Health Insurance Before Secretary Joseph A. Califano*, Washington, D.C., Oct. 4, 1977.

9 See "Abortion Clouds Real Hospital Issues," *Davenport Times-Democrat*, Mar. 7, 1976; K. Barker, "Catholic Hospital, Rejected for Howard County, Appeals," *Washington Post*, June 27, 1973; "Bishop Guilfoyle Says Abortion Has No Place in Perinatal Center Issue," *Williamstown (N. J.) Plain Reader*, June 9, 1977; and J. Undercoffler, "County Maternity Services Gets Heated Discussion," *Westchester Rockland Newspapers*, Oct. 5, 1976.

10 "National Guidelines for Health Planning," *Federal Register*, Jan. 20, 1978.

11 H. H. Marshall, acting president, Planned Parenthood Federation of America, comments on "National Guidelines for Health Planning," delivered to Office of Planning, Evaluation and Legislation, Health Resources Administration, Feb. 16, 1978.

12 The Alan Guttmacher Institute, *Eleven Million Teenagers: What Can Be Done About the Epidemic of Adolescent Pregnancies in the United States*, New York, 1976.

13 S. V. Roberts, "Funds to Help Pregnant Teenagers: An Idea Emerges and Gets in Budget," *New York Times*, Jan. 24, 1978.

14 Ibid.

15 Memorandum to the secretary from deputy assistant secretay for planning and evaluation, "Initiative to Address Adolescent Pregnancies and Related Issues—Decision Memorandum," Aug. 4, 1977.

16 M. Goldstein and H. M. Wallace, "Services for and Needs of Pregnant Teenagers in Large Cities in the United States, 1976," *Public Health Reports*, 93:46, 1978.

17 W. Delaney, "No Mention of Abortion in HEW Bill," *Washington Star*, May 9, 1978.

18   The following discussion is based upon material presented in D. Hart, "Fetal Research and Antiabortion Politics: Holding Science Hostage," *Family Planning Perspectives,* **7**:72, 1975.

19   *Planned Parenthood Washington Memo,* Aug. 13, 1975, p. 4.

20   L. Altman, "Birth Defect Suits Worry Doctors," *New York Times,* Jan. 23, 1979.

21   E. B. Hook, "Estimates of Maternal Age-Specific Risks of a Down-Syndrome Birth in Women Aged 34–41," *Lancet,* July 3, 1976, p. 33.

22   H. L. Nadler, "Prenatal Diagnosis of Inborn Defects: A Status Report," *Nursing Digest,* Fall 1976, p. 63.

23   National Foundation—March of Dimes, *Facts '78,* White Plains N.Y.: The National Foundation, 1977.

24   The average hospital stay for small babies is reported at 78 days and costs $15,000; in some cases, the bill exceeds $100,000. L. J. Butterfield, "Can Society Afford to Save These Babies?", *Contemporary Ob-Gyn,* **10**:110, 1977.

25   V. Cohn, "Geneticists Cite Lag in Testing Newborns, Pregnant Women," *Washington Post,* Feb. 14, 1978.

26   S. Hagard and F. A. Carter, "Preventing the Birth of Infants with Down's Syndrome: A Cost-Benefit Analysis," *British Medical Journal,* **1**:753, 1976.

27   Cohn, op. cit.

28   National Foundation, "Further Clarification on Genetic Services," memorandum to chapter chairmen from Arthur J. Salisbury, M.D., vice president for medical services, and W. R. Russell, vice president for chapters, Mar. 2, 1978.

29   National Foundation, "The March of Dimes in Genetics—Fact Sheet," distributed Mar. 14, 1978.

30   National Foundation "Pro-Life Agitation," memorandum to chapter executives from George P. Voss, vice president for public relations, Mar. 16, 1976, reprinted in U. S. Coalition for Life, "Who Will Defend Michael?", *Pro-Life Reporter,* Vol. 4, no. 11, 1976.

31   B. Williams, "The March of Dimes and Abortion," *Homiletic and Pastoral Review,* October 1973, p. 48; U. S. Coalition for Life, op. cit., p. 11; P. A. Mullan, "Why Is The March of Dimes Cutting Off Genetic Services?", *Ob-Gyn News,* Jan. 15, 1978; and B. J. Culliton, "Amniocentesis: HEW Backs Test for Prenatal Diagnosis of Disease," *Science,* **190**:537, 1975.

32   National Foundation, *Policies and Procedures Governing Medical Service Grants,* adopted May 18, 1972, cited in Williams, op. cit.

33   U. S. Coalition for Life, op. cit., p. 10.

34   Ibid.

35   Mullan, op. cit.

36   National Foundation, "Clarification of Policies in Medical Service Grants," memorandum to chapter chairmen from Arthur J. Salisbury, M. D., vice president for medical affairs, and W. R. Russell, vice president for chapters, dated Feb. 10, 1978.

37 "March of Dimes to End Birth Defect Test Support," *Washington Post,* Mar. 7, 1978.

38 B. J. Culliton, op. cit.

39 Comptroller General of the United States, *Preventing Mental Retardation—More Can Be Done,* Report to the Congress, Oct. 3, 1977.

40 *Beecker v. Schwartz* 46 N.Y.2d401, 413 N.Y.S.2d895, 386 N.E.2d 807 (1978) and *Berman v. Allen* U.S.L.W. 2026 (N.J.S.C. June 26, 1979).

41 L. Altman, 1979, op. cit.

42 "DHEW Ethics Board Considering U.S. Policy on 'Test Tube' Fertilization Research," *Planned Parenthood Washington Memo,* Oct. 6, 1978.

43 Harris Poll, September 1978, reported in *Parents Magazine,* November 1978.

44 V. Cohn, "Test Tube Baby Study Debated By HEW Panel," *Washington Post,* Feb. 4, 1979.

45 Ibid.

46 Department of Health, Education and Welfare, Ethics Advisory Board Meeting IV, statement of Rev. Paul J. Murphy, S. J., Boston, Oct. 13, 1978.

47 *Federal Register,* June 18, 1979, p. 35033, and Nov. 9, 1979, p. 65191.

48 *The New York Times,* Jan. 9, 1980, p. 9.

CHAPTER THIRTEEN
Déjà Vu

By 1975, religious differences in fertility-control attitudes and practices had all but disappeared in the United States.

The proportion of married Catholics using modern contraceptive methods was only a few percentage points lower than that of non-Catholics.[1] Fewer than 10 percent of Catholic couples married less than five years conformed to the Church's teachings on contraceptive methods.[2] Based on current reproductive rates, Catholics were expected to average 2.27 children per couple, compared with 2.17 among non-Catholics.[3]

In this context of converging reproductive norms and family-planning practices, it is difficult for many persons to remember—or to believe—that not long ago there was a raging religious controversy over the morality of contraception. Even as recently as 1960, as astute an observer of religious matters as the late John Cogley, who was widely regarded as the "dean of intellectual Catholic journalists,"[4] concluded that "Americans are hopelessly divided on the question of birth control."[5]

The conflict stemmed from the fact that the Catholic Church condemned—as unnatural and immoral—all forms of contraception except the rhythm method. But almost all non-Catholics and nonbelievers approved of contraception.

The long, bitter history of religious controversy over the *morality* of birth control has been well analyzed elsewhere.[6] It is not our purpose to repeat it. Starting in the mid-1950's, however, the conflict shifted to the *public-policy* issue of whether tax-supported institutions and programs—hospitals, health departments, welfare agencies, and foreign assistance—should provide birth-control services. This, of course, is exactly the same kind of public-policy issue raised by restrictions on Medicaid funding and public-hospital services for abortion.

The earlier controversy thus is relevant to the current debate for two principal reasons: first, the terms of the contraception argument in the 1950s and 1960s were almost identical to those of the abortion argument today. Second, the public-policy controversy over birth control was more or less satisfactorily resolved by the late 1960s—and so provides insights into how the abortion conflict might be resolved now.

The most effective contraceptives require a doctor's prescription. But in the 1950s, almost no tax-supported hospital or health department provided contraception to its patients, most of whom were poor. What is more, while high fertility was poverty's hallmark, few welfare departments allowed caseworkers to counsel their clients on contraception or to refer them to clinics where they could get it. In some instances, this ban was formalized in departmental regulations and manuals; in others, it was unwritten but no less effective.

The origin of these prohibitions is obscure. By the 1950s, however, they clearly were being sustained as public policy by the power and influence of the Catholic Church. When the noted obstetrician-gynecologist Alan F. Guttmacher came to New York, in 1952, and proposed to the hospitals commissioner that contraceptive services be initiated in the city's 15 municipal hospitals where they had been barred, he was told the issue was "untouchable," and he would "only be batting his head against a stone wall."[7] Louis M. Hellman, the chief of obstetrics at Kings County Hospital, the municipal hospital with the largest maternity service, said:

> The ban was attributed to the power of the Roman Catholic Archdiocese of New York, to the Mayor (a Catholic) and to the many Catholic members of local medical boards. Perhaps the strongest element of all was the fear of the staff doctors to speak out lest they offend their Catholic colleagues.[8]

The hospitals' patients, doctors, and nurses included Protestants, Jews, and nonbelievers as well as Catholics. The taxes that supported the hospitals were levied on citizens of all faiths. Many of the hospitals' non-Catholic doctors—and perhaps some Catholics—regarded contraception as an integral part of health care and prescribed it for middle-income patients in their private offices. But they were barred by unwritten policy from prescribing it for the poor whom they saw in the public hospitals.

The city hospitals, then as now, also served as teaching institutions for the city's half-dozen medical schools. So, professors of obstetrics and gynecology found themselves in the ignominious position of teaching a subject that they could not use or demonstrate in practice with their patients on the wards. In short, the municipal hospitals' policy, based on sectarian doctrines of one religious denomination, prevented doctors belonging to all religious groups from practicing medicine in accordance with their professional judgment.

These incongruities led some medical leaders to try to persuade city officials to end the ban. They worked quietly for several years through the prestigious New York Academy of Medicine, but their efforts were futile as long as the ban remained hidden from public view.

Then, in 1957, *New York Post* reporter Joseph Kahn wrote and published an award-winning series of articles documenting the existence of the unwritten ban.[9] When further efforts to resolve the conflict quietly and peacefully were unsuccessful, a public confrontation became inevitable.

The crunch came in July 1958, when the hospitals commissioner ordered Dr. Hellman not to fit a diaphragm for a diabetic Protestant mother of three children, whose two previous pregnancies had been delivered by Cesarean section.[10] The order was publicized in the newspapers. The issue now was open to public scrutiny.[11]

The debate that followed received prominent coverage in local and national news media; it lasted two months. The ban was defended by the hospitals commissioner, who maintained it was neither "the function or responsibility" of the city hospitals to provide birth-control services.[12] His position was supported by the Catholic archdiocese[13] and a handful of organizations that represented Catholic doctors and laymen. The Knights of Columbus, for example, congratulated the commissioner for his "prompt and forthright response to a pretext that gives rights to an ignorant and indecent practice."[14]

But the hospitals' policy was roundly condemned by almost everyone else. Led by the Protestant Council of New York and the American Jewish Congress, nearly all the city's major non-Catholic religious groups and many medical, civil-liberties, and civic organizations insisted the ban be revoked. Their views were summarized in a *New York Times* editorial, which found it "astonishing" that the matter still needed to be debated:

> Birth control is profoundly objectionable to many persons, and . . . their views must be fully respected. These views cannot be controlling in regard to other persons in the community who also use the city hospitals and to whom medical prescription of contraceptive devices presents no

moral or religious problem. Freedom of religion works both ways; and in this delicate area the city hospitals must certainly remain neutral, neither imposing birth control therapy . . . on one to whom it is morally repugnant nor withholding it from those to whom it is not.[15]

The controversy also was marked—unexpectedly—by a forthright public indication of dissent within Catholic ranks. In an important article in the liberal Catholic journal *Commonweal*, associate editor James Finn showed how Catholics could support a neutral policy and remain consistent with the Church's teaching.[16] He noted:

Constitutionally there is a clear distinction between the orders of competence of the Church and those of the State. This means that the State does not attempt to decide questions proper to the Church . . . and the Church does not ask the State to enforce ethical codes which are not themselves supported by the society at large . . . .

Pluralism imposes on both majorities and minorities a "self-limitation" that is "necessary for the ideal functioning of our society," Finn continued.

It is practical wisdom for Catholics—or anyone else—not to attempt to have laws enacted and directives established in accordance with their beliefs except where there is good reason to believe that there is, on the particular question, a consensus.

Within these general principles, Finn addressed the specifics of the birth control question:

Other citizens cannot expect Catholics to change either their beliefs or their practices . . . . But neither can Catholics expect to control the beliefs and practices of others . . . . If, in this controversy . . . Catholics were to rely on education, personal moral suasion, and indoctrination rather than on a civil directive which embitters and alienates many people, the Church would surely gain in the long run. For those who resent directives imposed by another group can scarcely examine the claims of that group with sympathy or objectivity . . . .

There are sound and compelling reasons why Catholics should not generally strive for legislation and directives which clash with the beliefs of a large portion of the society. In doing so, they not only strain the limits of the community, and actually lessen the persuasive force of their teachings, but they almost inevitably strengthen in the minds of non-Catholics the already present worries about Catholic power.

With almost the entire non-Catholic community and some sections of the Catholic intelligentsia aligned against the ban, the outcome, in retrospect, seemed inevitable: in September 1958, the board of hospitals voted 8-2 for a new policy:[17]

1. Where there are clearly defined medical conditions in which the life or health of a woman may be jeopardized by pregnancy, it is generally recognized by the medical profession that contraceptive measures are proper medical practice.

2. Municipal hospitals should provide such medical advice, preventive measures, and devices for female patients under their care whose life and health in the opinion of the medical staff may be jeopardized by pregnancy and who wish to avail themselves of such services.

3. Physicians, nurses, and other hospital personnel who have religious or moral objections should be excused from participating in contraceptive procedures.

This decision was hailed by the non-Catholic community and by Planned Parenthood. It was condemned by the Catholic archdiocese as introducing "an immoral practice in our hospitals that perverts the nature and the dignity of man. It uses public funds for corrupt purposes, contrary to the manifest will of a large number of taxpayers."[18]

The new policy embodied two principles that were the bases for much of the legislation and public policy on fertility control until the Hyde amendment was enacted in 1976:

(1) Public institutions would make available religiously controversial fertility-control services to persons eligible for these services, in accordance with the professional judgment of their staff; and (2) staff personnel and patients with religious or moral objections would be exempt from providing or receiving these services.

In succeeding years, similar battles were fought to remove birth-control bans in public-health programs in Chicago, Pittsburgh, Washington, D.C., Baltimore, Denver, and other cities.[19] The issue was escalated to the national level in 1959 when a study commission recommended that the U.S. foreign-assistance programs provide family-planning help to countries that requested it.

The Catholic bishops, appealing to "natural law," replied:

United States Catholics . . . will not support any public assistance, either at home or abroad, to promote artificial birth prevention, abortion, or sterilization, whether through direct aid or by means of international organizations.[20]

Attention immediately was focused on the extent to which the bishops' position would be binding on Catholic candidates in the 1960 Presidential elections, particularly John F. Kennedy. In an interview with James Reston of the *New York Times*, Kennedy deftly differentiated his views from those of the bishops, saying he thought it would not be "wise for the U.S. to refuse to grant assistance to a country," such as

India, that had decided to encourage birth control as "a policy it feels to be in its own best interest. To do so would be a kind of intervention in their national life."[21] Ten months later as the campaign drew to a close, Kennedy faced the church-state issue head-on in a key address to the Greater Houston Ministerial Association:

> Whatever issue may come before me as President—on birth control, divorce, censorship, gambling or any other subject—I will make my decisions . . . in accordance with what my conscience tells me to be in the national interest, and without regard to outside religious pressure or dictates.[22]

When the ballots were counted in November, Kennedy had won by a mere 118,000 votes, out of the 69 million cast. Many political observers were convinced he would not have won if he had equivocated on the church-state issue.

Six months before he was assassinated in 1963, President Kennedy endorsed increasing research in human reproduction to improve fertility-control methods and make them available to other nations.[23] It remained for his brother-in-law, Sargent Shriver, as head of the Johnson administration's antipoverty program, to administer the first federal-grant-support program for community family-planning services. It started in 1965. By 1967, local voluntary family-planning efforts were supported by both antipoverty and HEW funds; family-planning assistance was incorporated into foreign aid; and Congress had enacted specific legislation authorizing these efforts.

In 1970, Congress enacted the Family Planning Services and Population Research Act, which provided support for a large-scale national program that now serves more than four million low-income women including 1.3 million sexually active teenagers who come from all income groups.[24] By 1973, the proportion of low-income couples using the most effective, medically prescribed contraceptive methods exceeded that of higher-income couples—a reversal of the historical class differential in contraceptive practices. This reversal is primarily attributable to the impact of the federally supported program.[25]

These developments took place in spite of opposition—open or covert—from the Catholic bishops. They could not, or would not, distinguish programs that help eligible individuals act voluntarily in accord with their values from those that coerce people to follow state-imposed norms. The bishops opposed family-planning legislation in 1965 and in 1970.[26] Even in 1977, after the voluntary nature of the federal program had been demonstrated for a dozen years, Archbishop Joseph L. Bernardin, president of the National Conference of Catholic Bishops, denounced federal support for family planning as "an unprecedented and unacceptable intrusion into family life."[27] Yet the essence of the policy, from 1958 to the present, has been that the government neither requires nor prohibits contraceptive practices but provides contraceptive services, as it does other health and social services, to low-income people and other participants in public programs who need and want them.

The Catholic bishops' opposition to federal support of voluntary family-planning services has been rejected by five presidents—Kennedy, Johnson, Nixon, Ford, and Carter—and by every Congress since 1965, as well as by public officials of all faiths in all parts of the country. For more than a decade, until the 1976 elections, almost all U.S. political leaders avoided placing the government in the position of approving one moral position in fertility-control matters and imposing it on individuals and groups with different views. Their position was to support policies and programs that were justified on public-interest grounds and to allow individuals and groups to follow their own consciences. This approach proved successful, not only in advancing the social objective of assisting the poor to avoid unwanted pregnancies but also in moderating intergroup conflict. In short, pluralism worked.

Abortion, like contraception, is the subject of controversy between religious groups. It will facilitate analysis of the current public-policy issues on abortion to examine more closely the arguments advanced against public contraceptive programs and to compare them to Catholic bishops' and Right-to-Life arguments against abortion. As the representative quotations selected for the panels in this chapter clearly show, the two sets of arguments are remarkably close.

The Catholic condemnation of contraception is derived from the Church's traditional view, expressed in Panel 1, that procreation, according to "natural law," is the primary purpose of sexual relationships. Because this doctrine originates in "natural law," the Church holds that it is binding not just on Catholics but on all people, regardless of their faith. The bishops' opposition to public family-planning efforts thus is based on the corollary rejection of all other religious groups' views of the morality of contraception.

The Catholic condemnation of abortion also is considered binding not only on Church members but, the U.S. bishops assert, is universal in scope. True, they do not attempt to justify this stance as "natural law"—perhaps because this objection to contraception was "a puzzle to the average Catholic"[28]—but rather as "God's law." The Vatican's Sacred Congregation for the Doctrine of the Faith, however, continues to cite "natural law" in its demand that governments impose Catholic abortion doctrine on nonbelievers.

From the doctrinal base of "natural law," the next step in the argu-

PANEL 1:   The Scope of Natural Law

Contraception

"Prohibition to practice contraception is not regarded by the Catholic Church as one of its laws binding only Catholics. The Church proclaims this as a law of God which binds all human beings, whether they be members of the Catholic Church or not."
—Rev. Francis J. Connell, Catholic University of America, 1957[29]

"The Church has opposed as contrary to natural law—and must continue to oppose—the direct frustration of conception by artificial means."
—The Most Rev. Phillip M. Hannan, Vicar General, Archdiocese of Washington, D.C., 1964[30]

"[The conjugal act's] purpose is the fulfillment of the primary end of marriage in the procreation of offspring. The natural law commands that the married state . . . fulfill the function of the conservation of the human race. Artificial birth control frustrates that purpose. It is therefore unnatural. . . ."
—Archdiocese of New York, 1958[31]

Abortion

"Abortion is wrong. It is a grave sin and a crime against God's law. This applies to all men and women everywhere."
—The Most Rev. Gerald O'Keefe, Bishop of Davenport, Iowa, Pastoral Message, 1976[32]

"Abortion, the deliberate destruction of an unborn human being, is contrary to the law of God and is a morally evil act. . . . A just civil law cannot be opposed to moral teaching based on God's law."
—U. S. Catholic Conference, 1974[33]

"Many others hold that [abortion] is licit, at least a lesser evil. Why force them to follow an opinion which is not theirs, especially in a country where they are in the majority?. . . . It is true that it is not the task of the law to choose between points of view or to impose one rather than the other. But the life of the child takes precedence over all opinions. . . . The law . . . cannot act contrary to a law which is deeper and more majestic than any human law: The natural law engraved in men's hearts by the Creator. . . ."
—Sacred Congregation for the Doctrine of the Faith, 1974[34]

ment was to castigate contraceptive services in public hospitals as a perversion of the purposes of health care as indicated in Panel 2. "Preservation of life" was singled out as the sole valid purpose of health institutions and was contrasted with its "unnatural" prevention; "artificial" contraception was labeled nontherapy "since it cures no disease." These statements did not refer only to the policies of Catholic hospitals—which the bishops reasonably could expect to follow Church teachings—but also to public hospitals serving all faiths. It is striking

PANEL 2:   The Purpose of Health Care

Contraception

"It would be unfortunate if our hospitals and medical facilities, aimed for the preservation of life, should be perverted to seek for the prevention of life. Catholics cannot accept such a procedure [contraception], nor can any Catholic, in or out of our hospitals, condone or cooperate in assisting others to this unnatural and immoral practice."
—Archdiocese of New York, 1958[35]

"Medicine is concerned with treating disease and restoring function . . . the practice of prevention of conception by the use of artificial contraceptives is not a therapy, since it cures no disease."
—New York City Guilds of Catholic Physicians, 1958[36]

Abortion

"We are asked . . . to train our doctors and nurses also and equip our hospitals to destroy life as well. Our hospitals are working in one room to preserve life, while in another room they are working to destroy it."
—Rep. John M. Zwack (Minn.), 1974[37]

"It is inadmissible that doctors or nurses should find themselves obliged to cooperate closely in abortions and have to choose between the law of God and their professional situation."
—Sacred Congregation for the Doctrine of the Faith, 1974[38]

"Instead of just being a healer, [the doctor] now becomes an executioner as well. [Abortion for health reasons] provides him with a license to kill."
—Rep. Henry J. Hyde (Ill.), 1977[39]

"It is especially shocking to learn of attempts on the part of hospital planning councils and state health department officials to establish sterilization and abortion clinics within the confines of the Scranton diocese."
—Bishop J. C. McCormick of Scranton, Pa., 1975[40]

---

that virtually the same metaphorical juxtapositions have been employed against abortion by congressional supporters of the antiabortion cause: "Preserve life" versus "destroy it," "healer" versus "executioner," and "shock" that health officials would even consider putting sterilization and abortion facilities in community health institutions.

Having dismissed as unworthy of respect—or even serious

attention—the moral approval of contraception by most Protestant and Jewish groups, the Catholic bishops had no difficulty opposing public support for domestic and overseas family-planning programs, as indicated in Panel 3. They cited two reasons: first, contraception was "im-

---

PANEL 3:   Public Responsibility for Fertility Control Programs for the Poor

Contraception

"We do not think it is the function or duty of tax-supported institutions to issue such a contraceptive instrument when it is morally and religiously objectional to a large portion of the taxpayers' involved."
—National Federation of Catholic Physicians Guilds, 1958[41]

"Catholics . . . will not support any public assistance, either at home or abroad, to promote artificial birth prevention, abortion or sterilization."
—National Catholic Welfare Conference, 1959[42]

"The Church opposes vigorously the use of public funds for the purchase of contraceptive devices and their distribution among indigent mothers."
—The Most Rev. Phillip N. Hannan, Vicar General, Archdiocese of Washington, D. C., 1964[43]

"The Pennsylvania Catholic Conference |and National Catholic Welfare Conference| feels it its duty to state its conviction that the public power and public funds should not be used for the providing of birth control services."
—William Ball, 1965[44]

Abortion

"We are opposed to provisions in a national health insurance bill for contraceptive devices and sterilization for contraceptive purposes. We are also opposed to the inclusion of abortion services. . . . This would be a violation of the first and preeminent principle . . . that human life is inviolate at every stage of its being."
—National Conference of Catholic Charities and U. S. Catholic Conference, 1977[45]

"The American taxpayer will be forced to continue to finance and condone the mass killing of hundreds of thousands of unborn children of the poor under federal Medicaid and AFDC programs."
—U. S. Coalition for Life, 1975[46]

"A comprehensive pro-life legislative program must therefore include. . . . b) passage of federal and state laws and adoption of administrative policies that will restrict the practice of abortion as much as possible."
—National Conference of Catholic Bishops, 1975[47]

"What is more proper than for citizens . . . to oppose the payment of tax moneys for purposes they regard as homicidal?"
—Rev. J. T. Burchatell, C. S. C., 1977[48]

moral," as Church leaders repeatedly had stated. Second, Catholic taxpayers objected to having their taxes used for religiously objectionable purposes.

Today's arguments against public funding of abortion for the poor are strikingly similar: the immorality of abortion is asserted as a universal truth, despite the conscientious contrary positions of most Protestant and Jewish groups; and antiabortion taxpayers are cited as protesting the use of their taxes for immoral purposes. In the 1977 Hyde amendment debate in Congress, the latter point particularly was stressed and was equated with the position of people who tried to withhold taxes to protest the Vietnam War. What was *not* stated was that the courts invariably have rejected the nonpayment of taxes as a means to protest government actions deemed to be immoral.[49]

The Catholic bishops' opposition to public funding of contraception failed, ultimately, because it could not address this simple question: Why should public institutions, supported by taxpayers of all faiths, deny to Protestants, Jews, and non-believers health services they believe to be moral and necessary? This question was forcefully asked by New York's Protestant leaders in 1958, as indicated in Panel 4, and no satisfactory answer was forthcoming from the Catholic archdiocese or

PANEL 4:   The Other Taxpayers

Contraception

"There is no moral reason why a Protestant patient should be denied birth-control therapy by the City Commissioner of Hospitals. . . . The responsible use of contraceptive devices is . . . approved by most Christian leaders. . . . This is our belief and the position of Protestants generally, and Protestants have as much right to the kind of medical services they require as any other group of taxpayers. We recognize the fact that the Roman [Catholic] group has its point of view which should be respected for its own members, but we claim the right to equal respect for our convictions."
—Protestant Council of New York, 1958[50]

Abortion

"All legal means are considered justified [by those opposed to abortion] if they limit abortions, no matter what the human consequences for poor women and others—as in the recent efforts to deny Medicaid funds and to prohibit use of public hospitals for abortion services. . . . We believe it is wrong to deny Medicaid assistance to poor women seeking abortions. This denial makes it difficult for those who need it most to exercise a legal right, and it implies public censure of a form of medical service which in fact has the moral support of major religious groups."
—"A Call to Concern," 1977[51]

the city's hospitals commissioner. Essentially the same argument now has been put forward with regard to funding by signatories of a "Call to Concern." The Church's main response has been to reassert the universality of Catholics' condemnation of abortion as "murder" and to claim "it is plainly misleading to describe abortion as a 'medical service,' when in 99 percent of cases it has nothing whatever to do with anyone's health."[52]

The Catholic bishops' opposition to public funding of contraceptive services failed because it could not—and would not—address the rights and needs of "the other taxpayers" in a pluralistic society. It also failed because it became clear in the early 1960s that many individual Catholics opposed efforts of the institutional Church to use public law and public policy to enforce its birth-control doctrines. In the reappraisal fostered by Vatican II, the liberalism of Finn's *Commonweal* article prompted numerous articles and books articulating a Catholic position consistent with the principles of pluralism.[53] In 1965, a group of 57 prominent Catholic theologians, priests, and laymen signed a Statement on Public Policy and Family Planning, which the late Reverend Dexter L. Hanley, S. J., of Georgetown University released at a meeting of the American Bar Association (ABA). It stated:

1. In a legitimate concern over public health, education, and poverty, the Government may properly establish programs which permit citizens to exercise a free choice in matters of responsible parenthood in accordance with their moral standards.

2. In such programs, the Government may properly give information and assistance concerning medically accepted forms of family planning, so long as human life and personal rights are safeguarded and no coercion or pressure is exerted against individual moral choice.

3. In such programs, the Government should not imply a preference for any particular method of family planning.

4. While norms of private morality may have social dimensions so affecting the common good as to justify opposition to public programs, private moral judgments regarding methods of family planning do not provide a basis for opposition to Government programs.

5. Although the use of public funds for purposes of family planning is not objectionable in principle, the manner in which such a program is implemented may pose issues requiring separate consideration.

These opinions are submitted as being morally justified and in accordance with the traditional Catholic position on birth control. These opinions are expressed out of a concern for civil liberty and freedom, and are based upon respect for the sincere consciences of our fellow citizens in this pluralistic society.[54]

In testimony before Senator Ernest Gruening's committee hearings on the population crisis, Father Hanley acknowledged the religious controversy over the morality of contraception but said he believed a practical resolution was possible, based on clearly defined principles. He stated:

> The Government is not the proper organ to decide the truth of conflicting [religious and moral] views. The freedom of conscience in a democratic society extends not only to matters of revealed truth, but to basic moral decisions about which men of good faith may differ . . . . If it is to meet its own obligations . . . [the Government] must either remain inactive . . . or it must make available funds, information and materials in such a way as to permit full freedom of moral choice to each citizen . . . . In any program . . . the Government may not indicate a preference for any particular method.[55]

Father Hanley said a government program would not be justified merely to emancipate women, or aid in "personal choice" in childbearing matters. But it would be legitimate if it were based on government's

> concern about education, health and welfare in a rapidly expanding population . . . . Responsible parenthood [now] has social dimensions far beyond any which were thought of at the time the battlelines were first drawn concerning public support for family planning.[56]

In a later elaboration, Hanley particularly criticized the claim that public funding would constitute "promotion" of contraception. He said in 1966:

> I have always understood the words "to promote" as implying that the Government itself supports artificial birth prevention as being moral, that is, as taking sides on a moral question. Rather than promote a moral position, the Government can be concerned with a social problem; rather than take sides, it can remain neutral . . . . It must be prepared to allow full freedom of choice as to medically accepted means of family limitation.[57]

Because he believed that the birth-control position of both Catholics and non-Catholics are "religious decisions," Hanley grounded his views in the Vatican Council's Declaration on Religious Freedom. He said "the Catholic can support Government programs because of their legitimate social aims and because of the civic value of religious freedom and choice."[58]

Father Hanley did in fact exclude abortion from his pluralistic approach because he felt it was "in flagrant disregard of a most fundamental social value."[59] He testified, "I do believe because of the social dimensions involved in abortions that no Government program should support, directly or indirectly, the practice of abortion."[60]

This distinction between the "immoral" birth control that Hanley felt government could support and abortion, which it could not, was not completely understandable to Senator Gruening, who pointed out that religious groups quite clearly disagreed on the morality of both contraception and abortion.

Some presumably differentiate contraception from abortion, as Hanley did, because they regard abortion as murder. But they know that many of their fellow citizens in "sincere conscience" believe that abortion often is a moral course of action—and it was this recognition of comparable conscientious differences about morality that led them to initiate the ABA contraception statement.

These Catholic intellectuals also know, better than most, that for much of Church history both contraception and abortion were condemned as homicide; Noonan documented this equation in his landmark study of Church doctrine on contraception.[61] Indeed, Noonan pointed out that contraception was treated differently from abortion by Church officials *for the first time* in the Second Vatican Council's Declaration on The Church in the Modern World in 1965.[62]

The distinction appeared to be short-lived, however. In 1967, the Minority Report of the Papal Panel on Birth Control, which Pope Paul VI accepted as the basis for his 1968 encyclical *Humanae Vitae*, described contraception as "analogous to homicide," as Panel 5 shows. This led the Catholic scholar, Norman St. John-Stevas, to criticize *Humanae Vitae* for again linking abortion with contraception.[63]

The principles of public policy that Hanley outlined before the ABA for dealing with the controversial issue of contraception in 1965 nevertheless seem generally applicable to the abortion controversy today: religious groups differ sharply on the morality of abortion; the government is not the proper organ to decide the truth of these conflicting views; and for sound public-policy reasons government should assist poor people who desire abortions to obtain them, without either advocating or denouncing the choice.

The American Bar Association statement on family planning was signed by, among others, André Hellegers, of Georgetown University; Noonan of Berkeley; and Michael Novak, professor of religion at Syracuse University. If they disapproved of the Hyde amendment, they did not make their views public. None of them proposed an approach to Medicaid funding of abortion that is comparable to their ABA statement on public funding of family planning.

It may be a harbinger of cracks in the seemingly monolithic Catholic position on abortion funding that a few prominent Catholic intellectuals do dissent. The noted theologian Father Charles Curran, of Catholic University, supports public funding of abortion out of his "compas-

PANEL 5.   Homicide and Its "Analogues"

Contraception	Abortion

Contraception

"Something which can never be justified by any motive or any circumstances is always evil because it is intrinsically evil. It is wrong not because of a precept of positive law, but of reason of the natural law. . . . Theologians . . . have not said that contraception is evil because God said, 'Increase and multiply,' but because they have considered it in some way analogous to homicide."
—Papal Panel on Birth Control
    Minority Report, 1967[64]

"It can be scientifically proven that 'the pill' and the intrauterine devices . . . are not merely contraceptive but abortifacient."
—Msgr. Alphonse S. Popekin of
    Milwaukee, 1970[65]

"The anti-life forces . . .are succeeding, with their tools of birth control and contraception, to destroy the moral fiber of many people. . . . Will we have to conclude that the best science can come up with as a solution is the murder of the unborn?"
—Mrs. D. R. Mogilka *et al* of
    Milwaukee, 1966[66]

"The official position of the U. S. Coalition for Life . . . is one of opposition to the Family Planning and Population Research Act of 1973 and all similar measures . . . leading to a host of anti-life programs and practices."
—Randy Engle, 1974[67]

Abortion

"The child in the womb is human. Abortion is an unjust destruction of a human life and morally that is murder."
—National Conference of Catholic
    Bishops, 1970[68]

"Abortion is the calculated killing of an innocent, inconvenient human being."
—Rep. Henry J. Hyde (Ill.), 1977[69]

sion for the poor."[70] The signers of the "Call to Concern" include six Catholic professors of religion and ethics, who aver: "The affirmation of life in Judeo-Christian ethics requires a commitment to make life healthy and whole from beginning to end."[71]

References

1   C. F. Westoff and E. F. Jones, "The Secularization of U.S. Catholic Birth Control Practices," *Family Planning Perspectives*, 9:203, 1977, table 3.

2   Ibid., table 1.

3   C. F. Westoff and E. F. Jones, "The End of 'Catholic' Fertility," paper presented at annual meeting of the Population Association of America, Atlanta, April, 1978.

4   R. Van Allen, *The Commonweal and American Catholicism*, Philadelphia: Fortress Press, 1974, p. 193.

5   J. Cogley, "Foreword," in N. St. John-Stevas, *Birth Control and Public Policy*, Santa Barbara, Calif.: Center for the Study of Democratic Institutions, 1960, p. 3.

6   See, for example, J. T. Noonan, Jr., *Contraception*, Cambridge: Harvard University Press, 1965; A. W. Sulloway, *Birth Control and Catholic Doctrine*, Boston: Beacon, 1959; R. M. Fagley, *The Population Explosion and Christian Responsibility*, New York: Oxford University Press, 1960; J. Rock, *The Time Has Come: A Catholic Doctor's Proposals to End the Battle Over Birth Control*, New York: Knopf, 1963; A. F. Guttmacher, *Babies by Choice or by Chance*, New York: Doubleday, 1959; K. W. Underwood, *Protestant and Catholic*, Boston: Beacon, 1975; N. E. Himes, *Medical History of Contraception*, New York: Gamut (reprint), 1963; J. Fletcher, *Morals and Medicine*, Princeton: Princeton University Press, 1954; M. Sanger, *Autobiography*, New York: Norton, 1938; and G. Williams, *The Sanctity of Life and the Criminal Law*, New York: Knopf, 1957.

7   A. F. Guttmacher, op. cit., p. 122. Guttmacher met resistance even to a proposal to establish a contraceptive clinic at Mt. Sinai Hospital, a private institution, because a board member was afraid the hospital would lose Catholic financial support. The clinic was established but called the "Maternal Health Clinic" out of deference to Catholic sensitivities. (*Anatomy of a Victory*, New York: Planned Parenthood Federation of America, 1959, p. 3.)

8   L. M. Hellman, "One Galileo Is Enough," *The Eugenics Review*, 57:161, 1965.

9   J. Kahn, "Birth Control—New York's Untold Story," *New York Post*, Mar. 13-18, 1957. Kahn received the Albert and Mary Lasker Award in Medical Journalism for the series in April, 1959.

10   J. Kahn, "Jacobs OKs, Then Bars Birth Control Device at Hospital," *New York Post*, July 16, 1958, and R. Alden, "City Stops Doctor on Birth Control," *New York Times*, July 17, 1958.

11   See, for example, A. F. Guttmacher, op. cit., chap. 8; J. Rock, op. cit., chap. 11; L. M. Hellman, op. cit.; T. Littlewood, *The Politics of Population Control*, Notre Dame: University of Notre Dame Press, 1977, pp. 22–24.

12   J. Kahn, "Jacobs Admits City Bans Birth Control Data," *New York Post*, Oct. 31, 1957.

13   "Church Cites Pope on Birth Control," *New York Times*, July 24, 1958.

14 "Words Still Fly on Birth Control," *New York Times*, Aug. 3, 1958.

15 "The Birth Control Issue," *New York Times*, Aug. 1, 1958.

16 J. Finn, "Controversy in New York," *Commonweal*, Sept. 12, 1958.

17 E. E. Asbury, "Birth Control Ban Ended by City's Hospital Board," *New York Times*, Sept. 18, 1958. The resolution was apparently written largely by a Catholic member of the board of hospitals, Dr. Charles Gordon (L. Hellman, op. cit., p. 164).

18 E. E. Asbury, op. cit.

19 See T. Littlewood, op. cit., chaps. 3 and 5; Edgar May, *The Wasted Americans*, New York: Harper and Row, 1964, chap. 8; *Birth Control Services in Tax-Supported Hospitals, Health Departments and Welfare Agencies*, New York: Planned Parenthood Federation of America, 1963; Rev. T. J. Reese, "Catholic Charities and Family Welfare," and Rev. T. B. McDonough, "Distribution of Contraceptives by the Welfare Department: A Catholic Response," in *The Problem of Population: Practical Catholic Applications*, Notre Dame: University of Notre Dame Press, 1964.

20 Statement of the National Catholic Welfare Board, "Explosion or Backfire?", reported in *New York Times*, Nov. 26, 1959. For an extensive treatment of the foreign-aid issue, see P. Piotrow, *World Population Crisis*, New York: Praeger, 1973.

21 Interview with James Reston reported in *New York Times*, Nov. 28, 1959.

22 Speech to Greater Houston Ministerial Association, Sept. 12, 1960, reprinted in *The Speeches of Senator John F. Kennedy—Presidential Campaign of 1960*, Washington, D.C.: Government Printing Office, 1961, p. 210.

23 Press conference statement reported in *New York Times*, Apr. 25, 1963.

24 The Alan Guttmacher Institute, *Data and Analyses for 1978 Revision of DHEW Five-Year Plan for Family Planning Services*, New York, 1979; for details on the evolution of federal policy during the 1960s, see T. Littlewood, op. cit.; P. Piotrow, op. cit.; F. S. Jaffe, "Public Policy on Fertility Control," *Scientific American*, July 1973; F. S. Jaffe, "Family Planning Services in the United States," in R. Parke and C. F. Westoff (eds.), *Aspects of Population Growth Policy*, vol. VI of Research Reports of the Commission on Population Growth and the American Future, Washington, D.C.: Government Printing Office, 1972; and F. S. Jaffe, "Toward the Reduction of Unwanted Pregnancy," *Science*, 174:119, 1971.

25 "Improvement in Contraceptive Practice 1970–1973 Was Greater Among Low-Income Than More Affluent Couples," *Family Planning Perspectives*, 8:279, 1976.

26 Testimony of William Ball on behalf of the National Catholic Welfare Conference in Subcommittee on Foreign Aid Expenditures, Committee on Government Operations, U.S. Senate, 89th Congress, *Population Crisis—Part 2-B*, Washington, D.C.: Government Printing Office, 1965, p. 1295; and T. Littlewood, op. cit., pp. 55–56.

27 Speech to Knights of Columbus National Convention, Indianapolis, Ind.,

Aug. 16, 1977, reported in K. A. Briggs, "Catholic Prelates Organizing a Drive Against Abortions," *New York Times*, Aug. 17, 1977.

28 R. Van Allen, op. cit., p. 167.

29 Quoted in "Birth Control—New York's Untold Story," *New York Post*, Mar. 14, 1957.

30 Statement issued Mar. 7, 1964.

31 Statement on prohibition on contraceptive prescription in New York City municipal hospitals, *New York Times*, July 24, 1958.

32 Quoted in "Abortion Clouds Real Hospital Issue," Davenport, Iowa, *Times-Democrat*, Mar. 7, 1976.

33 Testimony before Subcommittee on Constitutional Amendments, Committee on the Judiciary, U. S. Senate, 93d Congress, *Abortion—Part 1*, Washington, D.C.: Government Printing Office, 1974, p. 185.

34 Sacred Congregation for the Doctrine of the Faith, *Declaration on Abortion*, Nov. 18, 1974, published by U.S. Catholic Conference, Washington, D.C., 1974, pp. 8–9.

35 Statement, op. cit., July 24, 1958.

36 J. C. Madden *et al.*, Statement of Guilds of Catholic Physicians, *New York Times*, July 24, 1958.

37 Testimony before Subcommittee on Constitutional Amendments, Committee on the Judiciary, U.S. Senate, 93d Congress, *Abortion—Part I*, Washington, D.C.: Government Printing Office, p. 145.

38 Sacred Congregation for the Doctrine of the Faith, op. cit., p. 9.

39 *Congressional Record, House*, Nov 13, 1977, p. H10969.

40 Quoted in "Change of Heart in Scranton Case," *Hawaii Catholic Herald*, Oct. 24, 1975.

41 Statement quoted in *New York World-Telegram and Sun*, July 23, 1958.

42 Statement, "Explosion or Backfire?", op. cit.

43 Statement issued Mar. 27, 1964.

44 W. Ball, op. cit., p. 1300.

45 Testimony on National Health Insurance before DHEW Secretary Joseph A. Califano, Jr., Oct. 4, 1977.

46 R. Engel, U.S. Coalition for Life, quoted in "Kennedy Anti-life Tirade Draws Pro-Life Condemnation," *The Wanderer*, Apr. 24, 1975.

47 National Conference of Catholic Bishops, *Pastoral Plan for Pro-Life Activities*, Nov. 20, 1975, p. 8.

48 J. T. Burchatell, "A Call and a Reply" (advertisement), *Christianity and Crisis*, 1977.

49 In a recent case, the U.S. Supreme Court refused to review a lower court ruling ordering a taxpayer to pay income taxes withheld to protest U.S. involvement in Vietnam *(Anthony v. Commissioner, certiorari* denied, May 22, 1978). The U.S. Court of Appeals for the Third Circuit stated the applicable rule:

"The sincerity of the taxpayer, which is not disputed, did not alter his obligation to share the common burden." (U.S. Court of Appeals, Third Circuit, *Anthony v. Commissioner*, No. 77-1159, decided Dec. 13, 1977.)

50 Rev. Dan M. Potter, executive director, Protestant Council of New York, in *New York Times*, July 31, 1958.

51 "A Call to Concern" (advertisement), signed by 218 Protestant and Jewish leaders, *Christianity and Crisis*, Oct. 3, 1977.

52 J. T. Burchatell, op. cit., p. 271.

53 See, for example, N. St. John-Stevas, op. cit.; T. B. McDonough, op. cit.; T. J. Reese, op. cit.; J. Leo, "The Catholic Church, Public Policy and Birth Control," in W. Birmingham (ed.), *What Modern Catholics Think About Birth Control*, New York: New American Library, 1964; J. Rock, op. cit.; W. Moran (ed.) *Population Growth—Threat to Peace?*, New York: Kennedy, 1965; Rev. J. O'Brien, "Let's Take Birth Control Out of Politics," *Look*, Oct. 10, 1961; W. V. D'Antonio, "Birth Control and Coercion," *Commonweal*, Dec. 2, 1966.

54 Statement on Public Policy and Family Planning released at American Bar Association convention, Miami, Aug. 9, 1965, reprinted in *Population Crisis—Part 2-B*, op. cit., p. 1137.

55 Testimony of D. L. Hanley in *Population Crisis—Part 2-B*, op. cit., pp. 1262–1263.

56 Ibid.

57 D. L. Hanley, S. J., "Population and Public Policy," an address for the Edward Douglas White lectures, Georgetown Law Center, Mar. 23, 1966, reprinted in Subcommittee on Foreign Aid Expenditures, Committee on Government Operations, U.S. Senate, 89th Congress, *Population Crisis—Part 5-B*, Washington, D.C.: Government Printing Office, 1966, pp. 1371–1372.

58 Ibid., p. 1372.

59 *Population Crisis—Part 2-B*, op. cit., p. 1264.

60 Ibid., p. 1267.

61 J. T. Noonan, Jr., op. cit., 1965, pp. 91–94, 232–237, 360–364.

62 J. T. Noonan, Jr., "An Almost Absolute Value in History," in *The Morality of Abortion*, Cambridge: Harvard University Press, 1970, p. 46.

63 N. St. John-Stevas, *The Agonising Choice*, Bloomington: Indiana University Press, 1971, p. 254.

64 Papal Panel on Birth Control Minority Report, as published in *National Catholic Reporter*, Apr. 17, 1967. St. John-Stevas states that it was not a "minority report" but a working paper drawn up by conservative theologians. (op. cit., p. 118).

65 Testimony of Msgr. A. S. Popekin in Subcommittee on Public Health and Welfare, Committee on Interstate and Foreign Commerce, House of Representatives, 91st Congress, *Family Planning Services*, Washington, D.C.: Government Printing Office, p. 310.

66 Statement opposing federal family planning programs of Mrs. D. R. Mogilka *et al.* (representing Civic Awareness Group of Milwaukee) inserted in *Congressional Record*, May 10, 1966.

67   *Pro-Life Reporter*, vol. 3, no. 6, spring 1974.

68   National Conference of Catholic Bishops, *Declaration on Abortion*, Nov. 18, 1970, reprinted in *Abortion—Part I*, p. 61.

69   *Congressional Record, House*, June 17, 1977, p. H6084.

70   F. Wessling, "Theologian Analyzes Abortion Positions," *Davenport Catholic Messenger*, Mar. 9, 1978.

71   J. T. Burchatell, op. cit., p. 271, and "Ethicists Defend Abortion, Criticize Catholic Bishops," *Crown Heights Christian*, Oct. 21, 1977.

CHAPTER FOURTEEN

"... Her Right to Be"

After enforcement of the Hyde amendment and its state counterparts began in August 1977, a number of cases challenging the legality and constitutionality of the legislation were filed by women denied Medicaid-funded abortions and by doctors and health institutions inhibited from performing abortions for their Medicaid-eligible patients. By the beginning of 1980, courts had enjoined the implementation of these laws in 13 states [1] and ordered those states to pay for medically necessary abortions (necessary, that is, in the light of physical, emotional, psychological, familial, and age factors "relevant to the well being of the patient" as defined by the Supreme Court in *Doe v. Bolton*). Most of these rulings did not address constitutional issues. Rather, the courts held that the Hyde amendment applied only to federal funding; states continued to be responsible under the Medicaid law to pay for medically necessary abortions, just as they were for other necessary medical services for eligible women. One district court, in Wisconsin, went so far as to order the state to pay for medically necessary abortions or to refrain from paying for *any* pregnancy-related services including childbirth and delivery.

Three federal circuit courts of appeals, however, ruled that the Medicaid legislation had in fact been altered by the Hyde amendment and that the *statute* did not require the states to pay for any abortions except those specified in the Hyde amendment, although they indicated that the amendment might be vulnerable on constitutional grounds.[2] In November 1979, the Supreme Court agreed to hear arguments on appeals from an Illinois district court decision that the state law, and the

Hyde amendment on which it was based, were unconstitutional because they deprived indigent women seeking medically necessary abortions of equal protection of the laws by treating them differently from poor women seeking other medically necessary care. The Court refused to stay the district-court judge's injunction that Illinois fund medically necessary abortions for Medicaid-eligible women.[3] And on January 9, 1980, the U.S. Court of Appeals for the Eighth Circuit reversed a lower-court decision that the state of Missouri need fund abortions only under those conditions specified in the Hyde amendment, also on the ground that such a resolution deprived poor women of their constitutional right of equal protection. The Hyde amendment restrictions, the court held, "single out for exclusion one procedure medically necessary to preserve health without furthering a legitimate state interest in doing so."[4]

One week later, on January 15, federal Judge John Francis Dooling, Jr., of the Eastern District of New York, issued an order that, for the first time, stopped enforcement of the Hyde amendment nationwide. After the Supreme Court refused to stay Judge Dooling's order, HEW notified the states that, pending a final Supreme Court decision, it would resume payments for medically necessary abortions for Medicaid-eligible women and that states participating in the Medicaid program were legally required to pay their share.

McRae v. Secretary of DHEW, the case on which Judge Dooling ruled, is the only suit to challenge the legality and constitutionality of the Hyde amendment directly. It represented a nationwide class action brought in 1976 by women in need of Medicaid abortions, physicians who wanted to provide such abortions for their poor patients, the Women's Division of the Board of Global Ministries of the United Methodist Church, Planned Parenthood of New York City, the New York City Health and Hospitals Corporation, and, as friends of the court, 18 religious and other organizations.

The trial lasted for more than a year; testimony was presented by 30 witnesses; the trial transcript took 6,000 pages, and included some 800 exhibits. Under these circumstances, it is perhaps not remarkable that Judge Dooling took 13 months to write his opinion, that it is 328 pages in length, and that it is accompanied by more than 300 additional pages of appendices and exhibits.

He ruled that the Hyde amendment did in fact amend the Medicaid law to exclude most medically necessary abortions from the services covered but that the exclusion violated the First Amendment guarantees of the free exercise of religion or conscience, and the Fifth Amendment rights of privacy, due process, and equal protection of the laws for poor women eligible under the program. He also found that poor women, and teenagers, have an even greater need for abortion on medical grounds than more affluent adult women because they run especially high health risks from continuation of a pregnancy. What is more, he stated, the conditions for payment for abortions specified in the Hyde amendment were framed in language alien to the medical profession and led to limitation of abortion to "crisis intervention," because doctors could not "divine what medical standards it implies,"[5] and, therefore, unduly burdened indigent women's constitutionally protected right to obtain medically indicated abortions. The judge held:

> A woman's conscientious decision, in consultation with her physician, to terminate her pregnancy because that is medically necessary to her health, is an exercise of the most fundamental of rights, nearly allied to her right to be, surely part of the liberty protected by the Fifth Amendment, doubly protected when the liberty is exercised in conformity with religious belief and teaching protected by the First Amendment. To deny necessary medical assistance for the lawful and medically necessary procedure of abortion is to violate the pregnant woman's First and Fifth Amendment rights. The irreconcilable conflict of deeply and widely held views on this issue of individual conscience excludes any legislative intervention except that which protects each individual's freedom of conscientious decision and conscientious nonparticipation.[6]

Judge Dooling's decision, which was appealed by the federal government to the U.S. Supreme Court, goes much further than other courts in citing constitutional—especially First Amendment—grounds and in detailing the background, the purpose, and the consequences of the 1976 Hyde amendment and its successors. Although the Supreme Court finally ruled the Hyde amendment constitutional, Judge Dooling's opinion requires careful review as an eloquent summation of a rational public policy in a society divided on the abortion issue by what Judge Dooling calls "an unbridgeable gulf of principle."[7]

Examination of the voluminous Congressional debates on the Hyde amendment in its various forms, Judge Dooling concludes, leaves no doubt that the only purpose of the legislation was to prevent as many abortions as possible. Its proponents, he said, wanted a constitutional amendment that would have prohibited all abortions. Frustrated in this effort, abortion opponents in the House of Representatives each year successfully held appropriations for the departments of Health, Education and Welfare and of Labor hostage in order to exclude almost all abortions from the otherwise comprehensive services paid for under the Medicaid program. Had Congress settled for restriction of Medicaid-paid abortions to those that were medically necessary, as the Senate wished, the judge notes that there would be no cause for action, since the Supreme Court had held that the state had a legitimate interest in using its funds to encourage normal childbirth and in protecting potential human life as against elective or nontherapeutic abortion. But the Congress specifically refused to accept such "medical necessity" language. Nor did it assert any possibly permissible state purpose in passing the Hyde amendment restrictions. Certainly, Judge Dooling wrote, "the impact of the Hyde amendment is not to influence the woman toward normal childbirth, for that is not medically possible . . . ."[8] (That is, a pregnancy that endangers the woman's health cannot by definition lead to "normal childbirth.")

In addition, he observed, "there is no federal policy of encouraging unwanted childbearing among the poor"[9]; on the contrary, federal policy is to help poor women avert unwanted childbearing through publicly funded family-planning programs. Nor can the Hyde amendment be construed as an economy measure, since it is "recognized that . . . the Medicaid and other costs of childbearing and nurture would greatly exceed the cost of abortion."[10] Finally, Judge Dooling found, the purpose of the legislation was not merely to shift the cost of paying for Medicaid abortions from the federal government to the states; rather it was to alter the Medicaid law so that neither would have to pay for abortions except under the narrow conditions specified.

This was, indeed, the effect of the Hyde amendment and its successors. Since its enforcement in the summer of 1977, Judge Dooling reported, the number of federally funded abortions fell by more than 95 percent [11]—from about 300,000 to about two thousand—almost all of them on the ground that continuation of the pregnancy threatened the pregnant woman's life—a standard in itself "not susceptible to any agreed definition among medical practitioners."[12] The other exceptions (promptly reported cases of rape and incest and, in 1977 and 1978, certification by two physicians that serious and long-lasting physical health damage would otherwise result) proved "illusory," Judge Dooling noted, since most doctors were unable or unwilling to certify abortions under the vague physical-health standard, and the reporting requirements for rape and incest were inappropriate and onerous.

Although nine states[13] and the District of Columbia continued voluntarily to pay for abortions for Medicaid-eligible women, and others were ordered to do so by the courts, most states, Judge Dooling concluded, passed laws similar to the Hyde amendment. Indigent women, he said, "have no significant alternative to Medicaid for legal abortions," either through "use of their necessarily exiguous 'personal funds,' or at free public hospitals or through philanthropic assistance or reduced clinical charge."[14] He found that, at the very minimum, the Hyde amendment worked to delay abortions and that such delay resulted in increased mortality risks.[15] He also noted that the restrictions caused some women to resort to illegal abortion.[16] He added that the dangers to poor women from such clandestine operations are probably greater than before 1973 since illegal abortions are no longer performed by physicians; as a result, "only the least qualified [remain] available to perform abortions for those most determined to obtain abortions and least able to pay for them."[17]

The Hyde amendment standards, Judge Dooling held, limit abortions "to crisis intervention . . . and preclude early safer use of the procedure in conditions in which professional judgment can reasonably find that termination of the pregnancy is medically necessary to the continued health of the pregnant woman."[18] He noted that they "exclude the greater part of the cases in which the professional would recommend abortion as a medically necessary procedure." He cited as examples a long list of physical ailments ranging from phlebitis to cancer, as well as conditions that endanger the mental health of the pregnant woman, possibly to the point where she would kill herself. He singled out cases involving teenagers, especially younger adolescents with unwanted pregnancies, who are physically and psychologically immature, poor, dependent, and at high risk of serious physical and psychological complications that threaten permanently to undermine their health and that of their fetuses.[19] He pointed out that poverty itself carries with it "enhanced health risks, nutritional deficiencies, and limitations on access to health care that make the incidence of medically necessary abortions markedly higher among the poor than among those who have the means to maintain a well-nourished life and regular health care." He indicated that the very fact that pregnancy is unwanted "is a factor deranging the management of pregnancy and aggravating the risks from otherwise controllable complications,"[20] as well as enhancing the risk of child abuse.[21] And the intentional exclusion of abortions upon prenatal determination of serious fetal defect, he noted, may result in "a grave threat to family stability and to the rearing of the defective child's siblings."[22] Such exclusions, Judge Dooling concluded,

> overrule the medical judgment, central as medical judgment is to the entire Medicaid system . . . [and constitute] an unduly burdensome interference with the pregnant woman's freedom to decide to terminate her pregnancy when appropriate concern for her health makes that course medically necessary . . . . [T]he disentitlement to Medicaid assistance impinges directly on the woman's right to decide, in consultation with her physician, to terminate her pregnancy in order to preserve her health. The interests of the state and the federal government . . . in the fetus and in preserving it are not sufficient, weighted in the balance with the woman's threatened health, to justify withdrawing medical assistance unless the woman consents to assume the risks to her health and essays to carry the fetus to term.[23]

Although, he reiterated, Congress "need not be neutral between normal childbirth and nontherapeutic abortion . . . it [must] be neutral among medically necessary procedures."[24]

Based on all this evidence, he found, "It must be concluded that the enactments in question are invalid under the Fifth Amendment."[25]

Is the Supreme Court's and Judge Dooling's broad definition of medical necessity, involving "all factors . . . relevant to the well-being of the patient" inconsistent with the high court's clear rulings that the government need not be neutral in preferring normal childbirth over nontherapeutic abortion? What is the difference between an "elective" and a "medically necessary" abortion? Were the congressional abortion opponents correct who charged that introduction of medical necessity into the Hyde amendment language would legitimate government payment for abortions on demand?

Judge Dooling took these questions seriously, as attested by the more than 50 pages in his opinion on the various health factors involved. Although he included mental health, teenage pregnancy, poverty, and unwantedness among the conditions that a physician should consider in evaluating whether an abortion is medically necessary, he did not suggest convenience of the woman or sex election of the child as coming within his definition of medical necessity. Medical judgment, he emphasized time and again, is paramount and irreplaceable. That judgment may be arguable, or even wrong, in the case of an abortion as in that of a hysterectomy or of brain surgery. But no closed list of conditions invented by Congress, Judge Dooling ruled, can substitute for the judgment of a doctor about a particular patient under the unique circumstances involved. Nor can concern about fraud be cited as a reason for substituting the judgment of Congress for that of the doctor. For example, he noted, exclusion of "mental health damage has no support in permissible legislative purpose. Fear of fraud . . . of feigned psychiatric problems, can hardly justify excluding a whole field of health damage from appropriate treatment."[26] Congress, he pointed out, was wise enough to leave decisions about medical necessity to doctors and their peer review organizations in framing the Medicaid law. Abortion cannot be made a special case.

Indeed, as we have shown, it is more than likely that most physicians are apt to deny certification that an abortion is medically necessary in circumstances they consider marginal.

While Judge Dooling essentially repeated the definition of a medically necessary abortion made by the Supreme Court in Doe v. Bolton, he went far beyond that brief reference in his exploration of the health reasons for performing an abortion, the place of medical judgment, and the appropriateness of the Hyde amendment standards. The Supreme

Court in *Maher v. Roe* had merely opened up the possibility that exclusion of medically necessary abortions from those covered by Medicaid might raise serious statutory (not constitutional) questions. This had been the premise on which a number of lower courts had required states to pay for medically necessary abortions, beyond those specified in the Hyde amendment. Three circuit courts of appeals, however, had ruled that the Congress *had* amended the Medicaid law through the Hyde amendment and that the statute no longer required the states to pay for abortions that the federal government excluded. Indeed, the Congress appeared ready (and the House had already passed) an amendment to the Medicaid law itself that specified that nothing in that law required states to fund *any* abortions.[27]

Judge Dooling noted the passage by the House of that legislation and found, at any rate, that the Hyde amendment had already modified the Medicaid law. Since it could not, by definition, be in violation of the statute it changed, he went directly to the overriding constitutional question.

To the members of Congress who framed the Medicaid amendments, and who considered abortion the unjustified taking of a human life, only a life-for-a-life standard of medical necessity was acceptable. (Rape and incest and serious and long-lasting physical health damage, Judge Dooling found, were added only grudgingly, when politically necessary, and as we have noted, proved "illusory," since virtually no abortions were paid for by Medicaid under these standards.)

Judge Dooling documented, however, that none of the Hyde amendment standards were "used by or familiar to the medical profession."[28] They were not the test for surgical intervention in any other procedure and could not rationally—or constitutionally—be made so in the single instance of abortion.[29]

Most doctors would agree that the Hyde amendment conditions hardly encompass all of the medically necessary reasons for performing abortions and that it would be impossible to supply Congress with a closed list even of life-threatening factors that could substitute for medical judgment under the special conditions and timing under which the abortion is sought. But, as we discussed in Chapter 5, many physicians have continued to balk at performing abortions, either because of moral objections or because of what they consider the "consumerist" definition of health implied in *Doe v. Bolton*. As one commentator put it, doctors are concerned lest they become "merely a set of powerful means . . . merely a technician and engineer of the body, a scalpel for hire, selling [their] services upon demand."[30]

As we have shown, the refusal of most physicians to perform abortions and of most hospitals to offer abortion services has led to a situation in which abortion provision is limited for the most part to those communities where the need for abortions is large enough to support a specialized clinic. The result is that in three-quarters of U.S. counties, containing one-half million women in need of abortion services annually, there is no doctor, hospital, or clinic providing any abortions. Poor, young, and rural women comprised the majority of those denied abortions because of lack of services even prior to enforcement of the Hyde amendment. At that time, three in 10 Medicaid-eligible women in need of abortion services could not obtain them simply because there was no nearby physician or medical facility that provided abortions. Although they constitute only one-tenth of all women of reproductive age, they account for one-fourth of those unable to obtain abortions in the year before the Hyde amendment was enforced.[31] Even if Judge Dooling's decision had been upheld by the Supreme Court, poor women would have continued to be disadvantaged by lack of access unless physicians and the institutions in which they practice accepted the responsibility with which the Supreme Court uniquely invested them to provide medically necessary services, including abortions, to the patients under their care.

There is one intriguing alternative. From the outset, abortion clinics offered a number of services besides abortion itself, including pregnancy testing, pelvic examinations, contraceptive counseling and services, Rh screening, and provision of immune globulin. Many centers have since added a wide variety of outpatient services for women, including screening and treatment for venereal disease, treatment of vaginal infections, sex counseling, simple surgery as well as prenatal care, and infertility advice. If doctors and hospitals remain reluctant to provide abortions in most counties, it is at least possible that such diversified abortion clinics might find it financially viable to offer abortion services in many communities currently without providers—and to offer these services (like the abortions themselves) at prices local health institutions would be unable to match.

Judge Dooling broke new legal ground when he declared that a poor woman who seeks payment under Medicaid for a medically necessary abortion not only exercises a right protected under the Fifth Amendment of the Constitution but is "doubly protected when the liberty is exercised in conformity with religious belief and teaching protected by the First Amendment."

The judge, a practicing Roman Catholic who sent his own five children to parochial schools, rejected the plaintiff's argument that the Hyde amendment violated the First Amendment's command against the establishment of a religion or that it advanced some religions and inhibited others. He held that its purpose, the prevention of abortions, reflected a traditionalist view more accurately than any religious view, even though its most vigorous spokesmen put their case in religious terms. He noted that the Hyde amendment "does not conform to or represent the moral teaching of the Roman Catholic Church,"[32] which allows no exception to its prohibition of abortion, even when the pregnant women's life is at stake. However, he pointed out, "the pro-life effort, of which the organized Roman Catholic effort has been the most active component, has made use of the political process and played a significant part" in securing enactment of the Hyde amendment and other restrictive abortion legislation. "The Roman Catholic clergy and laity are not alone in the pro-life movement, but the evidence requires the conclusion that it is they who have vitalized the movement, given it organization and direction, and used ecclesiastical channels of communication in its support."[33] He added that only the Roman Catholic Church, among the institutional religions, has sought to secure enactment of legislation that would forbid abortion, has organized educational and lobbying efforts to that end, and acted to mobilize popular support for its legislative goals.[34] The evidence, he said, shows "that an organized effort of institutional religion to influence the vote on [the Hyde amendment] was made and . . . the narrow votes in both Houses are open to the inference that in one or the other way the religious factor was decisive of the issue for enough legislators to affect the outcome of the voting."[35]

After a detailed analysis of Right-to-Life political activity and the role of the Catholic Church in supporting it, Judge Dooling concluded that whatever damage resulting religious confrontation may have done to ecumenism, and whatever incitement it may have offered to extremes of emotion and of its expression,

> it is clear that the healthy working of our political order cannot safely forego the political action of the churches, or discourage it . . . . [T]he spokesmen of religious institutions must not be discouraged, nor inhibited by the fear that their support of legislation, or explicit lobbying for such legislation, will result in its being constitutionally suspect.[36]

The judge found, nevertheless, that the Hyde amendment (which, as he noted, was heavily influenced by the efforts of institutional religion) violated the First Amendment rights of the free exercise of religious conscience of poor women denied Medicaid-funded abortions.

After an exhaustive examination of the views on abortion of different religions, Judge Dooling found that

> the major religions . . . all regard abortion as presenting religiously framed questions of moral right, moral duty and conscience, that they are in disagreement on the appropriate rules of conduct but in agreement that abortion is a morally grave undertaking in any circumstances, and that their sharpest disagreement concerns the role of civil government.[37]

The Roman Catholic position is that abortions are impermissible because the embryo and fetus have a value equivalent to a born human being, but most other religious groups disagree. For example, Judge Dooling notes, both Conservative and Reform Jewish teaching regard abortion as mandatory when it is necessary "to preserve the pregnant women's health"; the American Baptist Church "recognizes that abortion should be a matter of responsible personal decisions"; the United Methodist Church holds that "continuance of the pregnancy is not a moral necessity if the pregnancy endangers the life or health of the women or poses other serious problems concerning the life, health, or mental capability of the child to be."

The jurist concludes:

> These teachings, in the mainstream of the country's religious beliefs, and conduct conforming to them, exact the legislative tolerance that the First Amendment assures . . . . The liberty protected by the Fifth Amendment extends certainly to the individual decisions of religiously formed conscience to terminate pregnancy for medical reasons.[38]

Surely it is no accident that Judge Dooling framed his decision—that the right of a poor woman to obtain a medically necessary abortion paid for by Medicaid is "nearly allied to her right to be"—in language customarily associated with Right-to-Life claims of the inviolable human life of the unborn fetus. It must have been to make unmistakable his finding that although the government may in its payment policies give preference to the protection of the potential human life of the fetus over the right of the pregnant woman to obtain a purely elective abortion, it cannot do so when her health is at stake—when the denial of an abortion would violate "the most fundamental" of her rights, rights protected by the First and Fifth Amendments of the Constitution.

Read as a prescription for a rational public policy with regard to a controversial medical service, Judge Dooling's opinion has a certain ring of familiarity. Family planning is the other health service uniquely protected by the Constitution under several Supreme Court decisions, for married and unmarried women as well as for unwed minor teenagers.

Not so very long ago, as we detailed in Chapter 13, contraception was denounced in the same terms that abortion is today—as immoral, contrary to the laws of nature, akin to murder. Numerous criminal and civil laws restricted the sale, distribution, advertising, or use of contraceptives, often classified with abortifacients as "obscene" devices. Public funding of family-planning services for the poor was vigorously and successfully opposed on the grounds that use of tax funds to pay for family planning constituted "promotion" by government of a practice that many taxpayers found morally repugnant. This argument subsequently has been rejected by five U.S. presidents, by the Congress, and by most state and local legislatures. As laws restricting contraceptive use were toppled by the courts, a new public policy emerged. It recognized that the expenditure of public funds for a necessary (and a constitutionally protected) health service was not inconsistent with government neutrality as to the morality of contraception so long as those public funds were not used to require individuals to use contraception. Rather, the use must be confined to enabling those eligible to receive family planning services if they want and need them in light of their personal circumstances and their perceived religious and conscientious obligations.

The public policy developed in relation to family planning has worked: it has made it possible for poor people who want and need contraceptive services to obtain them and for those who do not want such services, for conscientious or other reasons, to ignore them. It has supported the provision of all methods of family planning, including periodic abstinence approved by the Catholic Church. Since the late 1960s, some two billion federal dollars have been expended for family planning services, and there is no instance on record in which an individual has been coerced to adopt a contraceptive method contrary to her conscientious belief or in which a religious institution has been forced to conduct a family-planning program against its wishes. The policy has fostered toleration of the integrity of each religious group in an area of morality and personal behavior that was still a matter of raging religious controversy less than 20 years ago.

The reasoning regarding governmental neutrality and use of taxpayers' funds that has been applied to family planning is as relevant, or perhaps even more relevant, to the issue of abortion. Some methods of contraception can be obtained from nonmedical sources, but the provision of abortion services is entirely controlled by the medical profession and health institutions. In our society, programs like Medicaid and institutions such as public hospitals are created by government to provide medical services to people who must rely on public assistance to obtain the medical services they need because they are too poor to afford private medical care. The fact that they have met the program's eligibility criteria means that in our collective judgment they do not have the resources to obtain those services elsewhere. When these programs and their physicians cannot provide abortions (now the most frequently performed surgical procedure for adults), recipients cannot obtain them from the sources on which they must depend for their medical care. When it denies funding, government is no longer neutral but is enforcing conformity with moral principles that eligible recipients may not share.

Judge Dooling's opinion, and past experience in developing a tenable governmental policy on contraception, provide the framework for constructing a reasoned and consistent public policy on abortion services appropriate in a pluralistic society. It is a policy in which the government neither encourages nor discourages abortion. It would protect the right of those morally opposed to abortion by offering adequate maternal and child-welfare services. It would protect the right of physicians, nurses, and ancillary workers with moral or religious objections to refuse to participate in abortion procedures and would exempt Catholic hospitals and those operated by other religious denominations opposed to abortion from such participation. It would also ensure the right to obtain abortions of women who, in consultation with their physicians, believe that termination of a pregnancy is necessary for preservation of their health and well-being; and it would protect the right of health-care providers, individual practitioners, and institutions to perform abortions. Publicly funded medical programs and institutions would be required to deal with abortion services in the same way as those programs and institutions deal with other necessary health services. They would neither promote nor prohibit abortions but leave the choice to the individual consciences of the patients and the professional judgments of their attending physicians. The government would regulate the safety and availability of abortion services in exactly the same way it regulates the safety and availability of other medical services. It would foster free and informed decision-making by providing information to patients about abortion and its alternatives, similar to the kinds of information it provides for other services (designed neither to encourage nor to discourage utilization of the service), and it would support research and training in abortion similar to that which it offers with regard to other medical and health services.

Such a public policy enables all persons to act in accordance with their conscientious beliefs and their perceived health needs. It avoids the imposition on any individual of conformity to a doctrine with which he or she may conscientiously disagree. It is the only kind of policy acceptable in a democratic, pluralistic society that contains many persons and institutions who hold and will continue to hold sharply divergent beliefs on the morality of abortion. It is the only policy that avoids using the power of government to preclude poor women—and *only* poor women—from obtaining medically necessary abortions, simply because they are unable to pay. Quite aside from its constitutionality, such a discriminatory policy as represented by the Hyde amendment is contrary to the public interest, since there is no conceivable advantage to be derived from forcing poor women to bear unwanted children. It represents a hazardous retreat from the philosophy of pluralism on which this democracy is based.

Judge Dooling's decision, even if it had been upheld by the Supreme Court, would not automatically have provided equal access to abortion services for poor women. That will not occur without recognition by physicians and health-care institutions of their professional obligation to provide abortion services in their communities as an essential element of necessary medical care. That is, unless, as we indicated, diversified abortion clinics step in to provide a range of reproductive health services in areas where there are no abortion providers. (Notably, it is free-standing clinics that now provide most of the family-planning services to poor women; such clinics are now found in nine out of ten U.S. counties.)

We can also expect the moral and political controversy over abortion to continue. Right-to-Life organizations will not give up their crusade to obtain a constitutional amendment to prevent the "slaughter of the unborn"; their adherents will probably continue to picket abortion clinics, confronting pregnant clients with posters displaying images of bloody fetuses; and members of Congress and Supreme Court justices will probably continue to receive their gifts of red roses every January 22d, the anniversary of the 1973 Supreme Court abortion decisions.

Is it too much to hope, however, that the level of rhetoric and invective might be diminished? As Father Richard McCormick pointed out in the Catholic magazine, *America*, the language of "murder" used by abortion opponents "is a conversation stopper . . . [and] is absolutely unnecessary in the defense of the traditional Catholic position on abortion." (Another talk-stopper, he noted, is the "unexamined assertion" by some feminists that abortion is justified because women have the right to control their own bodies.[39]) The level of discourse about contraception has become so civilized in recent years that many people do not realize that the Catholic bishops continue to speak out against public funding of contraception and sterilization, although most are aware that Pope John Paul II, like his predecessors, uncompromisingly condemns the use of all methods of contraception except for periodic abstinence.

May not discourse about abortion in time become as civilized as that about contraception?

Those who favor conscientious choice in matters of reproduction cannot expect abortion opponents to give up their deeply held convictions in the name of democratic pluralism. The emergence of some moderate voices on both sides of the abortion debate, and the example of the earlier debate over family planning, do suggest, however, the possibility that those who would prohibit abortion (as well as those who favor free choice) will act within the law, will respect the moral convictions of those with whom they disagree, and will forego the kind of invective that promotes divisiveness and encourages violent acts like the firebombing of abortion clinics.

References

1 California, Connecticut, Georgia, Illinois, Louisiana, Minnesota, Missouri, New Jersey, Ohio, Pennsylvania, Virginia, West Virginia, and Wisconsin.

2 591 F.2d 121 (1st Cir. 1979), *cert. denied, sub nom. Preterm Inc. v. King*, 47 U.S.L.W. 3748 (U.S. May 14, 1979), rehearing denied, 48 U.S.L.W. 3223 (U.S. Oct. 1, 1979); *Zbaraz v. Quern*, 596 F.2d 196 (7th Cir. 1979); *Hodgson v. Board of County Commissioners*, U.S. Ct. Appeals 8th Cir., Jan. 9, 1979, Case No. 79–1665.

3 *Williams v. Zbaraz*, No. 79–4, *Quern v. Zbaraz*, No. 79–5, and *U.S. v. Zbaraz*, No. 70–491, 48 U.S.L.W. 3350 (U.S. Nov. 26, 1970).

4 *Reproductive Health Services v. Freeman*, U.S. Ct. Appeals 8th Cir., Case No. 79–1275.

5 *McRae et al. v. Secretary, DHEW*, 421 F. Supp. 533 (E.D.N.Y. 1976), *vacated and remanded*, 433 U.S. 916 (June 29, 1977), p. 323 (hereafter referred to as *McRae*).

6 Ibid., p. 311.

7 Ibid., p. 165.

8 Ibid., p. 311.

9 Ibid., p. 314.

10 Ibid., p. 31.

11 Ibid., p. 293.

12 Ibid., p. 91.

13 Alaska, Colorado, Hawaii, Maryland, Michigan, New York, North Carolina, Oregon, and Washington. In the year following enforcement of the Hyde amendment, about 191,000 poor women obtained abortions paid for by the states (voluntarily or under court order), in addition to the 2,000 paid for by the federal government. This is about two-thirds the number obtained in the year before the Hyde amendment went into effect.

14 *McRae*, pp. 74–75.

15 Ibid., p. 158.

16 Ibid.

17 Ibid, p. 69.

18 Ibid., p. 159.

19 Ibid., pp. 315–316.

20 Ibid., p. 309.

21 Ibid., p. 129.

22 Ibid., p. 130.

23 Ibid., p. 313.

24 Ibid., p. 320.

25 Ibid., p. 323.

26 Ibid., p. 322.

27 The amendment proposed by Rep. Robert E. Bauman (Rep., Md.) was to the Child Health Assurance Act (HR 4962), a bill to expand Medicaid benefits for indigent pregnant women and their children. It specified that no funds authorized under Medicaid "shall be used to perform abortions except where the life of the mother would be endangered if the fetus were carried to term: *Provided however*, that nothing in this title shall be construed to require any state funds to be used to pay for any abortion." The amendment was passed by the House on Dec. 11, 1979, by a vote of 235–155.

28 *McRae*, p. 100.

29 Ibid., p. 321.

30 L. R. Kass, "Regarding the End of Medicaid and the Pursuit of Health," *The Public Interest*, No. 58, summer 1975, pp. 11–42.

31 The Alan Guttmacher Institute, *Abortions and the Poor*, New York, 1979, p. 13.

32 Ibid., p. 165.

33 Ibid., p. 238.

34 Ibid., p. 281–282.

35 Ibid., p. 271.

36 Ibid., p. 326.

37 Ibid., p. 280.

38 Ibid., pp. 327–328.

39 R. S. McCormick, "Abortion: Rules for Debate," *America*, July 22, 1978.

POSTSCRIPT

Closing the Door

On June 30, 1980, the Supreme Court by a one-vote majority affirmed the constitutionality of the Hyde amendment. In what seemed almost an apology for its decision, Justice Potter Stewart, summing up the majority's reasoning, declared:

> It is not the mission of this Court or any other to decide whether the balance of competing interests reflected in the Hyde Amendment is wise social policy. If that were our mission, not every Justice who has subscribed to the judgment of the Court today could have done so. But we cannot, in the name of the Constitution, overturn duly enacted statutes simply "because they may be unwise, improvident, or out of harmony with a particular school of thought."[1]

The Court virtually closed the door on further litigation of the Hyde amendment in any of its forms by ruling constitutional even its most restrictive version, the prohibition of federal funding of abortions except where the pregnant woman's life is threatened by carrying the pregnancy to term.

Justice Stewart delivered the opinion of the Court, joined by Chief Justice Warren E. Burger and Justices Byron R. White, Lewis F. Powell and William H. Rehnquist. Dissents were filed by Justices William J. Brennan, Thurgood Marshall, Harry A. Blackmun and John P. Stevens.

Although for different reasons, the Court agreed with Judge Dooling that Title XIX of the Social Security Act (the Medicaid law) did not require participating states to fund medically necessary abortions even if there were no federal reimbursement. The Court ruled:

The cornerstone of Medicaid is financial contribution by both the Federal Government and the participating state . . . Title XIX was designed as a cooperative program of shared financial responsibility, not as a device for the Federal Government to compel a State to provide services that Congress itself is unwilling to fund.[2]

It also agreed with Judge Dooling that the Hyde amendment did not run afoul of the constitutional prohibition against the establishment of religion. It found that while "the funding restrictions in the Hyde Amendment may coincide with the religious tenets of the Roman Catholic Church,"[3] their purpose is essentially secular. The Court dismissed the plaintiffs' arguments that the Hyde amendment deprived them of their First Amendment rights of free exercise of religion on the ground that they did not have proper legal standing to do so.

The Court majority rejected in a footnote Judge Dooling's contention that the Hyde amendment was unconstitutionally vague because the conditions it set for reimbursement were framed in language alien to the medical profession and doctors could not "divine what medical standards it implies."[4] The Court held that the language met conditions that it had previously imposed—that an "ordinary person exercising ordinary common sense can sufficiently understand and comply with [it], without sacrifice to the public interest."[5]

Most important, the majority of the Court rejected Judge Dooling's opinion that the Hyde amendment violated the Fifth Amendment rights of due process and equal protection of the laws for poor women denied medically necessary abortions.

In *Maher v. Roe*, the Court had held that the state could constitutionally express its preference for nontherapeutic, or elective, abortions over normal childbirth by subsidizing the latter, but not the former. In its June 30 decision, the Court extended the *Maher* ruling to include the right of a state or the federal government to subsidize childbirth while refusing to pay for abortion, even if the abortion is deemed medically necessary and its denial could endanger the health of the mother or the health (or even survival) of the baby that is finally born.

The Court reasoned:

[A]lthough government may not place obstacles in the path of a woman's exercise of her freedom of choice [of an abortion], it need not remove those not of its own creation. . . . The financial constraints [in the Hyde amendment] that restrict an indigent woman's ability to enjoy the full range of constitutionally protected freedom of choice are the product not of governmental restrictions on access to abortions, but rather of her indigency.[6]

The Court noted that "a substantial constitutional question would arise" if Congress attempted to withhold all Medicaid benefits from a woman who "exercised her constitutionally protected freedom to terminate her pregnancy by abortion."[7] Since this was not the case, it ruled that the Hyde amendment does not impinge on the freedom of choice of poor women to terminate their pregnancies by abortion as protected by the Due Process Clause of the Constitution. Whether such freedom of choice "warrants federal subsidization is a question for Congress to answer," the Court ruled, "not a matter of constitutional entitlement."[8]

Finally, the Court ruled that the Hyde amendment does not violate the right of equal protection before the law of poor women in need of medically necessary abortions. It argued that the guarantee of equal protection under the Fifth Amendment is not in itself a source of "substantive rights or liberties . . . but rather a right to be free from invidious discrimination in statutory classifications and other governmental activity."[9] If the statute does not violate any other constitutionally protected right, the equal protection guarantee only has force if the statute is wholly irrelevant to the achievement of a legitimate governmental objective, or if it is based on criteria that are constitutionally "suspect"—mainly on race.

The Court repeated its earlier assertions that "poverty, standing alone, is not a suspect classification."[10] (It rejected Judge Dooling's assertion that teenagers in need of medically necessary abortions represent a suspect class, arguing that the Hyde amendment restricts abortion funding for women of all ages.) And it held that the funding restrictions are rationally related to a legitimate governmental objective.

> [T]he Hyde amendment, by encouraging childbirth except in the most urgent circumstances, is rationally related to the legitimate governmental objective of protecting potential life. By subsidizing the medical expenses of women who undergo abortions (except those whose lives are threatened), Congress has established incentives that make childbirth a more attractive alternative than abortion for persons eligible for Medicaid. These incentives bear a direct relationship to the legitimate congressional interest in protecting potential human life. . . . Abortion is inherently different from other medical procedures, because no other procedure involves the purposeful termination of a potential life.[11]

The four dissenting justices expressed opinions on the constitutionality of the Hyde amendment in sharp disagreement with the majority of their colleagues. Justice Brennan (joined by Justices Marshall and Blackmun) charged that the Hyde amendment unconstitutionally coerces poor pregnant women to have babies that they do not want. He argued:

> By funding all of the expenses associated with childbirth and none of the expenses incurred in terminating pregnancy, the government literally makes an offer that the indigent woman cannot afford to refuse.[12]

Justice Brennan and his colleagues argued that "as a means of delivering health services . . . the Hyde amendment is completely irrational. As a means of preventing abortions, it is concededly rational—brutally so. But this latter goal is constitutionally forbidden."[13] They charged that the funding restriction

> is a transparent attempt by the Legislative Branch to impose the political majority's judgment of the morally acceptable and socially desirable preference on a sensitive and intimate decision that the Constitution entrusts to the individual. Worse yet, . . . it imposes that viewpoint only upon that segment of our society which, because of its position of political powerlessness, is least able to defend its privacy rights from the encroachments of state-mandated morality.[14]

These justices argued that the Court majority

> fails to appreciate that it is not simply the woman's indigency that interferes with her freedom of choice, but the combination of her own poverty and the government's unequal subsidization of abortion and childbirth. . . . [T]he discriminatory distribution of the benefits of governmental largesse can discourage the exercise of fundamental liberties just as effectively as can an outright denial of those rights through criminal and regulatory sanctions.[15]

In a separate dissent, Justice Stevens charged the majority with shirking a duty imposed on it by its 1973 abortion decisions—namely, that it cannot place protection of the potential life of the fetus before protection of the pregnant woman's own health:

> Because a denial of benefits for medically necessary abortions inevitably causes serious harm to the excluded woman, it is tantamount to severe punishment. . . . [T]hat denial cannot be justified unless Government may, in effect, punish women who want abortions. But as the Court unequivocally ruled in *Roe v. Wade*, this the Government may not do.[16]

Justice Stevens noted that some types of medically necessary treatment may reasonably be excluded from Medicaid reimbursement on fiscal grounds—"in order to preserve the assets in the pool and extend its benefits to the maximum number of needy persons."[17] Since the cost of abortion is only a small fraction of the costs attendant on childbearing, however, he points out that this cannot be the reason for excluding medically necessary abortions. Ironically, he adds, the exclusion harms all Medicaid-eligible individuals, not just those denied Medicaid-funded abortions, since it involves "draining money out of the pool that is used to fund all other necessary medical procedures."

Justice Stevens concluded:

> Having decided to alleviate some of the hardships of poverty by providing necessary medical care, the Government must use neutral criteria in distributing benefits. . . . It may not create exceptions for the sole purpose of furthering a governmental interest that is constitutionally subordinate [protection of the potential life of the fetus] to the individual interest that the entire program was designed to protect. The Hyde amendments not only exclude financially and medically needy persons from the pool of benefits for a constitutionally insufficient reason; they also require the expenditure of millions and millions of dollars in order to thwart the exercise of a constitutional right, thereby effectively inflicting serious harm on impoverished women who want and need abortions for valid medical reasons. In my judgment, these amendments constitute an unjustifiable, and indeed blatant, violation of the sovereign's duty to govern impartially.[18]

Justice Marshall also filed a separate dissent, charging that the majority decision "marks a retreat from *Roe v. Wade* and represents a cruel blow to the most powerless members of our society."[19] He took issue with the majority's finding that no "suspect" class was involved in the Hyde amendment that required Court scrutiny on equal protection grounds. He noted that "nonwhite women obtain abortions at nearly double the rate of whites," suggesting that minorities may be particularly harmed by the restrictions. He added that the state's permissible interest in normal childbirth cannot apply to conditions "where the fetus will die shortly after birth, or in which the mother's life will be shortened or her health otherwise gravely impaired by the birth."[20]

Justice Blackmun concurred with the opinions of Justice Brennan and Justice Stevens, and, in a brief separate dissent, repeated his earlier contention in *Maher v. Roe* that there is "another world 'out there,' the existence of which the Court, I suspect, either chooses to ignore or fears to recognize."[21]

Undoubtedly, in affirming the right of Congress to enact the Hyde amendment (while indicating that the restrictions are improvident and unwise public policy), the Court was impressed by the unprecedented amicus curiae brief submitted by 242 members of Congress—including the majority of the members of the House—asserting the right of Congress, as watchdogs of the public purse, to appropriate funds as it sees fit. At any rate, however much the majority of the justices disclaimed approval of their own ruling, however narrow the margin of decision, and however eloquent the dissents, the fact remains that after a brief four-month respite, indigent women are once more denied public support for abortions they want and need to prevent unwanted births—births that pose serious risk to their health and threaten to deepen their poverty and dependency.

As we noted in Chapter 14, even if Judge Dooling's decision had been upheld by the Supreme Court, poor women in need of abortion services would continue to be disadvantaged. This does not mean that the Supreme Court action will not make an important difference.

First of all, the impact of the Hyde amendment had never before been fully felt. Nine states and the District of Columbia that had provided 30 percent of all Medicaid-funded abortions prior to enforcement of the Hyde amendment continued to pay for medically necessary procedures out of their own funds; and another 13 states, that had provided 60 percent of abortions in the pre-Hyde era were ordered to do so by the courts. The result was that in the year following enforcement of the restrictions, some 194,000 abortions to Medicaid-eligible women were paid for out of public funds (even though only some 2,000 were paid for by the federal government). This figure represented about two-thirds of the 295,000 publicly funded abortions reported in the year before the Hyde amendment went into effect.[22] Even prior to enforcement of the Hyde amendment, there were about 133,000 Medicaid-eligible women in need of publicly subsidized abortion services who were unable to obtain them because of inaccessibility of services and local restrictive policies. Thus, in the year following passage of the Hyde restrictions, the unmet need for publicly funded abortion services rose by more than 100,000.

Many indigent women managed somehow to raise the funds necessary to pay for their own abortions—even if this meant delaying the rent check or holding back on needed food and clothing. Nevertheless, studies by The Alan Guttmacher Institute and Princeton University in Georgia and Ohio found that about 20 percent of women who had been able to obtain Medicaid-funded abortions in those states prior to enforcement of the Hyde amendment could not do so afterwards. A similar study by the Center for Disease Control (CDC) in Texas found that 35 percent of the Medicaid-eligible women were unable to obtain abortions after the cutoff.[23]

The nine states and the District of Columbia currently paying for medically necessary abortions for poor women voluntarily are certain to come under tremendous pressure from Right-to-Life groups to conform to the restrictive standards of the Hyde amendment. Even if these states resist those pressures, however, and if 75 percent of women in the other states who obtained Medicaid-funded abortions prior to enforcement of the Hyde amendment manage to obtain abortions on their own, the number of poor women unable to obtain abortions at all can be expected to reach nearly 200,000—the overwhelming majority of whom will be forced to have unwanted births. (Although, based on past experience, only a small proportion are likely to resort to illegal or self-induced abortions, it should be recalled that four deaths have been attributed to the Hyde amendment restrictions, and this number may be expected to increase severalfold.) Thus about half of the 427,000 Medicaid-eligible women estimated to need and want abortion services annually will be unable to obtain them.

The health, social and economic costs of this denial to poor women forced to bear unwanted children, and to the children who are born, have been documented here, and cited by Judge Dooling and the Supreme Court dissenters.

Congress has "chosen" to prefer unwanted childbearing over wanted and medically necessary abortions for poor women, and for poor women only. The Supreme Court has held that the choice is constitutional (even if unwise and improvident). The question may be asked whether Congress has chosen as consciously to pay the bill which will be rendered—probably more than a half-billion dollars the first year just for medical and welfare costs attendant upon these unwanted births—more than 10 times the cost of Medicaid-funded abortions for these same poor women.

It is all too likely that when these costs begin to register, we will once again hear denunciations from Congress and the state legislatures of poor women alleged to be having babies just to get on the welfare rolls. (It is notable that many if not most of the members of Congress who voted for the Hyde amendment also oppose legislation to extend health and welfare aid to pregnant women and young children.)

Individuals and groups interested in protecting the reproductive choices of poor women in the wake of the Hyde amendment would probably be well-advised to concentrate their efforts on increasing the geographic and economic availability and accessibility of abortion services—that is, getting services into as many as possible of the three-quarters of U.S. counties currently without an abortion provider, advertising the availability of low-cost clinic services widely through media, classified directories and referral services; reducing the cost of abortion services through private subsidy or billing Medicaid for ancillary services such as pregnancy testing and gamma globulin.

While The Guttmacher Institute and CDC studies do not provide information on the subject, it is highly likely that most of the Medicaid-eligible women who managed to pay for abortions in states that adopted the Hyde amendment restrictions lived in communities where low-cost clinic services were accessible and advertised and where payments could be deferred or reduced by billing Medicaid for ancillary services.

While litigation will probably be pursued in a few states such as New Jersey and California where state constitutional issues are involved, the Supreme Court has probably definitively closed out further litigation on federal constitutional grounds.

It is almost certain that antiabortion forces will be encouraged by the Court's decision to drive for a constitutional amendment to outlaw all abortions, both through the congressional and constitutional convention routes. However, even Congressman Henry Hyde, who gave his name to the restrictive amendment, is doubtful about passage—in the short term—of any constitutional amendment. (In a recent television interview, he predicted that there might be enough Senate votes amassed for passage of a Right-to-Life amendment after the 1982 elections.) Meanwhile, an estimated 1.5 million women obtained legal abortions in 1979; the number increases each year. And, as we noted in Chapter 8, public support for legal abortion for all reasons increased in 1980, after declining slightly in 1978.

Without a major shift in public attitudes about abortion, the chances of a constitutional amendment appear slim.

Certainly, the June 30th Supreme Court decision gives antiabortion forces new heart, after their disappointment with the Dooling decision. It serves to legitimate not only the Hyde amendment, but the various other restrictions Congress has imposed on federal funding for abortions (e.g., in the Department of Defense, the Peace Corps and Legal Services). And it will encourage Congress, and state legislatures, to proliferate such restrictions. It absolves the states of any responsibility to pay for abortions under Medicaid or any future federal-state cost sharing programs where the federal government does not pick up its share of the costs. Although the probability of enactment of National Health Insurance legislation is unlikely in the country's current budget-cutting mood, the Court's decision presages a similar outcome for any public sharing of abortion costs as occurred with Medicaid—given continuation of the current attitudes and makeup of Congress.

Abortion politics continue. The June 30th Supreme Court decision serves to make them less accessible to moderation and to a solution that is tenable in a pluralistic society.

References

1 *Harris v. McRae,* 48 U.S.L.W. 4949 (U.S. June 30, 1980).

2 Ibid., p. 4944.

3 Ibid., p. 4947.

4 Ibid., p. 4945, see fn. 17.

5 Ibid.

6 Ibid., p. 4946.

7 Ibid., see fn. 19.

8 Ibid., p. 4947.

9 Ibid., p. 4948.

10 Ibid.

11 Ibid., pp. 4948–9.

12 Ibid., p. 4951 (BRENNAN, J., dissenting).

13 Ibid., p. 4950, see fn. 4.

14 Ibid., p. 4950.

15 Ibid., p. 4951.

16 Ibid., p. 4956 (STEVENS, J., dissenting).

17 Ibid.

18 Ibid., p. 4957.

19 Ibid., p. 4952 (MARSHALL, J., dissenting).

20 Ibid., p. 4954.

21 Ibid., p. 4955 (BLACKMUN, J., dissenting).

22 R. B. Gold, "After the Hyde Amendment: Public Funding for Abortion in FY 1978," *Family Planning Perspectives,* 12:131, 1980.

23 J. Trussell, J. Menken, B. L. Lindheim and B. Vaughan, "The Impact of Restricting Medicaid Financing for Abortion," *Family Planning Perspectives,* 12:120, 1980; Department of Health and Social Services, Center for Disease Control, "Effects of Restricting Federal Funds for Abortion—Texas, *Morbidity and Mortality Weekly Reports,* Vol. 29, No. 22, 1980, p. 1.

INDEX